THE EDUCATIONAL THEORY OF
JEAN JACQUES ROUSSEAU

The Educational Theory of
JEAN JACQUES
ROUSSEAU

BY

WILLIAM BOYD, M.A., B.Sc., D.Phil.

NEW YORK
RUSSELL & RUSSELL · INC
1963

FIRST PUBLISHED IN 1911

REISSUED, 1963, BY RUSSELL & RUSSELL, INC.

L. C. CATALOG CARD NO: 63—15150

PRINTED IN THE UNITED STATES OF AMERICA

PREFACE

ROUSSEAU is a man about whom it is almost impossible to write with perfect detachment. When in the flesh he excited the most violent feelings of love or of hate in all who came in contact with him, and even after a century and a half he tempts the reader of his works to the same partisanship in milder forms. At the moment I cannot remember a single important writing on his life or his doctrines which does not betray some bias either for or against him. Personally I cannot lay claim to the spirit of neutrality which others lack, and I have no desire to do so. My interpretation of his view of life is based on a discriminating but firm faith in the essential nobility of the man and in the greatness of his thought. I believe, further, that the *Emile* with all its faults is the most profound modern discussion of the fundamentals of education, the only modern work of the kind worthy to be put alongside the *Republic* of Plato. This appreciation, however, must not be taken to imply discipleship on my part. I certainly am in agreement with Rousseau in all that is most vital in educational philosophy, but the extent of my disagreement is almost as great as the extent of my agreement. I am only a disciple in the sense that I have learned and continue to learn a great deal from him. Whether agreeing or disagreeing, I have found no other thinker on educational questions so stimulating or so enlightening. Under his guidance, it seems to me, one gets to the very heart of the great problems of democratic education which are still perplexing us.

It was my first intention to follow the practice of most of those who have written about Rousseau's views on education, and make the *Emile* the central theme of my book. I was the more inclined to this course, because it seemed (and still seems) to me discreditable that in spite of all that modern education owes to Rousseau there should still be lacking any adequate exposition of this epochmaking work in the light of subsequent thought and practice; and I aspired to the honour of making good the deficiency. But as I grew more intimate with his writings, I was reluctantly forced to the conclusion, already indicated by Rousseau himself in one of the last of his Dialogues, that the right method of approach to his theory of education is not through the *Emile* but through his whole social philosophy. For this reason I postponed the idea of writing a treatise on the *Emile* and set myself to give the account of the development of his educational ideas which is here presented.

I think the result justifies the change of plan. Once the *Emile* ceases to monopolise attention, everything is seen in better perspective. Though it is the most detailed and authoritative statement of Rousseau's educational doctrines, it represents only one of the two points of view with regard to social institutions between which his mind constantly oscillated. The common idea that it is a complete expression of his thought inevitably results in a one-sided view of his educational theory, which lacks the rich suggestive-

ness of his whole thought. What is perhaps worse
is that it leads to a wrong estimate of his influence
on the later developments of education by laying
undue emphasis on his opposition to ordinary practice.
To understand him we must get away from this
narrowness, and realise that the contradictions which lie
implicit in his theories are the very contradictions which
became explicit in the controversies of the last century
between the old education and the new. Rousseau's
greatness shows itself in the fact that he was not
merely the protagonist of the new education, the
advocate of the child against society, but that with
penetrating vision he saw the essential truth in old
and new alike, and sought to do justice to both
child and society.

The extent of my indebtedness to those who have
preceded me in the study of Rousseau will be evident
in my references. A deeper indebtedness, though one
which will only be obvious to the philosophical
reader, is that to my former teachers, the late
Master of Balliol and Professor Henry Jones, his
worthy successor in the chair of Moral Philosophy
in Glasgow University. To them I owe in large
measure the view of life which underlies both my
exposition and my criticism, and I gladly take this
opportunity of acknowledging how much I am their
debtor.

WILLIAM BOYD.

October, 1911.

CONTENTS

CHAPTER I

CHAPTER II

CHAPTER III

CHAPTER IV

CHAPTER V

CHAPTER VI

CONTENTS

CHAPTER VIII

CHAPTER IX

NOTE ON THE REFERENCES TO THE *EMILE*

THE absence of any subdivisions in the Books of the *Emile* makes reference to particular passages inconvenient. To get over this difficulty I have followed the numbering of the paragraphs in Dr. Sallwürk's German translation. It is to these numbers I refer in quoting. Thus *Emile*, ii. 95 is a reference to the 95th paragraph in the Second Book. Slight variations in the paragraphing of different editions of the text, and the uncertainty about the best method of numeration for those sections containing dialogues, make even this way of reference somewhat imperfect; but the student who numbers the paragraphs in his own copy and turns up a few references will readily make the necessary allowances for differences so caused.

THE EDUCATIONAL THEORY OF
JEAN JACQUES ROUSSEAU

CHAPTER I

WHAT ROUSSEAU LEARNED FROM HIS OWN BOYHOOD

1. *Rousseau's Ancestry.*—Jean Jacques Rousseau was born in Geneva on the 28th of June, 1712. His father, Isaac Rousseau, a watchmaker and a dancing-master by turns, traced his descent from a Protestant bookseller who had fled from Paris about the middle of the sixteenth century when the wars of religion were raging in France, and had established himself in Geneva. His mother, Susanne Bernard, was a woman of more than ordinary refinement and culture. One of her uncles was a Calvinist minister,[1] and both by birth and fortune she belonged to a grade of society somewhat superior to that of her husband. Both of them, as Rousseau is proud to recall, were citizens of Geneva.[2]

---

[1] In the *Confessions*, Rousseau says that it was her father who was a minister. Later inquiry proves that this, like many of the details of the *Confessions*, is wrong. As the accuracy or inaccuracy of Rousseau's autobiography is of no particular consequence here, I shall make the necessary corrections of his story without comment.

[2] "Je suis né à Genève en 1712 d'Isaac Rousseau, citoyen, et de Susanne Bernard, citoyenne."

Beyond the fact that Rousseau had the French book-seller for an ancestor several generations removed, we have little definite knowledge as to the racial stock from which he sprung. But it is no extravagant con-jecture that, like most Swiss people, he had both Gallic and Teutonic blood in his veins. The Genevese, in spite of strong affinities with the French, in spite even of constant intercourse with France, are certainly not French. Their racial warp may be French but the woof is German; and it is more than an ethnological fancy that sees in Rousseau and his distinctive genius the result of such an admixture of races. One might go further in the way of speculation and find here one of the factors that determined his chequered career. "To be born a Frenchman, with a foreign character," says Rousseau's countrywoman and disciple, Madame de Staël, "with French tastes and habits, and the ideas and feelings of the North, is a contrast which ruins one's life."[1] But in Rousseau's case, the combination that spoiled the man undoubtedly made the artist. With the peculiar endowments due to his mixed ancestry, Rousseau made Cosmopolitanism articulate in finding expression for himself, and created at once a new litera-ture and a new view of life.

2. *Rousseau's Home Education.*—Unfortunately for Rousseau, his mother died a few days after his birth. "I cost my mother her life," he remarks, "and my birth was the first of my misfortunes." Here Rousseau spoke more truly than he was aware. Though we know little of the character of the unhappy mother, we may assume that his home training would have followed a different course if she had lived to direct it. As it was, the household was kept together by the help of one of his

[1] Texte, *J. J. Rousseau and the Cosmopolitan Spirit in Literature*, p. 91.

father's sisters, who made a kindly enough foster-mother
to the boy, but proved quite unfit for the difficult task
of educating him aright. Beyond giving him the taste
for music that was to play a very large part in his later
life, she was too weak to influence appreciably the self-
willed boy, and from his earliest years he seems to have
enjoyed the dangerous satisfaction of doing as he
pleased.

Till the age of ten, Jean Jacques had no teacher
except his father: the best of fathers, says Rousseau;
the worst of fathers, say most of Rousseau's critics.
Even on the most charitable judgment of him, it must
be said that he was in many respects a weak and foolish
person, with a limited sense of paternal obligations.
Like his great son, he was a man overflowing with
sentiment, ready to tear a passion to shreds on the
slightest provocation. "Jean Jacques," he would say to
the boy, "let us talk of your mother"; to which Jean
Jacques would make the naïve reply, "Yes, father, but
then, you know, we shall cry." "And," adds Rousseau,
"immediately the tears would start from his eyes." It
was a misfortune for himself and for his family that his
fine sentiments generally exhausted themselves in good
intentions.

To do him justice, however, it must be said that he
showed an unusual devotion to young Jean Jacques,
and took a great interest in his early education. When
the boy reached his sixth year, he taught him to read,
choosing for text-books some of the romances which
had belonged to the dead mother. In some ways, the
choice of reading matter was an unfortunate one. As
Jean Jacques acquired facility in reading, the lesson
gradually lengthened into a debauch of novel-reading.
"The interest became so keen that we went on reading

in turns whole nights together, and could never stop till we had reached the end of the volume. Sometimes my father, hearing the swallows in the morning, would say in a shamefaced way: 'Let us go to bed. I am a greater child than you.'" Looking back on this reading some fifty years later, Rousseau found in it the explanation of the extravagant views of life which, he confesses, subsequent experience and reflection had never been able to eradicate. It may be doubted, however, whether even so precocious a boy as he suffered much harm from the reading of the romances. Probably the greatest mischief was the drain on nervous energy that premature emotional stimulation always entails. A high-strung boy like Jean Jacques, not very robust at the best, was certainly a bad subject for such excitement.

The next venture was equally strange but more satisfactory. Having come to an end of the mother's collection of romances by the time the boy reached the age of seven, father and son forthwith applied themselves to certain books that the mother had inherited from the uncle who had been a minister; and day after day, as the father sat at work, the boy sat beside him reading from the learned volumes with as much eagerness as he had felt in reading the works of fiction. The collection included Le Sueur's *History of the Church and the Empire*, Bossuet's *Discourses on Universal History*, Plutarch's *Lives*, the *History of Venice* by Nani, Ovid's *Metamorphoses*, La Bruyère, Fontenelle's *Worlds* and his *Dialogues of the Dead*, and a few volumes of Molière. If Rousseau was really only seven when he read these books with appreciation, he is not far wrong in saying that his literary taste was very uncommon for one of his years.

This reading left its mark on Rousseau's mind in two

ways. In the first place, it introduced him to the
literature of the seventeenth century, from which at
a later time he got his models for the distinctive
style that startled his readers into attention by a
certain quaint old-world flavour. In the second place,
and far more important, it acquainted him through
Plutarch with the great men of ancient Greece and
Rome. "Plutarch," he says in one of the *Reveries* [1] of
his last days, "was the first reading of my childhood
and will be the last of my old age. He is almost the
only author from whom I have continued to draw some
fruitful thought at every reading." Just how much this
romantic new world of ancient history meant for the
boy is a difficult matter to decide. One is always
inclined to suspect that in reminiscence many of the
thoughts and feelings of later years have been read
back into the haloed experiences of boyhood; and
Rousseau is specially open to suspicion on this score.
But even if in this case there has been some antedat-
ing of enthusiasms, it cannot be gainsaid that the first
reading of the great biographer exercised a decisive
influence on the susceptible boy. "Incessantly occupied
with Rome and Athens, living as it were with their great
men, myself born the citizen of a republic, the son of a
father whose ruling passion was the love of his country,
I was set on fire by his example. I would fancy myself
a Greek or a Roman, and enter into the character of the
personage whose life I was reading. Carried away by
stories of constancy and courage, my eyes would flash,
and my voice grow firm. One day when narrating the
adventures of Scævola at table, I gave every one a fright

---

[1] *Les Rêveries du Promeneur solitaire ; Quatrième Promenade. Cf.*
also a letter to Madame d'Epinay (1756) : " Voilà mon maître et con-
solateur, Plutarque."

by going forward and holding my hand on a hot chafing-dish in imitation of his action."

To the credit of the father, let it be noted that it was his talks with the boy which brought Plutarch's tales into relation with the life around him, and established in his mind the sense of a community of spirit between the city states of Greece and Rome and the little republican township of Geneva. As a further illustration of the father's conversational teaching, there may be instanced the interesting episode that Rousseau introduces into a note near the end of the *Letter to M. d'Alembert* on the theatre, in support of his contention that the Spartan festivals might well serve as models for the modern world. The regiment of Saint Gervais had been going through their exercises in Geneva, and after supper officers and men had begun to dance among themselves. This unusual spectacle brought all the people to their windows, and soon women and children were hurrying down to mingle with their men folk, and the impromptu dance came to an end in caresses and general mirth. "My father, as he embraced me, was filled with an excitement that I can almost feel and share to this day. ' Jean Jacques,' he said to me, ' love your country. Look on these good Genevese. They are all friends and brothers, and joy and concord prevail among them. Some day you will see other peoples, but even if you travel as far as your father has travelled,[1] you will never see their like.' " The critic, if he will, may condemn this as empty sentiment on the part of a man whose enthusiasm for humanity began and ended in sentiment. But, at any rate, it was effective enough from the edu-

---

[1] The father, like some other members of Rousseau's family, was a man of unsettled habits and fond of wandering. He had even reached Constantinople on one occasion, ostensibly in the practice of his hereditary trade of watchmaker

cational point of view. Whatever the inconsistency of Rousseau or Rousseau's father, it is undeniable that throughout Rousseau's writings there is a sound insight into certain aspects of ancient life, and a comprehension of their relation to modern life no less sound, which can only be ascribed to this paternal teaching.

3. *Rousseau under Tuition.*—This easy-going method of education came to an end when Rousseau was about ten years of age. His father, who was a quarrelsome man, had wounded an ex-captain of the Polish army in a brawl, and rather than undergo the penalty imposed by the Lords of the Council of Geneva, fled the country, leaving Jean Jacques under the charge of his brother-in-law. Jean Jacques' uncle, who had a son about the boy's own age, sent them both off to be educated by a minister named Lambercier in the little village of Bossey, and there for the space of two years Rousseau had the only systematic training in his life. The main study was "Latin with all the useless stuff that goes along with it"; but in spite of that, the burden of study seems to have been light. M. Lambercier, their teacher, Rousseau tells us, was a very reasonable man, who did not neglect their instruction and yet never made their tasks irksome. Altogether, this was one of the happiest times in an unhappy life. The very restraints of study gave play a new zest, and the two boys, busy with their gardens and their outdoor games, found complete satisfaction in a friendship that lasted unbroken for many years. To this time Rousseau dates back the love of country life which continued to the end one of his most absorbing passions. "As I decline into old age," he declares in the *Confessions*, "I feel the memories of these times reawaken with a force and charm that gather fresh strength every day—as though

I felt life slipping away and sought to seize it again at its beginnings. I recall every circumstance of time, place, and person. I see the maid or footman busy in the room, a swallow entering by the window, a fly perching on my hand as I said my lesson."

But the unkind fate that seemed always to be on Rousseau's heels brought this time of happiness to an abrupt finish. He was charged one day with some petty offence and punished for it in spite of his protestations of innocence. Henceforward, he says, his state was like that of the first man in the Garden of Eden after the Fall: the situation appeared to be unchanged, but in reality everything was different. The affront rankled in his mind and poisoned the wellsprings of life. "Even while I write this, I feel my pulse quicken, and were I to live a thousand years that time would still be fresh in my memory. This first experience of violence and injustice remains so deeply graven in my soul that every idea relating to it brings back my first emotions. But now," he adds (at the time of writing the *Confessions*), "this feeling which had its origin in myself is so detached from every personal interest that my heart is as much inflamed at the sight or the tale of any unjust act as though I myself were the sufferer."

Though the boys continued their studies with M. Lambercier for some time longer, the good relations between teacher and pupils that had made learning a pleasure were at an end, and both parties were relieved when the time came for the boys' return to the uncle's house in Geneva. Here Rousseau spent a few months free from the restraints incidental to education; for neither his uncle nor his aunt were willing to take any trouble with his training. In a way these were months of idleness, but, as Rousseau takes care to point out, the time was by no means wasted. It was intended that his cousin should become an engineer, and with that in view he got lessons in drawing and the elements of Euclid, which Jean Jacques shared. Drawing and colouring, indeed, were their chief occupations. For the rest, their leisure was abundantly filled with handicrafts of all kinds. They made cages, flutes, kites, drums, houses, pop-guns, and crossbows, and spoiled their grandfather's tools making watches in imitation of him. So busy were they with themselves and their own concerns that they had no need of other acquaintances, and held themselves aloof from the rest of the boys in the town.

4. *Rousseau's Unfinished Apprenticeship.*—But this could not go on for long. Jean Jacques had to find means of earning a livelihood, and the question of his future occupation came under debate. He himself would have liked to be a minister, but the money left to him by his mother was insufficient to carry him through the necessary course of training; so, much against his will, poor Jean Jacques was sent off to the office of the city registrar to become a clerk. But the experiment was a failure, and before very long Rousseau was turned out of the registrar's office as a hopeless fool, "only fit to handle a file."

A second experiment proved no greater success. This time he was bound apprentice to an engraver. But the master was a hard man who believed in keeping apprentices in their proper place; and under a course of repressive treatment Rousseau gradually went from bad to worse, in spite of his fondness for the work. Before long he had acquired all the typical sins of the apprentice. He learned to "covet, to dis-

semble, to lie, and finally to steal." [1] "Despite my
good education," he confesses, "I must have had a
strong tendency to degenerate; for I went to the bad
with the greatest ease. Never did so promising a
Cæsar so quickly become a Laridon." [2]

The unhappy experience came to a sudden end. On
Sunday nights, after sermon time, Rousseau and some
of his companions were in the habit of wandering
outside the city walls, and twice over he had been
shut out the whole night. The third time this mis-
adventure occurred he was too much overcome with
fear to return to face his master's anger, and taking
his courage in his hands, he set off on his travels to
seek whatever fortune might bring him. Thus at the
age of sixteen he abandoned the attempt to earn a
living in the ordinary way and embarked on a career
of temporary vagabondage, certainly not a very auspi-
cious ending for his boyhood nor a very promising
beginning for his youth. Well might Rousseau look
back on this time and speculate on the different course
his life would have taken if he had continued at his
craft. Nothing, he affirms, would have suited his disposition better, or more surely have led to happiness,
than the obscure and peaceful condition of a good
artisan. [3] "This estate, being lucrative enough to yield

[1] ". . . fantaisie qui jusqu'alors ne m'était pas venue et dont je
n'ai pu depuis lors bien me guerir."

[2] This statement has frequently been quoted against Rousseau's doctrine of the primitive innocence of children and of uneducated men.
The criticism proceeds on a wrong view of what Rousseau meant by
innocence. He himself recognises as readily as his critics the facts of
heredity, and finds no difficulty in reconciling his own statements
that some children are well born and other children ill born with the
view that it is society that is responsible for *moral* evil. See the discussion of this topic in the Letter on Education in the *New Heloïse*,
v. 3.

[3] This should be connected with what Rousseau says about the advantages of an artisan's life in *Emile*, iii. 138.

me an easy subsistence if not a fortune, would have limited my ambition for the rest of my days, and satisfied me in my own sphere without giving me any opportunity of leaving it. I should have lived quietly and peacefully in the bosom of my religion, my country, my family, and my friends. I should have been a good Christian, a good citizen, a good father, a good friend, a good workman, and a good man in every respect." Whether a man of Rousseau's temperament could have settled down to the humdrum routine of an ordinary life under any circumstances may fairly be doubted. Probably he would have contrived to make himself miserable whatever his condition. But such speculations serve no good purpose. Rousseau decided his destiny for himself by running away from the trade that stood for ordinary respectable life, and the world of letters has no cause to regret what happened. Genius must have its *Wanderjahre*. Rousseau's began on the night when he found the gates of Geneva barred against him, and he turned away to seek his fortune in the untried world.

5. *The Personal Basis of Rousseau's Educational Method.* — In narrating the story of his boyhood, Rousseau notes with the greatest care the various circumstances that determined the appearance and development of all the special characteristics constituting his distinctive personality — his passion for music, his chastity of life, his love of nature and of country conditions, his sense of justice, his interest in handicraft, his thievish propensities, and so on. And the student of his educational doctrine will do well to keep in mind the importance of this biographical material—to be found for the most part in his re-

markable *Confessions*—for the light that it throws on
the details of his educational scheme.

The fact is that Rousseau is the most personal of
writers and is constantly drawing on his own experience
for the materials out of which to build up his theories.
It has not inaptly been said that the second half of
his life was spent writing about the first half.[1] This is
true whether we consider the copious autobiographical
writings and those romances of which the hero is
Rousseau himself in ineffective disguise,[2] or his more
impersonal writings on sociological subjects. Through
them all we have a constant sense of contact with the
personal experience of the writer, sometimes stated as
an individual opinion, more often put in the form of
a generalisation.

In the *Emile*, his main educational work, which is
partly a romance, partly a treatise, the disguise under
which the personal element is concealed is very thin.
The discussion of educational matters is hung on a
slender framework of plot, bringing in as the two chief
characters the boy Emile and his tutor. It is almost
unnecessary to say that both are created in the
image of Rousseau: the tutor is Jean Jacques at
fifty, busy with the education of a Jean Jacques of
ten, fifteen, or twenty as the case may be. The difficulties attendant on the working out of this idea are
obvious; and it cannot be said that Rousseau has
managed to avoid them all. But, on the whole, this
reproduction of himself in tutor and pupil is a success.

---

[1] Chuquet, *J. J. Rousseau*, p. 192.

[2] " En tous ses écrits, Jean-Jacques est le peintre de Rousseau et son
constant héros. Saint-Preux, épris de vertu et d'amour : Émile, né
bon, sauvage et citadin : le vicaire savoyard, détracteur des philosophes
et raisonneur, croyant et incrédule : Julie, prêcheuse touchée de piété
attendrie . . . sont un même personnage."—BRÉDIF, *Du caractère intellectuel et moral de J. J. Rousseau*, p. 194.

In spite of an occasional touch of caprice in the boy
that is not quite the caprice of a boy, and in spite of
an excess of sentimentality on the part of the tutor
which leads him at times to adopt very questionable
methods, the relations of teacher and pupil are set
forth with psychological truth. The boy is a genuine
boy, with the ignorance and stupidity of the boy, and
not merely a miniature man;[1] and the teacher is a
genuine teacher, generally conscious of how the world
looks to his pupil and taking appropriate action to
direct him aright. Both are clearly expressions of
actual experience. The creator of Emile and of the
tutor had himself been a boy and a tutor, and had
understood the characters of both with an insight that
shows itself in his imaginative projection of them in
the story of the *Emile*.

But it is not merely in matters of detail such as
appear in the portraiture of Emile and his tutor that
the *Emile* shows the influence of Rousseau's own
history. To that history he owes his whole view of
education. The *Confessions* indeed prepare us for this:
"If ever child received a sound and reasonable education," he says, "it was I." If one can say this with
conviction, what need to go far afield in the search for
new methods to displace the old? The most obvious
course for Rousseau, when he came to discuss education, was to adapt the method which seemed to him
to have worked so well in his own case by giving it
a form that made it suitable for children in general;

---

[1] It is interesting to compare Emile in this respect with his future
mate Sophie, whose education is discussed in the Fifth Book of the
Emile. It is difficult to discern any of the characteristics that distinguish the girl from the woman in Rousseau's presentation of her.
Rousseau could understand women up to a certain point; but there is
no evidence that he could appreciate the girl's point of view.

and this in the main is what he has done in the
Emile. Except for the two years spent with M. Lambercier—no very serious exception—Rousseau had no
teaching of the kind commonly given in schools and
colleges. Most of what he learned was learned in a
quite casual way without any consciousness of effort.
He read books after his own heart and talked about
their contents with his father; he played at gardening
and at country work; he "wasted paper and colours";
he busied himself with tools of various kinds. Occupied with these boyish tasks, he reached the age of
thirteen or fourteen without ever needing to learn
anything he did not want to learn. And this is
substantially Rousseau's educational programme for
boyhood, which, as he says in the *Emile,* ought to
be wholly spent in "games and sportive amusements."[1]
The only important difference between Emile's discipline and Rousseau's own is that Rousseau was left
almost entirely to his own resources, while Emile was
kept under the constant supervision of a tutor. But
so far as the occupations of boyhood are concerned the
difference is of little consequence. It is not the teacher's
function in the romantic world of the *Emile* to give
what Rousseau calls "the ordinary kind of lessons,"
which must be mastered whether the pupil wishes or
not. Emile's tutor gives the boy the largest possible
measure of freedom, and confines himself to directing
this free activity in such a way that the pupil learns
the lessons of experience better than he would have
done if left entirely to himself.

6. *The Meaning of Education for Rousseau.*—The
principles underlying this method of informal education
by free activity are explicitly set forth in the preliminary

[1] II. 287.

statement of Rousseau's views on education which serves as preface to the story of Emile; and before going on to the further discussion of what Rousseau learned from his own experience as a boy, it will be well to make ourselves clear about the meaning he attaches to the word "education," by a consideration of the following passage:[1]—

"We are born feeble and need strength. We are born devoid of everything and need help. We are born stupid and need judgment. All that we lack at birth and need when grown-up is given us by education. This education comes to us from nature, from men, or from things. The internal development of our faculties and organs is the education of nature. The use we are taught to make of this development is the education of men. And the acquisition of personal experience with regard to the objects that affect us is the education of things. . . . Now, of the three educations, that of nature does not depend on us at all, and that of things only depends on us in certain respects. The education we get from men is really the only one over which we have any control. And even this is not absolutely true; for who can hope to have the entire direction of the speech and actions of all the people surrounding a child?"

Here it is necessary to get through a certain crudity of expression to reach Rousseau's thought.[2] He does not really mean to say that there are three distinct educations capable of being carried on independently of

---

[1] *Emile*, i. 5, 6, 8.
[2] The crudity of expression is the result of a crudity of thought—which, however, it exaggerates. Rousseau is led to speak of the three educations because he sometimes thinks of the natural development as capable of taking place independently of the other factors. In the *Emile*, however, he generally avoids this error.

one another, but that in all true education three factors
need to be taken into account : (a) the internal impulse
to growth in certain determinate directions depending on
the original nature of the child; (b) the shaping influence of physical environment making itself felt
through personal experience; (c) the modification of
the child's nature by means of teaching, with a view
to social ends. Or, paraphrasing this into the language
of modern biology, the growth of the child under social
conditions, which we call education, is, like every form
of growth, the result of the operation of the three
concomitant factors of inheritance, environment, and
function.[1] Let us consider quite briefly Rousseau's
account of education in the three different aspects thus
suggested.

In the first place, the analogy of plant culture and
human education, with which the *Emile* begins, implies
that education is essentially a process of growth, following a definite course prescribed by the nature of the
growing being. From this point of view, inheritance
(or, as Rousseau calls it in this passage, "nature") is the
first constant with which the educator must reckon.
The child comes to him with a fixed equipment of
capacities, which follow a fairly well defined order in
the times and seasons of their appearing and coming to
maturity. To this extent, at least, education is outwith
his power to control. He must take the child as he
finds him—dull and stupid, or alert and intelligent, of
good disposition or of bad; and he must await the

---

[1] The interpretation of what Rousseau says about the three educations in terms of biology is warranted by the context. The preceding
paragraph begins thus : " Plants are shaped by culture and men by
education"; and the analogy is developed at length. The whole
passage is noteworthy as the first occurrence of this comparison in
modern educational thought. Plato had already suggested it (*Republic*,
491D–492A).

nascence of his powers, conscious that he is as little able to hasten their unfolding by a single hour as he is to add one jot or tittle to the inherited capacities.

In the second place, education in its external relations is a process of adaptation to environment. From this new point of view, it is the ordered course of physical nature that presents itself to the educator as a constant. The world of things into which the child enters as soon as he acts, responds to each of his actions with a constant reaction. If he touches fire, he is inevitably burned. If he goes about bareheaded and lightly clad, he becomes habituated to extremes of heat and cold. Once the train of causes has been laid by his action, whatever it be, the appropriate result follows sure and invariable in every case. Right living, therefore, calls for the proper adjustment of the growing individual to the things around him. On the child's side, it is a gradual process of learning about things by experience of their effects on himself. On the teacher's side, it is a method of selecting and emphasising the most valuable of these educative experiences, and excluding those which are bad or dangerous.

In the third place, considered as a means of preparing the child for society, education is the modification of his "nature" for social ends. In a sense this is only a particular phase of the whole process of adjustment to environment; but Rousseau is so much impressed by the differences between the physical and the social environment that he makes a sharp distinction between the relative forms of education. The adaptation of the child to the physical world, he seems to think, is not incompatible with the natural development of organs and faculties; but he is by no means sure that the same can be said of "the use we are taught to make

of our developing organs and faculties" in preparation
for social life. He is even inclined at times to regard
the "use" to which the child's capacities are put as
inconsistent with the native impulses to self-realisation.
Quite apart from that, there is on his view a very considerable difference in the method of education in the
two cases. Adaptation to the physical environment he
regards as primarily a matter for the learner, the social
adaptation primarily a matter for the teacher. The
child might conceivably become familiar with the world
of things by his own unaided efforts, but the social order
is so much more complex that he is perfectly helpless
in it apart from adult direction.

7. *Education as Individual Experience.*—If this
account of education as the progressive adaptation of
the child's nature to his whole environment, and especially to his physical environment, be kept in mind,
Rousseau's assertion that his own upbringing was eminently "sound and reasonable" will lose some of its
strangeness. It must be admitted that if judgment were
passed in accordance with the standard of the schools, a
boy like Rousseau, left to his own resources, could not be
said to be educated at all. But everything turns on what
is meant by education. Rousseau is obviously giving the
word a far wider significance than is usually attached to
it when it is confined to the lore of school or college.
The pedagogue thinks primarily of "lessons." Rousseau
thinks rather of all those manifold agencies by means of
which the child is brought into conformity with natural
and social conditions; and among these, lessons and
books play but a small part compared with the personal
experience of men and things outside school.

It is scarcely necessary to say that there is no real
opposition between the formal lessons of the schools and

the informal lessons of experience; and no one is better aware of this than Rousseau himself. Nevertheless, there is a very considerable difference in point of view between him and the ordinary teacher. By the very nature of his office, the teacher is tempted to minimise the worth of what is self-learned or learned apart from his instruction. The wisdom of the adult community which it is his business to impart seems to him, as a matter of course, of far greater consequence than what the child learns for himself through self-chosen occupations; and he is ready on occasion to force it on his pupil, "for his good," without respect to the pupil's interests or capacities. Against this narrowness of view it is necessary to present the conception of education as co-extensive with the whole process of learning, and not limited to the comparatively small segment of it that must be carried on under adult guidance and teaching; and this in effect is what Rousseau has done in holding up as a model for the educator the free and easy *régime* under which his own boyhood was spent.

If we are to get at Rousseau's meaning here we must not read too much into the commendation of his own freedom from the schoolmaster's yoke. We must not, for example, infer that he would leave the boy to follow his own bent without let or hindrance from parent or teacher. The main implication is that the most important part of what a boy learns is not acquired from the schoolmaster or any other person, but comes to him without any consciousness of learning in the course of the spontaneous activities of play. This, it should be noted, does not involve the denial of the worth of the ordinary education that prepares for complete living as a member of society when it comes at the proper time. But in Rousseau's view of human development the proper time for social education is not boyhood but youth. The boy he regards as a creature of the senses, without conscience or reason, and therefore incapable of the intelligent relationship with society which is the pre-condition of an adaptive education. The child confined within the world of the senses has only a physical environment; and any attempt at education that ignores this limitation by introducing him prematurely to the fundamental human interests is foredoomed to failure. "Our real masters," says Rousseau, "are experience and personal feeling; a man never appreciates what is proper to manhood until he is actually in its relations. A child knows that he will one day become a man, and all the ideas he can have of man's estate are occasions of instruction for him; but concerning the ideas of that estate which are beyond his comprehension, he ought to remain in absolute ignorance."[1] If, then, the child is to be educated at all, it must only be with reference to his physical environment; and here nature has made ample provision for his education in the constant promptings to activity that lead him to explore his immediate world and to perfect his senses at the same time. The wise educator will follow nature's lead.

But it may be asked: If the boy learns best when he plays, what need for the educator at all?. If it is so important that he should learn for himself by personal experience, why not leave him to the guidance of instinct, to learn as primitive man learns? To these questions Rousseau has two answers of conflicting import.[2]

[1] III. 64. The words "*sentiment*" and "*sentir*" occurring in this passage have something of the meaning of the words "*Anschauung*" and "*anschauen*" in the Pestalozzian usage, and suggest the first-hand acquaintance with reality which, according to both Rousseau and Pestalozzi, is the pre-condition of all real learning.

[2] The reader will find both answers in the *Emile*. The first appears, *e.g.*, in i. 2. The clearest statement of the second is to be found in the Letter on Education in the *New Heloïse*, v. 3.

The one is that if the boy lived under primitive conditions he might be safely left to follow the path marked out by instinct, but that as a matter of fact he is born into a society which either perverts the native impulses or makes them of no avail. On this view, the prime function of the teacher is to save the boy from society by removing the social obstacles to his natural development. The other answer is that the child, though a non-social being, will one day be a member of society, and that with this in view the teacher must not merely preserve the original impulses of his nature from baneful change, but must seek to bring them to perfection by giving them a socially useful form not inconsistent with their own character. The one is a negative answer, the other a positive, but both, it will be observed, show that Rousseau recognised the need for the directing and regulating work of the teacher quite as much as those whose methods he condemned.

In point of fact, the difference between Rousseau and the old school of educators is not as to whether the boy should be left to educate himself. Whatever Rousseau may say to the contrary in erratic moments, he is generally in no uncertainty as to the need the child has for adult guidance, in all save a few elementary activities like walking and eating, in which instinct is quite sufficient. The real question at issue between the protagonists concerns the form that this direction and guidance is to take. Generally the direction given is casual and intermittent—as in Rousseau's own case, and in the case of the ordinary schoolboy. The boy gets so many tasks, and that is all. Rousseau, full of the idea that every moment of the child's life from the very day of birth is educationally important, is not content with anything less than complete supervision in accordance with a clearly defined plan.[1] Emile's tutor devoting his whole time for twenty-five years to the education of the boy is the perfect embodiment of his view. The boy knows no impulses to action save those that have their origin in his spontaneous interests and activities, and the only check on impulse of which he is conscious is that which comes when he breaks the law that is in the nature of things; yet all the while the course of his life is being determined by the tutor towards the appointed end. It is wrong, therefore, to say, as some of Rousseau's critics do, that Rousseau leaves the boy free to do as he pleases. Indeed, if fault is to be found with the method of education proposed in the *Emile*, it should be not with its excessive freedom but with its excessive restraint. The Plan of the teacher is really a new addition to the constants of the boy's life.

Whether Rousseau is consistent with himself in regarding his own education as thoroughly satisfactory, despite the absence of the omniscient tutor to administer an inflexible law in the name of nature, is another question. The parallel between himself and Emile undoubtedly breaks down at this point; for, even with the greatest stretch of imagination, it can scarcely be maintained that the direction given to Rousseau's own education by his father and by M. Lambercier is at all

---

[1] The idea of education conducted according to a pre-arranged plan is one of which Rousseau was rather fond. His first educational writing—the *Project for the Education of M. Sainte-Marie*—was intended to give a working scheme for the education of a pupil of his own. Again, in his letters to the Prince of Wirtemberg concerning the education of his infant daughter (written after the publication of the *Emile*), he suggests that the child should be entrusted to a governess with the same absolute power over the pupil as Emile's tutor, but subject to a prescribed Plan.

comparable with the rigid rule of Emile's master. M. Compayré is so much impressed by the contradiction between Rousseau's own education and that of Emile that he finds " the fancies of Emile's education in formal opposition with the realities of Rousseau's existence" at this and many other points. " I do not know . . . one of our great writers whose childhood and youth were to such a degree lacking in guidance. He cannot, indeed, be said to have had a family: his mother died in giving birth to him; his father, after having spoiled him, deserted him. Nobody brought him up. . . . How after that could the temptation be avoided of imagining a situation quite the reverse, by which Emile is given a tutor who does not lose sight of him for a second, a mentor who will accompany him and protect him in his every action right up to the threshold of the nuptial chamber ? " [1] Against this, one can only quote Rousseau's remark about his own " sound and reasonable education," in view of which it is difficult to believe that it was any sense of defect in his own education which provoked the idea of the foreseeing tutor deliberately working out the plan of Emile's life. After all, the resemblances between Rousseau's own education and that of Emile are so much greater than the differences that there does not seem to be any special need to explain the differences in this way. Probably Rousseau's critics (including M. Compayré) exaggerate the closeness of the tutorial supervision. Rousseau himself speaks of the method of the *Emile* as one of " well-regulated *liberty.*"

8. *The Community as Educator.*—Whatever view may be taken as to the difference between the education

---

[1] G. Compayré, *Rousseau and Education from Nature* (Eng. tr.), pp. 15, 16.

of the boy Emile and of his prototype the boy Rousseau, it would be a mistake to suppose that the informal learning done by a boy who has been allowed to pursue his own line of interest is entirely aimless because there has been no teacher to direct it. Such a conception, from whatever quarter it come, betrays an individualism as extreme as that which leads Rousseau to make the education of Emile depend entirely on the individual thought and effort of his tutor. The truth is that in every case, whether the education be formal or informal, the real educator is society itself, sometimes acting through a teacher who owes his status to his representative character, sometimes bringing about the development of mind and character without the mediation of a teacher, by means of those institutions in which the child or youth participates. It is wrong, then, to say that the boy who has not gone to school, nor had his studies directed by some adult, is necessarily uneducated or even badly educated. He will certainly not be so completely developed as he would have been if he had been properly taught; and if it should happen that his home is a bad one, or that his work makes no demand on intelligence, or that he lives in a town or country unable to call forth his patriotism, his education will indeed be a sorry one. But, on the other hand, if the relationships of home and neighbourhood and country are fruitful in interests that inspire him to noble thoughts and worthy deeds, his whole life will be one continuous learning; and his education, if lacking somewhat in completeness, will be no more devoid of order than those institutions which have formed him for their service.

This is something like the view that stands vaguely behind Rousseau's commendation of his own untutored boyhood, and finds a somewhat uncertain expression in some of his minor educational writings. So far as his own boyhood is concerned, the conception of the educational function of social institutions appears most definitely in a remarkable letter to Dr. Tronchin,[1] that was written in elucidation of some remarks he had made about the simple games of the workmen of Geneva in his *Letter to M. d'Alembert*. He begins by directing attention to the marked difference between the citizens of Geneva and those of other countries. A watchmaker of Geneva, he says, is fit to take his place in any society: a Parisian workman, on the other hand, can talk of nothing but watches. The reason for the difference is simply that the Parisian workman is only trained to use his hands. Unlike his Genevan fellow whose head and heart are formed by his civic functions, he lacks opportunity for the worthy exercise of mind and character, and never rises above the narrow interests of his trade. Rousseau then goes on to apply this to his own case. He himself belonged to the artisan class of Geneva. In that class he was born, and in it (but for the chances of life) he should have lived: it was his misfortune that he ever left it. "In it," he goes on to say, "I received this *public education*, not from any formal instruction but from those traditions and precepts handed down from generation to generation, which impress on young people at an early age the knowledge and sentiments they ought to have." In answer to the objection that on this method of education the children are virtually left to themselves, he proceeds to supplement his remarks about public education by calling attention to the important part played by the home in the upbringing of the Genevan

[1] *Correspondance*, Nov. 27, 1758.

child. "It is there," he says, "the children ought to be educated, the girls by the mother, the boys by the father. This is exactly the education suited for us,[1] midway between the public education of the Greek republics and the domestic education of monarchies in which all the people have to remain in isolation with nothing in common save obedience." The education of the people of Geneva, then, on Rousseau's account of it, has two aspects. It begins in the family circle: that is the guarantee that the child will be rightly directed and trained. It culminates in the common life and duties of citizenship: that provides an abundant content of spiritual experiences. And the proof of its goodness and efficiency is that it makes not merely workmen but citizens and men.

9. *The Two Tendencies in Rousseau's Thought.*—It is interesting to note that the *Letter to Dr. Tronchin* was written in the year 1758, just about the time when Rousseau was beginning the composition of the *Emile*. The two writings are in their different ways attempts to interpret and to generalise Rousseau's own experience as a boy; and they are so far at one that they both take as their starting-point the assumption that, if properly employed, a boyhood left free from the restraints of the schoolmaster is perfectly satisfactory from the educational point of view. But, in spite of this common ground, their respective views of the nature and method of education differ very considerably.

In the *Emile*, on the one hand, we find (especially in the earlier books) a deep-seated distrust of social actions and institutions. It seems to be taken for granted that social organisation is in the main inimical to the individuals who make up society, and it is not obscurely

[1] That is, the people of Geneva.

suggested that prejudice and convention are so powerful in shaping men's lives that natural men, faithful to their innate personality, are rarely if ever to be met. It is implied, further, that the natural education which produces such men is only possible under quite exceptional circumstances; and in the discussion of the methods of education in accord with nature, elaborate precautions are taken to screen the natural man in the making from most of the ordinary social influences. The individualistic spirit of the *Emile* is most perfectly illustrated by the extraordinary tutor who directs the educative process. He stands out a solitary figure, dedicated by his own choice to the task of educating one boy for perfect manhood. His whole attitude to society is one of suspicion. He lives in constant fear of the malign influences that surround his pupil, holding himself ever ready to interpose a situation of his own creation to save him from them. He rarely looks to society for any help in his work. The best he seems to hope for is that society may not in the end prove too much for him, and that, by dint of unceasing effort and watchfulness, he may succeed in keeping one soul unspotted from the world.

How different, on the other hand, is the spirit of the *Letter to Dr. Tronchin!* Instead of the attitude of distrust that characterises the *Emile*, there breathes through it a sturdy faith in the power of home and country to direct men's lives to noble issues. Instead of the disbelief in social influences, there is a firm conviction that a social education which is in the highest degree natural is not only desirable but possible. Why, we may ask, the difference? The reason is plainly to be found in the fact that here Rousseau is not thinking of education as it is commonly practised, but of the education imparted in the little city State in which he himself had been born and brought up. Looking on Geneva with patriotic love, he found in its social life a happy exception to the common evils of other communities. In the well-ordered life of the city, with its fine theocratic tradition, custom and law did not destroy the spontaneity and goodness of individual aspirations as they seemed to do elsewhere. On the contrary, its citizens found themselves not worse but better men for the share they had in its communal activities, a fact that seemed to Rousseau to justify the hope of finding like conditions for the whole human kind. In the *Letier to Dr. Tronchin* he was led by this line of thought to a view of education fundamentally different from that of the *Emile*. According to this view, the end of man's life is only truly realised when he is educated by the state to play his part as the citizen of a free community which has in it a fitting place for each of its members.

Following Rousseau in his diverse interpretations of his own education as a boy, we thus end with two views to all appearances contradictory. The reason for this will become evident as we follow the course of Rousseau's mental development.

CHAPTER II

ROUSSEAU'S YOUTH AND EARLY MANHOOD

1. *Conversion to Catholicism.*—In the *Confessions* Rousseau dwells on the delight with which he looked forward to the life of adventure that was to follow his escape from the bondage of apprenticeship. "Here was I," he says, "while still a child, about to give up my country, my friends, and my resources; to leave an apprenticeship half finished, before I had learned enough to make my living by my trade; to expose myself to all the temptations of vice and despair at an age of feebleness and innocence; to go out in search of evils, misfortunes, slavery, and death. That was the picture I ought to have drawn for myself. It was a very different one I actually did draw. The independence I seemed to have gained was the one thought that possessed me. I was a free man and my own master, and nothing seemed impossible for me. I entered the vast arena of the world with perfect confidence." It is a brave picture this, of the young Rousseau, just turned sixteen, going out boldly to face unknown dangers. Unfortunately, the strength of mind and character it suggests is not confirmed by his own record of the events that followed his running away. For some days he lingered about the outskirts of Geneva, taking advantage of the hospitality of some peasants of his acquaintance; and even when he could

stay with them no longer and set off from the city, he got no further than Confignon, a little village in Savoy about five miles from Geneva, where his slender resources came to an end.

In this extremity he bethought him of the welcome the Catholics of Savoy were ready to give to wanderers like himself, and with all the confidence of extreme youth walked boldly into the proselytising trap by paying a visit to the Vicar of Confignon. Having been brought up in ultra-Protestant Geneva, he had up to this time regarded Catholicism as a system of the grossest idolatry. But as his heart grew warm with the viands and wine set before him by the Vicar, his scruples vanished, and he became willing to be considered a possible convert, and fell in with the arrangement made to send him to Annecy to enjoy the hospitality of a certain Madame de Warens, who was wont to extend her bounty to "curs disposed to sell their faith." The plan, it is true, was not altogether to his liking, and only his poverty made him consent. Prepossessed with the picture of Madame de Warens as a stern devotee of advanced years, he lingered on the journey as long as he could in order to delay his arrival at Annecy. What was his surprise to find her a young and beautiful woman of twenty-eight, with "a face of perfect charm, fine blue eyes full of tenderness, a ravishing complexion, and a neck of enchanting contour." From the first moment of their meeting he became her proselyte, convinced that a religion preached by such a missionary must certainly lead to Paradise.[1] Madame de Warens, for her part, was

---

[1] Rousseau is right in calling himself her proselyte. That he continued a good Catholic for twenty-six years was largely due to his intimate association with her for the first half of the time. Under

scarcely less pleased with the lad, and would fain have
given him a permanent place in her household; but
considerations of propriety, it seemed, were against the
idea, and after a short sojourn in her house Rousseau
was sent on his travels again, this time over the Alps
to Turin, where there was an institution for the instruction of proselytes. Here, if his own story is to be
credited, he was shut up as in a prison, and after four
months' argumentation was cajoled into renouncing the
faith of his fathers, and then turned adrift in the streets
of Turin with a parting gift of twenty francs.

So long as the money lasted Rousseau was perfectly
happy, wandering about and seeing all the sights of the
town. Then he set himself to look for work. After
a vain attempt to turn his training as engraver to
account,[1] he was obliged to take service as a uniformed
lackey with the Countess of Vercellis, and continued
in her service till her death a few months later. After
some weeks of idleness and dissipation, during which he
lived on a gift of money received on leaving the Vercellis household, he entered the service of the Comte de
Gouvon. Here, as he says with some bitterness, he was
still a lackey; but he had little real cause for complaint.[2]

other circumstances his Catholicism would have been allowed to drop
off after he had exhausted its temporal advantages. That at any rate
was his first intention.

[1] At this point in the *Confessions* Rousseau enters into a long story
about one of his interminable love affairs. As it is quite impossible to
give anything like a proper view of his relations with women without
going into the subject at too great length, I have passed over this
feature of his biography altogether. Except for its bearing on the discussion of the education of women, it is not specially relevant to our
present purpose.

[2] It seems to me that M. Lemaître in his excellent book on Rousseau,
in working out an idea suggested by M. Girardin, exaggerates the permanent effects on Rousseau's view of life, of the humiliation felt by him
when he had to serve as lackey. According to M. Lemaître, it is
" l'ancien laquais qui écrira le *Discours sur l'Inegalité* " (pp. 20–22).

He won the good opinion of his employers, and the
Abbé de Gouvon, his master's son, finding he knew some
Latin, undertook to teach him more and other things
beside. "Thus," he comments, "by one of those oddities
which have occurred so often in the course of my life, I
was pupil and lackey in the same house, and though but
a servant, had a teacher whose birth would have qualified
him for that office even with the children of kings."
What the intentions of this family were with regard to
Rousseau is uncertain. Probably Rousseau guessed
rightly when he thought they wished to train him to be
a confidential secretary and agent. Whatever their plans,
they were frustrated by his impatience. "My foolish
ambition only sought fortune along a path of adventure,
and as I saw no woman in it all, this way of getting on
struck me as slow and painful." Rather than endure
the restraint, he deliberately set himself to provoke
dismissal, and with some difficulty finally succeeded
in accomplishing his purpose.

2. *Madame de Warens.*—All the time Rousseau was in
Turin he had kept in touch with Madame de Warens by
an interchange of letters. Immediately he was free again
his thoughts turned to her, and off he set to walk back
to Annecy. This time Madame de Warens made no
difficulty about taking him into her house. "People
may say what they like," she said. "Providence has
sent him back, and I am determined not to turn him
away." And now began a season of pure delight for
Jean Jacques. "From the first day, the sweetest
familiarity was established between us, and it lasted
without change for the rest of her life. She called me
'Little One,' I called her 'Mamma'; and so we continued to do even after the passing of the years had
almost effaced the difference of age. It seems to me

that those sweet names exactly indicated the spirit of
our life, the simplicity of our manners, and above all the
relation of our hearts." The time certainly passed very
agreeably for Rousseau. He acted as a kind of secretary
for his patroness, helped her in her alchemic experiments, and entertained her motley gathering of guests.
Part of his leisure was spent, with much profit to himself, among the books he found in his room. Of these,
he notes, the one that pleased him most was the
Spectator.[1]

In the meantime Madame de Warens had been
making plans for his future, with which (as he says
himself) he could easily have dispensed, since their
execution meant the ending of this time of idyllic
happiness. On the advice of one of her kinsmen, he
was sent to the Lazarist Seminary at Annecy to be
trained as a priest. Here he began once more the
study of Latin, but failed to make progress;[2] and
finally was sent back to his patroness with the un-
flattering report that, though a good enough boy and
free from vice, he was unfit for the priesthood. Undis-
couraged by this failure, she next sought to find him a
vocation in which his musical interest might be turned
to account, and sent him off to reside with the choir-
master of the cathedral, and to be instructed by him.
At first this venture promised well; but in the end,
largely through the fault of the master, it stopped
before Rousseau's studies were near completion, and
by an unhappy combination of circumstances, into

[1] " The point of interest to us is that Rousseau understood and loved
an Addison whose genius, in common with his own, possessed a rare
and precious quality of moral elevation."—TEXTE, *J.-J. Rousseau*
p. 124.

[2] " It is singular," he comments on this, " that though I have a good
enough understanding, I have never been able to learn anything with
any masters except my father and M. Lambercier."—*Confessions*, iii.

which there is no need to enter, separated him from Madame de Warens for two years.

3. *Rousseau's Wanderings.*—During these two years Rousseau lived a roving life, gaining a precarious livelihood by devices that were not always above reproach. His wanderings, which included a visit to Paris that disappointed his expectations, probably did something to confirm the tendency to vagabondage and unsettled habits which he had got from his father,[1] and certainly provided the future writer with experiences of the greatest value. It was during his long walks through "one of the finest countries in the world" that the love for wild nature and for the ways of simple country folk, which coloured all his subsequent thinking, took possession of him. To these years of later adolescence, indeed, rather than to his childhood (as he himself suggests), are to be attributed the beginnings of the passion for nature which made him the chief pioneer of the modern romantic literature of Europe. The sentimentalism of the later writings is already manifest in the Rousseau who makes a three or four days' pilgrimage to the birthplace of Madame de Warens on the Lake of Geneva, and, melting with tenderness, sighs and weeps like a child in the happiness of melancholy. Perhaps we may also find in the experiences of this period the source of some of his revolutionary thoughts about the constitution of society. There is little doubt that it was in the course of his wanderings he obtained for

---

[1] "Le vagabondage est chez lui une passion. Il aime vivre au hasard. Apprenti greffier, graveur, laquais, valet de chambre, séminariste, employé au cadastre, maître de musique, on peut dire que, dans les longs intervalles de ces diverses occupations, il redevient volontairement et autant qu'il peut, un errant, un chemineau. C'est son gout dominant. . . . C'est à cette vie errante dans un des plus beaux pays du monde . . . que Rousseau doit son intelligence et son amour de la nature."—LEMAÎTRE, *J.-J. Rousseau*, p. 19.

himself an insight into the lives of the common people
of France, and saw the sufferings inflicted on them by
misgovernment and oppression;[1] and when he came
to write on social questions this made itself felt in
a certain strain of bitterness that had in it more of
sympathy with the unfortunate poor, whom he knew
and loved, than the sense of personal wrong.

4. *Rousseau's Studies.*—For the history of the next
eight or nine years, up to the time of his departure for
Paris, the reader must be referred to the *Confessions*
or to any of the numerous biographies of Rousseau
which amplify and correct his own story. Apart from
interludes, of which there were not a few, the greater
part of these years was spent in the company of Madame
de Warens at Chambéry. The changing of occupations
still went on as before. Beginning as a clerk in government employ, he subsequently tried to earn a living
as a teacher of music, then became Madame de Warens'
steward, and later on the tutor of the two sons of M.
de Mably, the provost of Lyons.[2]

So far as his mental history is concerned, the most
important feature of this period was the course of study
on which he entered during and after a serious illness,
which threatened his life when he was about twenty-
four.[3] He has left a curious record of his reading in a
doggerel poem entitled *Le Verger des Charmettes* which
he wrote about this time. The list of authors to whom

---

[1] It was on a journey to Lyons that there occurred the well-known
incident of his meeting with the peasant who had concealed all signs
of wealth for fear of the unscrupulous exactions of the tax-gatherer.

[2] Those who regard Rousseau as a degenerate, may find some support for their opinion in the fact that frequent change of employment
is common among degenerates. See A. Marro, *La Pubertà, studiata
nell' uomo e nella donna.* Torino, 1898.

[3] This at any rate is his own account. A less kindly critic diag-
noses his case as one of hypochondriacal melancholia.

reference is made in it is peculiarly instructive when the poem is read in connection with the subsequent development of his thought.[1]

Confining our attention to those authors who exercised a marked influence on his educational views, we note, in the first place, as specially significant, the names of Locke and of Pope. In spite of the fact that it was not till a later time that he read *Robinson Crusoe* and the *Essay on Man*—the two books which have most definitely left their mark on his educational doctrine—we may regard the reading of the two English writers at this period of his life as decisive influences in determining his whole intellectual point of view. Not only were his thoughts turned in the direction of teaching as his life work by his reading of Locke's *Thoughts on Education*, but these two writers and the author of the *Spectator*, which he had read at an earlier time, encouraged in him what he and his contemporaries recognised as the distinctively English

---

[1] It may be worth giving a few extracts from it:

" Là, portant avec moi Montaigne ou La Bruyère,
Je ris tranquillement de l'humaine misère ;
Ou bien, avec Socrate et le divin Platon,
Je m'exerce à marcher sur les pas de Caton.

. . . .

Tantôt avec Leibnitz, Malebranche et Newton,
Je monte ma raison sur un sublime ton ;
J'examine les lois des corps et des pensées ;
Avec Locke je fais l'histoire des idées ;
Avec Képler, Wallis, Barrow, Raynaud, Pascal,
Je devance Archimède, et je suis l'Hospital.
Tantôt, à la physique appliquant mes problèmes,
Je me laisse entraîner à l'esprit des systèmes :
Je tâtonne Descarte et ses égarements.

. . . .

O vous, tendre Racine ! ô vous, aimable Horace !
Dans mes loisirs aussi vous trouvez votre place :
Claville, Saint-Aubin, Plutarque, Mézerai,
Despréaux, Cicéron, Pope, Rollin, Barclai,
Et vous, trop doux Le Mothe, et toi, touchant Voltaire,
Ta lecture à mon cœur restera toujours chère."

attitude to life.[1] "To French thinkers of the seventeenth century, to Pascal and Descartes, it had seemed that the object of life was something outside life itself, that human thought found its dignity in projecting itself, if one may say so, without limit. Baconism confined thought and science to the present existence."[2] Baconism, in this wide meaning of the word, is the philosophy of Rousseau, and its influence is written large over the *Emile* and his utterances on education generally. The recurrence of the utilitarian depreciation of knowledge for knowledge' sake, and the constant insistence on the idea that human happiness can only be attained by teaching the child or the man to confine his desires and imaginations within modest limits,[3] serve to provide some measure of the greatness of Rousseau's debt to England and her thinkers.[4]

[1] The service that Locke and the other English writers rendered to Rousseau was not so much to give him new ideas as to enable him to bring his own view of life to clear consciousness. The people of Geneva, as M. Texte so admirably points out in his exposition of the relations of French and English thought in the eighteenth century (*J.-J. Rousseau*, Part I. chap. iii. : Part II. chap. ii.), are the mental kin of the English rather than of the French ; and it was consequently no alien mode of thought that Rousseau found in the writings of the great Englishmen. This does not mean, however, that he has not borrowed largely from them. The *Confession of Faith of the Savoyard Vicar* (*Emile*, iv.), for example, gives ample evidence of the greatness of his debt to English deism, especially as expounded in the *Essay on Man*.

[2] Texte, p. 84.

[3] See, for example, *Emile*, ii. 26. With this may be compared a passage quoted by M. Texte as exemplifying the " English" point of view : " ' When a man employs himself,' writes Johnson, ' upon remote and unnecessary subjects, and wastes his life upon questions that cannot be resolved, of which the solution would conduce little to the advancement of happiness : when he lavishes his hours in calculating the weight of the terraqueous globe, or in adjusting successive systems of worlds beyond the reach of the telescope ; he may very properly be recalled from his excursions by this precept [Know Thyself] and reminded that there is a nearer being with which it is his duty to be more acquainted.' " *The Rambler*, xxiv., quoted p. 85.

[4] It should be added here that it was Voltaire whose works first turned Rousseau's attention to the English writers. He " informs us

In the second place, the extent of Rousseau's acquaintance with works of science, as evidenced by the poem is worthy of note. The interest in science which dates back to this time continued unabated all through his life, and helps to explain the fact that Rousseau is the first educational thinker to recognise the vast importance of scientific matter and scientific method in the work of education. Beyond the names of the authors he professes to have read, we know nothing about the course of study he followed; but his treatment of the teaching of science in the Third Book of the *Emile* shows that he had a clear comprehension of the experimental method and of its meaning and value. Whether for that he owes most to the English scientists who were pioneers in this line of work, or to the alchemic experiments with drugs and chemicals which he wrought in conjunction with Madame de Warens, it is not possible to say on the evidence before us. But it seems probable that his appreciation of the scientific method was due to the uncommon combination at this period of his life of reading and experimental work of a personal kind.

5. *Rousseau's Choice of Teaching as his Vocation.*— The *Emile* was published in 1762 : according to its author, after twenty years' reflection and three years' labour. Counting back twenty years, we discover as the experience from which Rousseau's educational doctrine took its rise the year of tutorship spent in the household of M. de Mably. As a matter of fact, Rousseau's interest in education dates still further

that in the days when his character was forming, nothing which Voltaire wrote escaped him, and that the *Philosophical Letters*, that is *Letters on the English*, were what first attracted him to study."—MORLEY, *Voltaire*, p. 335.

back, as we learn from a letter written to his father when he was about twenty-four years of age. His father had been expostulating with him on the foolishness of his constant changes of employment, and had pointed out that though he had reached man's estate he was still unable to maintain himself. To this criticism Jean Jacques replied by detailing his plans for the future.[1] There were three careers open to him, he said : Music, which had already served him and might still serve him till a better turned up ; a secretarial post in the household of some nobleman—his talents of style, his prudence, his faithfulness and his discretion all fitted him well enough for the discharge of this function ; and finally, the one he would prefer, the office of teacher in a good family—his scientific and literary studies, and the special attention he had paid to those pursuits that are fitted to shape the heart to wisdom and virtue, had prepared him for this difficult task.

If now we ask what led Rousseau to put educational work first in order of preference, we may perhaps find an answer in the fact that this letter was written about the time when Rousseau was most busy at his studies. The French translation of Locke's *Thoughts on Education*, with which Rousseau was acquainted, was published in 1728, some seven or eight years before this,[2] and Rousseau had certainly read it in 1741. It is surely a reasonable conjecture that a book which impressed him so considerably as we know the *Thoughts* did,[3] was read at this period of study, and served to

---

[1] *Correspondance*, 1736.

[2] The first French translation was published in 1695, two years after the book had appeared in England, but the copy which Rousseau used, as he informs us in the Preface of the *Emile*, was dated 1728.

[3] See especially the Preface to the *Emile*.

turn his mind in the direction of educational work
when the practical problem of finding a suitable vocation was pressing upon him. At any rate it is worth
pointing out that Rousseau's work as a tutor was not
a mere *pis aller*, or taken up because of some accident
of circumstances, but a more or less deliberately chosen
employment in which he hoped to find the main
business of his life.

6. *The Education of M. de Mably's Sons.*—Three
years passed, however, before he was able to give effect
to his choice of vocation. After recovery from his
long illness, he continued to live with Madame de
Warens; and it was not till a certain coldness had come
between them, owing to various changes in her household which did not meet with Rousseau's approval, that
he again began to think seriously of taking steps
towards earning his living independently of her. In
this mind, he gladly accepted the invitation, which she
procured for him, to become the tutor of the two sons
of M. de Mably, the eldest brother of the famous
Condillac and of the Abbé de Mably, whose philosophical views coincided in many respects with those
subsequently held by Rousseau himself.

He entered on the work of tuition with every confidence in his own powers. He had almost the necessary amount of knowledge for a tutor's needs, as he
remarks in ingenuous self-depreciation; and he believed
that he had the capacity for teaching. But a year spent
with M. de Mably's sons sufficed to disabuse him of this
conceit. The two boys between them succeeded in
proving to him that he was unfit to be a teacher.
Sainte-Marie, the elder of them, a boy of eight or nine,
was very quick and intelligent, but too full of mischief
to attend to lessons. Condillac, the younger, on the

contrary, was too stupid to learn anything, and "as stubborn as a mule." If the story Rousseau tells of his work in the *Confessions* is to be believed, he completely failed to make any impression on either of them.[1] "At times I was so much affected in dealing with Sainte-Marie that I could not refrain from tears, and I hoped to provoke the same feeling in him, forgetting that the child was not capable of real emotion. At other times I exhausted myself talking reason to him, as if he could understand me; and as he occasionally used very subtle arguments in reply, I concluded he must be rational because he was a reasoner. The little Condillac was still more embarrassing. He understood nothing, answered nothing, was interested in nothing, and never got the better of me so completely as when he made me angry. Then he was the sage and I was the child."

Why this unexpected failure? Partly, Rousseau admits, the fault was in his own disposition. He had a natural kindliness with children, was thoroughly interested in his work and had made a careful study of the individual characters of his pupils. Yet in spite of all these things which should have given success, he failed completely. The reason for this failure, in his own opinion, was the hastiness of his temper. "When things went well and I saw my efforts meeting with success," he remarks, "I was an angel; but when they went wrong I was a devil. If my pupils did not under-

---

[1] In the *Confessions* Rousseau shows a perverse delight in exaggerating his own defects and failures. The reader must make allowance for this in reading this story. Probably his failure with M. de Mably's sons was not quite so complete as he represents it. Nevertheless, it was a failure. Cf. *Emile*, i. 71. "I once made a trial at the work of teaching, sufficient to convince me that I was unfit for it." The apologetic note in the *Projet pour l'Éducation de M. de Sainte-Marie* (*vide infra*) is convincing enough testimony that things had not gone well with him in his teaching venture.

stand me, I raged at them; and when they became mischievous, I could have killed them. My behaviour was certainly not calculated to make them either good or wise." He puts forward as another explanation of his lack of success his inability to understand the child's point of view. The only instruments he could use in governing the boys, he says, were sentiment, reasoning, and anger, all of them "always useless and often pernicious in dealing with children." Of the folly of a method that employs these instruments there can be no question; but the real reason for his failure was where he found it first himself—in the defects of his own temperament. Probably enough he made things worse for himself and his pupils by forgetting the essential differences between children and adults: that is a common fault of the ignorant or inexperienced teacher, and is generally cured by widening knowledge and experience. But what no knowledge or experience could cure in Rousseau's case was the morbid introspective cast of mind which led him to regard offences due to mere thoughtlessness or stupidity as affronts to himself, and which produced outbursts of irritability subversive of all discipline. Too much taken up with himself ever to forget himself in the subjects he taught or to give himself up wholeheartedly to his pupils' interests, his personality was the kind that provokes opposition and conflict. Even the many admirable teaching gifts, with which his discussions of educational method show him to have been endowed, could not save him from the consequences of his neurotic disposition.[1]

7. *The Project for the Education of M. de Sainte-*

---

[1] It must not be thought that Rousseau's failure as a teacher was an exceptional phenomenon. Any hyper-subjective teacher provokes the same unrest in a class as Rousseau experienced with his pupils. *Cf.* Findlay, *Principles of Class Teaching*, p. 390.

Marie.[1]—This educational experiment went on for rather more than a year and then came to an abrupt end for some unknown reason.[2] Just before the end, Rousseau drew up an elaborate memoir for the use of M. de Mably, setting forth his views on education and making plans for an extended course of study for the elder of the two boys—subsequently published under the title, *Projet pour l'Éducation de M. de Sainte-Marie.* Though the document gives no particular indication of later genius either in the contents or in the style, it is of some considerable interest as his first writing on the subject of education. Moreover, it shows that even at this period he was reaching out in the direction of his characteristic doctrines, and it is therefore of importance in studying the development of his thought.

The opening sections are mainly personal. Rousseau admits partial failure in his dealings with the boys and attempts an indirect justification of himself. The reason for his lack of success he finds in the fact that he has had to share a divided authority with the father; and he suggests that it would be better if for the future he were given entire control. This, it is to be noted, is very different from what he says in his retrospective account of the facts in the *Confessions.* But though his explanation here removes the blame from himself and puts it on the conditions under which he worked, it need not be regarded as merely the special pleading of the self-apologist on that account. The principle that underlies his request for complete responsibility re-

---

[1] Translated in my *Minor Educational Writings of Rousseau.*

[2] Rousseau himself creates the suspicion that he was dismissed by the care he takes to remove the suspicion of dismissal. The *Project*, which was written almost immediately before he gave up his duties, takes for granted his intention to continue as the tutor of M. de Sainte-Marie for several years.

appears in the *Emile* in the demand made by the tutor, that since he is discharging the parental function, he should enjoy the full parental authority. "Emile," he says, "is virtually an orphan.[1] That he has a father and mother is a fact of little importance. Charged with their duties, I inherit all their rights. The boy should honour his parents; only to me does he owe obedience."[2] Stating this in a more general form, we get the idea that in a right education there should be one and only one person with the right to determine the various conditions of a child's development—the father when the circumstances are "natural," the tutor or instructor under the more artificial conditions that arise when the father delegates his duties to another.

From this more or less personal consideration, he goes on to a statement of what he regards as the object of education. "The end the teacher should set before him in the education of a young man," he says, "is to form the heart, the judgment, and the mind, following the order given"—which, in spite of essential difference in point of view, is a definite anticipation of the very important doctrine that mental development takes place in a series of stages which the good educator should endeavour to follow. Then in a passage which reproduces Locke's general standpoint, he goes on to point out that most teachers, and especially the pedants, regard the acquisition and accumulation of knowledge as the sole

---

[1] I have inserted the word "virtually" to prevent a mistaken interpretation of the passage which is very common with critics eager to find absurdities in Rousseau.

[2] *Emile*, i. 88. Compare also the advice given to the Prince of Wirtemberg to the effect that the governess to whom his daughter's education was entrusted should enjoy 'absolute power.' See chapter viii. (*infra*).

object of a good education, while on the other hand most fathers, being doubtful of the value of all that goes by the name of studies, are quite satisfied if their sons learn physical exercises and acquire a knowledge of the world; but that for his part he hopes to find a mean path between the two extremes by establishing his pupil in good morals before going on to impart to him the different forms of learning. There is, however, nothing specially worthy of note in this statement of the educational end, unless perhaps it is the rather vague generality that conduct is more important than knowledge, which is only a particular form of a view that appears consistently all through his writings to the effect that knowledge is worthless in itself and gets what worth it has from the conduct or action to which it leads. The most outstanding fact is that even in this first discussion of educational questions, Rousseau has broken quite definitely with the Renaissance tradition, without however going very much beyond what had already been said by Montaigne, Locke, and a number of others.

Then he comes to the question of curriculum, and here he lays special claim to novelty in what he has to say. Again, however, the novelty is only relative to existing practice. Most of what he says had already been said by others, and his detailed programme of studies is practically identical with that set forth by Locke in his *Thoughts on Education*. He begins by insisting on the importance of an informal education in religion and morals. In particular, he protests against the multiplication of precepts as unlikely to inspire the pupil with lasting principles of conduct. It is not by burdening the memory with lists of laws and of duties beyond his comprehension, he says, but by directing

mind and heart to know and experience them in a
personal way, that the principles of religion and morality
are really to be mastered; and this is best done by
treating such matters in the course of ordinary conversation, when the opportunity presents itself, rather
than by definitely prescribed studies. The same thing
holds good in the formation of a sound judgment on
social usages.[1] The method he proposes is even easier of
execution in this sphere. Let the father or the tutor
invent some special social situation and invite the boy to
say what he thinks the best course to be followed in it,
and it will not be long till he acquires an intelligent
apprehension of "the science of human affairs." "He
will learn more in two hours by this method than he
would do in a year by ordinary instruction." This whole
view, it will be seen, is based on his own experience as a
boy, and is reproduced to some extent in the peculiar
methods of the *Emile*.

The ordinary studies of the boy he proposes to limit
for the first two or three years to history, geography,
and the elements of Latin.[2] "With regard to Latin,"
he says, "I do not propose to train him by a too
methodical study, and intend to avoid the composition
of themes altogether. Themes, according to M. Rollin,[3]
are children's crosses; and in pursuance of my intention
to make his studies agreeable to him, I shall take good
care to let him escape this cross. A young man,
especially if intended for the army, studies Latin to
understand it and not to write it; and indeed will

---

[1] Rousseau seems to mean here judgment on social matters and not
judgment in the intellectual sense. He occasionally uses the word in
the same way in the *Emile*.

[2] His pupil was about eight years of age at the time.

[3] Rollin: *Treatise on Studies* (First two volumes, 1726: the next
two, 1728).

not need to write it once in a lifetime. It is enough, therefore, for him to translate the ancient authors and to acquire the taste for good Latinity and for literature through reading them." At a later stage the pupil will study natural history, "the most interesting of all the sciences cultivated by mankind." Then since it is not possible to go very far in physics without a knowledge of mathematics, he will get a year's mathematics. This will serve the further purpose of teaching him to reason logically and to fix his mind on his work. At a still more advanced age he will come to the study of moral and natural law through the reading of Puffendorf and Grotius, combining with this as the most important of all studies the first principles of historical method. For the rest, Logic, Rhetoric and the scholastic philosophy, which are generally reckoned as educationally valuable, are quite superfluous. When the boy is old enough he will read the Port Royal Logic and Lami's *Art de Parler;* and in the case of the latter, there will be no need to go too much into the details of tropes and figures. All that is really worth learning in what goes under the name of literature—meaning by that "the knowledge of books and authors, criticism, style, poetry, eloquence, the theatre, in a word all that helps to form the taste"— will not be learned as a serious study but as a pleasant recreation.

This curriculum, as we have noted already, is substantially the same as that proposed by Locke, with certain omissions and modifications of no great consequence. The similarity indeed is the most significant thing about it. For when we look at it in this light we see that, though very different from the educational scheme of the *Emile,* it is really a first study for the

Emile. Locke broke away from the ordinary methods
of instruction inherited from the teachers of the later
Renaissance and tried to get a method that would take
account of the nature of the learning mind as well as
the materials of knowledge—dwelling, for example, on
the somewhat crude idea which Rousseau repeats after
him in the *Project*, that the child's studies should be
agreeable to him.[1] But his attempt to modify the
traditional curriculum of studies in the same direction
was a failure. To protest against the harmful pre-
dominance of the dead languages and to broaden
out the course of study to include the sciences and
the arts, as he did, was a very necessary piece of
work for the redemption of education from its aloof-
ness from actual life; but from the point of view of
the child, which was the point of view from which
Rousseau considered both curriculum and method
in the *Emile*, the new subjects proposed by Locke
were no better than those he had rejected. To make
them acceptable to the child, the motive for learning
had still to be found in considerations extraneous to
the matter to be learned.[2] In a word, Locke began
a revolution which he did not complete. He adapted
the methods but not the subjects of instruction to the
child. It remained for Rousseau to take up Locke's
problem at the point at which it had been left by
Locke, and to develop its logical consequence by a
complete reconstruction of the curriculum, as well as

[1] "None of the things they are to learn should ever be made a
burden to them, or imposed upon them as a task."—LOCKE, *Thoughts
on Education*, § 73.

[2] The criticism which Rousseau passes on Locke in a brief footnote
in the Letter on Education in the *New Heloïse*, v. 3, is perfectly
sound: "He says more of what should be required of children than
of the means needed to obtain it." That is, he discusses curriculum
much more than method.

by fundamental changes in the methods of teaching. The *Project*, in which he is at the standpoint of Locke, shows him at the beginning of his task. If there had been no *Project*, in all likelihood there would have been no *Emile*.

CHAPTER III

THE DISCOURSE ON THE SCIENCES AND THE ARTS

1. *Rousseau in Paris.*—After the unhappy outcome
of the educational venture with M. de Mably's sons,
Rousseau returned once more to Madame de Warens;
but the attempt to re-establish their old relationship
proved a failure. After a few months of blackest
melancholy, spent chiefly among his books, he resolved to make trial of his fortunes in Paris. His
thoughts had been turned Parisward by his discovery
of a new method of musical notation embodying
the principle of the movable Doh of the modern
Tonic Solfa.[1] The discovery coming at this crisis
led him to hope that he might win fame and fortune
by bringing his system before the notice of the
leaders of thought in the city. Behold him then in
Paris in the autumn of 1741 at the age of twenty-nine
with fifteen louis of silver, a comedy which had been
written some years before, and his musical project, as his
entire resources!

He was not long in discovering that fame and fortune
were more difficult to win than he had imagined. The
people to whom he went with letters of introduction
from his late employer wished him well but could do
nothing for him; and the musical system that was to
make so great an impression on the world was damned

---

[1] In his system the musical notes were represented by figures.

with faint praise by the Academy and almost entirely ignored by the public. For a time indeed Rousseau must have had a tough battle with poverty, though no record of its details remains even in the pages of the *Confessions*. But gradually his talents and his personality won for him a certain meed of recognition. His dealings with the Academy in the matter of the musical notation, though a disappointment in themselves, helped to bring him into touch with various men of letters, notable among whom was Diderot, with whom he began a friendship that lasted several years.[1] Of more immediate practical consequence, however, was the patronage of some of those great ladies who held literary court in their *salons* and were always ready to give countenance to a man of promise. As a result of the influence of one of them he received an appointment as secretary to the French ambassador in Venice. For a time, he achieved quite an unwonted success in his new career. The business of diplomacy, with the outlook it gave on the problems of government and of society, interested him greatly, and set going in his mind trains of thought which continued long after he had abandoned this occupation and ultimately issued in the *Contrat Social*. It almost seemed as if he had found his vocation at last; but in the end the usual thing happened. He quarrelled with the ambassador and had to make his way back to Paris as well as he could, arriving there after eighteen months' absence without a franc in his pocket and with one more failure

[1] " Sa liaison avec Diderot, esprit si inspirant et si facile, devait fortifier encore plus ce goût pour les lettres, et on peut regarder les cinq ou six années que Rousseau passa dans cette société, avant d'être célèbre, comme un préparation à tous ses ouvrages."—VILLEMAIN, *Dixhuitième siècle*, p. 228. For a good comparison of the two men, see Lanson, *Histoire de littérature française*, p. 763.

added to the already long list. In the circumstances, it was some little consolation to find his old friends with one or two exceptions still well disposed to him.

2. *Thérèse Le Vasseur.*—Rousseau was not long in finding another consolation for himself.[1] Returning to the little inn where he had stayed when he first came to Paris, he was led to form an alliance with a young servant-maid named Thérèse Le Vasseur in consequence of a mild knight-errantry on her behalf. The alliance was not marriage, nor yet was it libertinism. In order (as he says in the *Confessions*) to show himself absolutely delicate, he made formal declaration to Thérèse that he would never leave her and would never marry her; and thus began a relationship which was marriage in all but name, and which lasted till Rousseau's death more than thirty years after. He only departed from this under-taking to the extent of going through a form of marriage in the last unhappy years of his life when Thérèse and he were wandering from place to place in the search for a settled abode.

There is no need to pass judgment on Rousseau in the matter of Thérèse Le Vasseur. So far as social class goes, she was in no way his inferior; but even by his own account of her she was a strange mate for an intelligent man. Despite all his efforts to teach her, she never learned to speak or read or count even passably well, and she could only write with much difficulty; she could not tell the time by the clock nor be quite sure about the proper order of the months of the year. But with all these defects, she satisfied Rousseau: "I lived with my Thérèse," he says, "as pleasantly as with the finest genius in the world."

If the story ended at this point, we might wonder at

---

[1] The expression is Rousseau's own.

Rousseau's strange taste and consider the case as one of
those unexpected partnerships which no one professes to
understand, but which may none the less be quite satisfactory to those concerned. Unfortunately there is a
lamentable sequel. In course of time a child was born.
To rid himself of this "new embarrassment," Rousseau
sent it off to the Foundling Hospital, seemingly in spite
of the mother's protests. The same thing was repeated
five times in all; and so little care was taken to make
subsequent identification possible that even when search
was made for the children some years after by one of
the ladies of Rousseau's acquaintance, no trace could be
found of them. Altogether, the story is such a sordid
one that Rousseau's admirers from his own day to this
would fain disbelieve it. Indeed the hypothesis has been
put forward at different times that the whole episode is
a fiction, and that Rousseau never had any children.[1]
Into this tangled tale we need not enter, beyond saying
that in view of all that Rousseau himself has said either
by way of extenuation or in expression of penitence, the
attempt to raise the burden of guilt in this way seems a
vain one. If Rousseau was not guilty, he believed himself to be guilty. The one fact is almost as damaging to
his reputation as the other. The student of the *Emile*,
consequently, can only read the noble words that recall
fathers and mothers to their obligations as parents and
educators, with a sense of amazement that one who saw
the path of duty so clear and well-marked should himself
have failed to walk in it.

[1] Two lines of argument have been followed, the one medical, the
other more general. The reader will find the latter at its best in Mrs.
Macdonald : *Jean-Jacques Rousseau, a new criticism*. The question is
discussed very fairly by Lemaître and by Beaudouin, judgment being
given against Rousseau by both. The chief passages in which
Rousseau refers to the matter are : *Confessions*, vii., *Emile*, i. 64,
Reveries, ix.

3. *Rousseau in the World of Letters.*—Meanwhile
Rousseau was gradually making a place for himself
among the men of art and letters of the day. These
formed a kind of guild whose members continually met
each other at the same *cafés* and in the houses of a few
of the wealthy farmers of taxes whose wives delighted
to act as patrons of the arts. The life of the Parisian
man of letters was indeed not one for which Rousseau
was well fitted. His whole upbringing had tended to
make him shy and retiring. In manners, he was somewhat clumsy and boorish; and his hypersensitive mind
exaggerated his social deficiencies until he was ready to
suspect himself at fault in the simplest speech or action.
Again and again in his *Confessions* and his *Dialogues,*
he bewails his *gaucherie* at excessive length. He can
only utter commonplaces without any force or precision
or delicacy of wit. He cannot take up fine points and
has never his answer ready. When by some happy
chance he manages to hit on a good remark, he spoils it
by endless repetition.[1] So with wearisome iteration
proceeds the confession of social helplessness.

"Barbarus his ego sum, quia non intelligor illis,"
he quotes with a morbid appropriateness as the title
motto of his *Dialogues;* and the words are written large
over the whole tale of his life in Paris. When we think
of him moving about in the world of *salons,* constantly
galled by being in the midst of a quickness of thought
and conversation in which he could take no part,
we are reminded of the description he gives of his
Emile as "a savage made to live in cities." This Rousseau who makes clumsy bows and artificial compliments

---

[1] *Rousseau juge de Jean-Jacques,* ii. D'Alembert, referring to
Rousseau at this time, speaks of him as "circonspect, timide et presque
flatteur" (*Jugement sur Émile*). Rousseau's diagnosis of his own case
in the *Emile,* iv. 406, is perfectly sound.

is so obviously out of place in the gay world that we do not wonder at his fretting and fuming throughout his intercourse with it.

4. *The Writing of the First Discourse.*—For some years Rousseau managed to eke out what must have been a scanty enough livelihood by teaching music and doing secretarial work of one kind or another, without in any way raising himself out of the common rut.[1] When fame came, it came, appropriately enough for a man of Rousseau's unsettled character, quite unexpectedly. As the incident marks the turning point of his career, it is worth telling in some detail.

One hot summer afternoon[2] in the year 1749, Rousseau —then at the "ripe age" of thirty-seven—was walking along the road from Paris to Vincennes on a visit to Diderot, who was imprisoned there. To moderate his pace, he was glancing through the *Mercure de France,* when he chanced on the question proposed by the Academy of Dijon for a prize essay: "Has the progress of the sciences and the arts tended to the purification or the corruption of morals?" "The instant I read this," he says, "I saw a new world, and became a new man." "If ever anything was like a sudden inspiration," he remarks in another account of the incident,[3] "it was the impulse within me at this reading. All at once, I felt my mind dazzled with a thousand lights. Crowds of

---

[1] It is interesting to note that one of his casual employments was the tutoring of the son of Madame Dupin, his chief patroness and employer, on one occasion when a regular tutor was not available. He was no more successful here than he had been with the sons of M. de Mably: "I passed eight days in such torments as nothing but the pleasure of obeying Madame Dupin could make endurable." The story of the headstrong child told by way of illustration in *Emile*, ii. 171, has reference to this episode.

[2] So Rousseau says in the *Confessions.* It was actually in October.

[3] *Quatre Lettres à M. de Malesherbes : lettre II.*

vivid ideas came thronging upon me with a force and confusion that threw me into an inexpressible bewilderment. . . . Not being able to breathe and to walk at the same time, I cast myself beneath one of the trees of the avenue, and there spent half-an-hour in such agitation of soul, that when I rose the whole front of my coat was wet with tears, though I had not been conscious of shedding them." In that half-hour under the trees, if we are to believe his statement, there had come into his mind a clear idea of all the evils wrought by society. " If only I could have written even a quarter of what I saw and felt under that tree," he says in a passage that reads back later reflections into this conversion time, but which may nevertheless be taken as generally true to the facts, " with what clearness would I have set forth the contradictions of our social system : with what power would I have exposed the abuses of its institutions : with what directness would I have shown that man is naturally good and that it is these very institutions that make him bad."

Full of this ferment of ideas, he hastened to Vincennes and there discussed the project of becoming a candidate for the prize, with Diderot. Following his advice, he set himself to write the *Discourse*. Night after night, as he lay sleepless, he turned over the periods in his mind until they had taken proper shape, then committed them to memory, and got Thérèse's mother to write them out at his dictation the first thing in the morning ; and after a vast labour succeeded in completing the essay, and sent it in to the Academy. After a long time of waiting, when he had almost forgotten about it, the news came that he had been awarded the prize ; and in the excitement, all the violent anti-social thoughts that the subject had provoked in him at first returned with new force, and completed the change in his attitude of mind towards society. Henceforward, he was determined to devote himself to exposing the evils of society.

The attempt has been made to suggest that the *Discourse on the Sciences and the Arts* was a mere literary *jeu d'esprit*, and that it was only its unexpected success which led Rousseau to follow the criticism of social institutions into new fields: that, in fact, Rousseau became the censor of society by what one writer calls a process of auto-intoxication.[1] Those who take this view can quote in favour of it Diderot's version of the story.[2] One day, he says, when he and Rousseau were walking together, Rousseau told him about the Academy's question and said that he was eager to treat the subject. "'What side will you take?' said I to him. 'The affirmative,' he answered. 'That is the bridge for the asses,' I told him: 'all the mediocrities will take that road and you will find only commonplace ideas on it, whereas the opposite view opens up a fresh rich field for philosophy and eloquence.' 'You are right,' said he, after a moment's reflection, 'and I shall follow your advice.'"

As a matter of fact, there is no real contradiction between the two stories. It is likely enough that Rousseau thought of following the more obvious course, for in spite of the aggressive self-assertion that he showed at times, there was an element of timidity about him which made him reluctant to leave the beaten path until he was very sure of himself; and the relations of the two men being what they were, it is likely enough that it was Diderot's advice which gave him confidence to venture for the first time on a line of expression that

---

[1] Lemaître, *J.-J. Rousseau*, p. 92.
[2] Marmontel, *Mémoires*, vii.

put him in opposition to the established order of things.[1]
But it is absurd to think that Rousseau adopted the
misanthropic *rôle* merely for rhetorical purposes, and
then deliberately followed up the success achieved by
doing so. On the contrary, it was the note of reality in
the misanthropy of the *Discourse* which forced it on the
attention of the age and saved it from the fate its
rhetoric invited. It is not to be denied that Rousseau
could have written quite a good essay from the orthodox
point of view; for Rousseau had a remarkable power of
thinking himself into the position of others, even when
he had no real sympathy with them. But for him that
would certainly have been the " asses' bridge "; and the
essay thus produced would inevitably have shared the
common fate of prize essays. As it was, he chose with
a wisdom greater than he knew, and found himself and
his vocation by entering on what was at first merely an
academic discussion. The *Discourse* only needs to be
read in connection with his life history to show how
much the writer owes to the man.

The dialectical element indeed is not wanting in the
Discourse. Rousseau himself has indicated its weakness
perfectly when he says in the *Confessions* that though
full of force and fire it lacks logical order, and that of
all his works it is the weakest in reasoning and the
most lacking in balance. But its rhetoric and paradoxes, it must be repeated, are only superficial characters.
The fact never to be forgotten about it is that its essential
ideas express the very spirit of Rousseau's life. Behind
the rhetoric and to some extent obscured by it is an

---

[1] At a later time, he attributed the violence of certain passages in
this *Discourse* and its successor to his association with Diderot. It
was his influence, he explains, which gave his writings a harsh tone and
an air of misanthropy, which they lost as soon as Diderot's influence
ceased. *Confessions*, viii.

indictment of civilisation drawn up by a man whose
whole life gave him cause to speak with a sense of
personal grievance against civilisation.[1] Consider the
terrible destitution of Rousseau in all the vital human
relations. Whether as child or man, he had never
known what real home life meant. Again and again, he
had sought congenial employment, and had always failed
to establish himself as a worker. He was proud to call
himself a citizen of Geneva, yet was condemned by
circumstances to live in permanent exile from it. And
even the kindly relations of neighbourliness, which sometimes go a long way to make good other social deficiencies,
were denied him by his own unhappy nature. Surely
no one was ever more a solitary in the midst of society
than he. If detachment from one's fellows is the main
characteristic of the man of nature, Rousseau's claim to
be the veritable man of nature must surely be admitted.[2]
It was, then, no accident that made Rousseau the
spokesman of nature against institution. Who could
more effectively lead the attack against social life than

[1] " Il n'y a pas seulement dans ce discours, comme dit la Harpe, le
dépit de n'avoir pas été invité chez madame Dupin le jour où elle
donnait son diner de gens de lettres : la blessure de Rousseau remonte
plus loin. On sent l'irritation d'un homme supérieur tenu longtemps
en dehors de la société: il y a le souvenir de sa miserable jeunesse
d'apprenti, de sa fuite sans asile et sans pain, de sa conversion forcé, de
ses métiers de laquais, de séminariste, de pauvre musicien, de
trucheman d'un moine quêteur, de copiste, de secretaire, et enfin de
commis de caisse à Paris sans pouvoir arriver à rien qu'à vivre à force
de travail."—VILLEMAIN, *Dixhuitième siècle*, p. 221.

[2] Rousseau expressly claims to be the man of nature in *Rousseau
juge de Jean-Jacques*, iii. : " A retired and solitary life, a fondness for
reverie and meditation, the habit of turning back on one's self in the
search for the primitive traits which most men have lost : these are
all necessary for the re-discovery of these traits. In a word, one man
had to depict himself in order to show us the primitive man ; and if
the author had not been as singular as his books, he would never have
written them." It is rather interesting to find a modern critic endorsing
the claim. " L'homme de la nature, le sauvage, il l'a été, il l'a vécu,
avant de le décrire."—LANSON, *Histoire de la littérature française*, p. 763.

one who owed so little to the great social institutions
of family, profession, and state that mean so much for
more ordinary men ?

5. *The Discourse on the Sciences and the Arts.*—A
curious mistake occurs in the account given in the
Confessions of the question proposed by the Academy of
Dijon for discussion.   The question, says Rousseau, was
as to the effect of the *progress* of the sciences and the
arts.   The actual subject was a much narrower one:
"Has the *re-establishment* of the sciences and the arts
made for the purification of morals ? "   The difference is
more than verbal.   The Academy's question invited a
discussion of the moral effects of the Renaissance.   But
Rousseau's quarrel was not with the Renaissance so
much as with his own age.[1]   Unless when he is engaged
in maintaining the comprehensive thesis of the first
Discourse that culture in every form is an evil, he makes
exception in favour of the classics and the Italian poetry
modelled on them that were the special studies of the
Renaissance.[2]   But though his real attack was on the
sciences and the arts of his own day, it would have been
impolitic to advance too directly to the attack in a
Discourse on which an Academy of learning was to sit in
judgment.   Accordingly, to avoid decrying the Renaissance and at the same time to express his opinion of his
contemporaries in a form not overtly offensive, he was
compelled to broaden out his problem in such a way as

[1] The suggestive sketch of Rousseau's educational views in Quick's
Educational Reformers gives quite a wrong impression on this point.
The *effect* of Rousseau's teaching was the destruction of the Renaissance
tradition, but that was only an incidental result of his attack on
civilisation in every phase.   So far was he from having a special
animus against the Renaissance that he regarded the classics as more
valuable than any modern writings.
[2] Note especially his views on the literature most suitable in the
education of the adolescent.   *Emile*, iv. 462 *seq.*

to make the Renaissance only a special case of an evil
inherent in all human institutions. He was then able
to draw his illustrations with seeming impartiality from
both the ancient and the modern world.

"It is a great and noble spectacle," he says in the
opening words of the First Part, "to see man by his
own efforts rising, so to speak, out of nothing, dissipating the darkness in which he had been enveloped
by nature by the light of his reason and rising above
himself." It must not be thought, he goes on to say,
that this has only happened once in the course of
human history. As a matter of fact, these marvels
are repeated every few generations. The revival of
the sciences and the arts which came about when
"the fall of the throne of Constantine brought to
Italy the debris of ancient Greece," and subsequently
"enriched France with these precious spoils," is but
one phase of a movement that is as old as mankind
itself.

But the progress of learning is only a blessing when
contrasted with the barbarism of an age that has sunk
into an ignorance more degrading than the first state
of man. In itself it is a curse. The direct expression of needs which reveals the nature of untutored
man in its original simplicity is crushed out for the sake
of an illusory uniformity. Art fashions the manners of
men and teaches their passions to speak a borrowed
language, until all minds, originally so different, look
as if they had been cast in a common mould.[1] The

---

[1] Rousseau returns to this theme repeatedly. For a striking elaboration of it, see *The New Heloïse*, ii. 17, in which Julie's lover describes
Parisian society to his mistress. "No one dare be himself. *One must
do as others do*—that is the first maxim of social wisdom. *Every one does
this* or *does not do this*—that is the last word on all subjects." Every
possible situation, he goes on to say, has its rule. It is settled to a

inevitable result of this change is the corruption of morals; and the further the sciences and arts advance towards perfection, the more are the souls of men corrupted.

Is this intimate connection between learning and depravity not abundantly proved by the fate of the great empires of the past? Think of Egypt, the mother of philosophy and of the fine arts, conquered by one nation after another; of Greece, once peopled by heroes, falling before Macedonia when luxury and the arts had corrupted her morals; of Rome, losing her primitive virtues and becoming degenerate from the time of her first poets; and of Constantinople with a black record of crime in spite of her pre-eminence in the arts and sciences. Or coming to a modern instance: "There is a large country in Asia where literature is held in such honour that the highest posts in the State are in the hands of literary men. If the sciences really helped to make men more moral and more devoted to their country, then the people of China ought to be free, wise, and invincible. But what is the actual state of matters? There is no vice which does not flourish among them, no crime with which they are not familiar." The counter-proof is afforded by the few cases in which nations have retained their innocence and their vigour by saving their citizens from the plague of learning: the ancient Persians, the Scythians, the Germans, the Romans in the days of their poverty and ignorance, the savages of America, and, most notable of all, Sparta,

nicety when one should call and when only a letter need be sent; when one ought to be at home; the offers it is right to make and to accept; the length of time one should be absent from town after a bereavement; the exact degree of sadness to be shown on the death of different people. All do precisely the same thing in the same circumstances as if they were so many soldiers or marionettes.

"that republic of demi-gods rather than of men, as famous for its happy ignorance as for the wisdom of its laws."

After laying the foundations of his thesis on this pseudo-history,[1] Rousseau proceeds in the Second Part to show in some detail what evils learning has wrought, and mentions the fostering of luxury, the corruption of art and science themselves, the loss of the military virtues and the depraving of youth by means of a bad education. There is no need to follow him through the confused medley of this part of his discussion. It will be a sufficient illustration of its tenor to quote his remarks on education.

"If the cultivation of the sciences is prejudicial to the martial qualities of a people," he says, "it is still more so to the moral qualities. From our very first years, an absurd education bedecks our minds and corrupts our judgments. On all hands I see immense institutions, where young people are educated at great expense and taught everything but their duty. Your children do not know their mother-tongue and yet speak others that are used nowhere. They can compose verses which are almost beyond their comprehension. Without being able to distinguish truth from error, they have the art of confusing others by specious arguments. Yet they do not know the meaning of words like 'magnanimity,' 'equity,' 'temperance,' 'humanity,' and 'courage.' The sweet word 'fatherland' never falls on their ear; and if they hear God mentioned, it is as a being to be dreaded rather than reverenced. To repeat the words of one wise man: 'I would rather my pupil passed his time

[1] It must be remembered that, as Morley points out, " Rousseau was entirely wanting in either taste or serious regard for history " (*Voltaire*, p. 293), and that he fashions it to suit his argument.

playing at ball. If he got no other good, his body at
any rate would be more nimble.' I am aware that
children need to be kept busy and that idleness is the
danger most to be dreaded in dealing with them.
What, then, should they learn ? That really is a fine
question ! Let them learn what they must do when
they come to be men, and not what they had better
forget." [1]

It has been necessary to follow the line of thought in
the *Discourse*, not for its intrinsic merits, which indeed
are but moderate, but because it is scarcely possible to
understand the various applications of Rousseau's social
philosophy unless we see it in its origin. Let us be
clear, then, about its import. Ostensibly it is an attack
on all forms of culture which are comprehended under
the terms " science " and " art." [2] In reality, it cuts down
to the very roots of civilisation. For if we ask what
is the gravamen of the charges brought by Rousseau
against culture, we find as the fundamental offence that
the varied forms assumed by culture are all products
of the human reason. " Are we to say that the evil
wrought by the sciences and the arts is peculiar to our
own age ? " he asks. " No, gentlemen ! the evils caused
by our vain curiosity are as old as the world." Here in
a phrase we get to the very core of Rousseau's doctrine
of man and society. The sciences and the arts, everything in which society ministers to more than the
physical being of man, is but the product of a vain
curiosity. Reason, in dissipating the darkness in which

---

[1] Rousseau adds a long quotation from Montaigne—the " wise man "
to whom he refers—about the education of the Spartans.

[2] In this connection, it is significant that Rousseau uses the words
"the sciences and the arts " as a stock phrase, and makes no attempt
to discuss the two constituents of it separately. In other words, he is
not really discussing the " sciences " and the " arts," but the culture
of which they are typical expressions.

nature had enveloped man, did him the momentous disservice of raising him "above himself." "Himself," on this view of things, was in the first instance a creature with merely corporeal wants, a body without soul or mind. Then somehow or other the meddling intellect appeared on the scene and added the mental to the purely animal wants; and urged on by this vain curiosity which made it impossible for him to confine himself within his original limits, man gradually created for himself various social institutions to satisfy these new wants. All this indeed is but hinted at in the *Discourse;* for there is a striking absence of the psychological analysis which is one of the most valuable features of his subsequent writings. But even in the absence of explicit analysis, it is not difficult to discern the later psychology taking shape. The vain curiosity that works such mischief in man's life is reason deserting its primary function of ministering to animal wants and setting up fresh wants of its own which are really alien to man's nature; and the sciences and the arts which come into being as a result of this illegitimate extension of the operations of reason are but exaggerated forms of the deeper disease of social life.

In short, what we have here is the dominant antithesis of Rousseau's philosophy of life, the antithesis of nature and society, in its first crude form. The opposition, indeed, is not stated anywhere in the *Discourse* in so many words. One might almost say that the conception of a state of nature in which man could live truer to himself than is possible under ordinary social conditions had not yet taken form at the time when the *Discourse* was written. Once or twice he refers to "nature," but he makes no attempt to define or explain it. Seemingly the idea of a state of nature meant for him at this time nothing more than the primitive animal condition, the condition of man apart from society; nature was only that-which-is-not-society. In other words, the fundamental motive of his thought in the discussion of culture and civilisation in the *Discourse* was a mere negation. He writes out of a deep sense of dissatisfaction with all the institutional products of the human spirit, and the result is criticism and condemnation unrelieved by any touch of idealism from a faith in a possible better. Like the Preacher, he can see nothing but vanity in all the works that men do under the sun: all is but "vanity and striving after wind." Not that Rousseau is a misanthrope in the ordinary sense of the word. That charge he would have repelled with indignation.[1] Even though the saving distinction between the goodness of the individual and the badness of society that plays so large a part in the later writings is not to be found in the *Discourse*, there is certainly nothing in its argument contrary to the spirit of the distinction. Towards his fellows, Rousseau shows no bitterness. Now as always, his complaint is against the evils inherent in the constitution of society. But, misanthrope or no misanthrope, his *Discourse* is the expression of a most thorough-going cynicism. Regarding all the developments of man's reason as so many excrescences on his nature, he is forced to think of the ideals of humanity as wholly due to a disordered imagination which creates a vain unrest and then seeks a futile satisfaction in culture; and ultimately he is led to deny the worth of

---

[1] In a letter written to a correspondent who thought of renouncing society altogether, in the very year when the *Discourse* was written (1749), he calls the misanthropes " the mortal enemies of the human race." *Cf.* also *Rousseau juge de Jean-Jacques*, ii. : " The real misanthrope, if a being so contradictory can exist. . . . " For real misanthropy, however, see his *Correspondance*, Oct. 13, 1758.

all the social relationships save those that are concerned with the beggarly rudiments of physical existence. Diogenes in his tub was not more out of touch with the common life of men than Rousseau attacking the sciences and the arts.

6. *The Permanent Cynicism in Rousseau's Thought.*— It is not possible for a person with a sane mind to continue permanently in a merely negative attitude. Sooner or later the attempt to give voice to dissatisfaction leads one beyond it. This is what happened in Rousseau's case. In the second *Discourse* he set himself to define with exactness the implicit ideas of the *Discourse on the Sciences and the Arts;* and later on he proceeded to a constructive application of his principles which led him beyond the crude cynicism of this period to some kind of reconciliation of the conflicting ideas of nature and society. And yet, though he was led by the evolution of his thought and experience to modify his attitude to society, the change was never entirely completed. Even with the recognition of social institutions as in some sense natural, or at any rate as not wholly unnatural, there persists some of the anti-social bitterness of the first *Discourse*, which leads to the constant intrusion of ideas difficult to reconcile with those more true to the later point of view. The consequence is a certain lack of unity about all the later writings. Like some great building begun in one age and finished in another, in which old style and new appear in discordant combination, they can never be made wholly harmonious. This must always be kept in mind by the student of the *Emile* and the other writings of the later and worthier period when he finds adjacent ideas in patent contradiction.

The explanation of this conflict of old and new is

comparatively simple. In the first place, it must be remembered that Rousseau was nearly forty years of age before finding utterance for his deepest thoughts.[1] Under any circumstances, ideas that have behind them the experience of well-nigh a lifetime are almost certain to form a static element in the structure of mind, which resists change of any kind; and when these ideas do not come to clear consciousness till an age when the mind has lost the plasticity of youth—as in Rousseau's case—it is almost inevitable that they should maintain themselves in something like their first form whatever changes a wider experience may have brought. In the second place, Rousseau was, as a rule, little distressed by the appearance of inconsistency in his arguments. Marvellously acute and rigidly logical in the development of any idea that interested him, his was the intuitive rather than the logical type of mind, the mind that does not easily grasp the relation of the ideas with which it is dealing to other ideas outside its immediate interest. It was a right judgment he passed on himself when he said that he did not think in wholes. Absorbed in the ideas immediately before him, he rarely attempted to bring his thoughts on different subjects into the unity of a system.[2] His thinking was more a process of musing

---

[1] In his comments on the *Emile* at the time of its publication, Grimm rightly refers to this as a fact that helps to explain Rousseau's attitude to life: " Un des grands malheurs de M. Rousseau, c'est d'être parvenu à l'age de quarante ans sans se douter de son talent." *Correspondance litteraire*, v.—June 1762.

[2] In reply to d'Alembert, who had charged him with inconsistency, he urged that the truth changes its form according to time and place, and that what might be said in Paris should perhaps not be said in Geneva. The Marquis of Mirabeau wrote to him : " Vous êtes toujours vrai selon votre conscience momentanée." Compare also Diderot's judgment on him : " Sa philosophie, s'il en a une, est de pièces et de morceaux."—BRÉDIF, pp. 41, 52.

than of active reflection, and he was generally content
to let the argument carry him along with it, indifferent
to a paradoxical ending or even to a flagrant inconsistency. It is obvious that with a mind like this, which
felt its way to the truth rather than forced experience
to yield up its meaning to the demands of thought,
the co-existence of two irreconcilable views of life was
possible without causing any serious inconvenience.[1]

The best demonstration of this characteristic double-
mindedness of Rousseau is furnished by the detailed
study of a treatise like the *Emile,* in which he is
dealing with a subject like education, which forces
him to abandon his first social philosophy and yet
provides continual temptation to relapse into it. As
it is important to realise how much the attitude of
mind that crystallised in the attack on the sciences
and the arts affected his subsequent thought, one or
two illustrations may be given from the later views
on education.

The first will be a curious story from the *Memoirs*
of Madame d'Epinay, sometimes told as illustrating
Rousseau's general educational position, but more cor
rectly taken as marking the transition to his later views.
" I was conversing with Rousseau and M. de Margency,"
she writes to Grimm in 1757, " on the method that Linant
[the tutor] was following with my son. . . . All at once
it occurred to me to remark that it was a very difficult
matter to educate a child. 'I agree with you, madame,'
Rousseau replied, ' seeing that nature has not made
fathers and mothers to educate, nor children to be
educated.' This reply of his bewildered me. ' What

[1] The student may get some light on the mind of Rousseau by
reading carefully the brilliant self-analysis of *Rousseau juge de Jean-
Jacques,* ii.

do you mean?' said I. Margency burst out laughing, and added what I had not dared to add: 'You have an educational scheme of your own in your head, have you not?' 'That is quite true,' replied Rousseau in the same matter-of-fact tone."

Here in this story we have the conflicting ideas presented in the briefest compass. Rousseau begins with the unqualified assertion that education as part of the whole system of social life is essentially an artifice that has no basis in the original nature of parents or children; and then, with a complete turn round, admits that he has an educational plan of his own, which would presumably be "according to nature."

When we come to the *Emile*, in which this educational scheme was embodied, we find the same phenomenon. For example, consider the fact that the tutor takes the boy away to a country village to get a suitable environment for him. Why does he do so? Rousseau suggests two answers which presuppose fundamentally different views of the relations of men in society. The first is that under the conditions of village life is to be found the closest approximation to complete isolation that can be got in a civilised country.[1] Even in a village, of course, he will not escape the perverting influences of society. "But where are we to put the child to bring him up as an unintelligent automaton?[2] Shall we keep him in the moon or on a desert island?

[1] For the point of view, compare *Rousseau juge de Jean-Jacques*, i., " In human society, all that the wise man can do is to withdraw himself from the world as much as possible, and to remain where chance has placed him, satisfied that by doing nothing he avoids running into harm and falling into new errors."

[2] This is only an exaggerated expression of the principle of negative education. Rousseau's view is that until the boy reaches the age of fifteen, when intellect and conscience both begin to function, the boy is virtually an automaton in conduct.

Are we to separate him from every human being? If he lives in the world, he will constantly have before him the spectacle and example of others. He will see other children of his own age, he will see his parents, his neighbours, his governess, his lackey, and even his tutor, who after all will not be an angel. This objection is a weighty one." [1] But there is another answer to the question, which may be taken as the mature conviction of Rousseau when his judgment was not perverted by the prejudice left in his mind by the earlier anti-social view which he had for the most part outgrown. It is that the tutor took the boy to a village, not with the intention of attempting the impossible task of escaping from society, but for the purpose of finding a community of a simple order which he could so far control that every factor in it might be made to promote the right development of his pupil as a member of society.

Let us take another example from the *Emile*. In the Second and Third Books Rousseau decrees that the boy is not to study history till he reaches adolescence. Here again in his various utterances we find the same mixture of motives. On the one hand, there is the sound principle that abstract subjects demanding the mature mind of the adult for their comprehension are out of place in the curriculum of the child, whose mind is largely confined within the world of the senses. This, for the most part, is the argument used for the exclusion of the humanistic subjects from the primary education. But, on the other hand, another argument, hinted at rather than developed, is that history, consisting of the records of social life, is *ipso facto* an evil thing calculated to give a wrong bias to the immature mind. So

---

[1] *Emile*, ii. 70.

far as this idea enters into the discussion, we have a lapse into the cynicism of the first *Discourse*.

Further illustration will be provided by our study of the *Emile*. It may only be noted in conclusion that, taken as a whole, the *Emile* shows the same undecided attitude of mind. We may, if we will, regard the *Emile* as the application of the cynical view of social relations in the sphere of education. That is the common view. Or, again, we may see in it an attempt to bring about a reconciliation between nature and society in a phase of life that is related to both nature and society. That is the view which does more justice to Rousseau's intention. But probably we come nearest the truth if we recognise that Rousseau's outlook is not single but double, and that his advance towards the truth is always hampered by the persistence of earlier error.

CHAPTER IV

THE DISCOURSE ON INEQUALITY

1. *The Maturing of Rousseau's Genius.*—The judgment of the Academy with regard to the *Discourse on the Sciences and the Arts* was promptly confirmed by the interest of the public. "Its success is quite unprecedented," wrote Diderot to the author. From obscurity, Rousseau at once passed into the full light of literary fame. A flattering number of writers hurried forward to the defence of the sciences and the arts, including no less a man than Stanislaus, King of Poland. To have a king for an adversary, as M. Beaudouin says, is an honour which does not come to a man of letters every day; and Rousseau duly appreciated the honour. Though protesting against the time wasted by the task, Rousseau replied at length to Stanislaus and the more important of his other critics; and though he made no substantial addition to the ideas already expounded, he revealed himself even more than in the *Discourse* as the master of a clear, incisive style of writing, and showed a surprising genius for controversial exposition.[1] It was more than ever evident that a new force had appeared in French literature.

The effect of this success was nowhere more manifest than in the change that came over Rousseau himself.

---

[1] Rousseau, says Villemain, had in the highest degree "le génie de la controverse et de l'à-propos." *Dixhuitième siècle*, p. 281.

The increasing directness and forcefulness of his controversial utterances was indicative of a profound change in his outlook on life. After long waiting, with the heart growing ever more weary, he had found himself; and the discovery declared itself in the growing certainty of expression and in the rapid ripening of all his powers. "From the lively effervescence which began in his soul at this time," wrote Rousseau about himself long afterwards, "there burst forth flashes of genius that lighted with brilliance everything he wrote through ten years of fever and delirium; and for a season he astonished Europe by productions in which common souls saw only eloquence and wit, but which won the recognition of the noblest and best as worthy to rank with their own." [1]   This is indeed an extravagant claim, but assuredly not too extravagant, as the reader of the extraordinary series of books produced in rapid succession in these ten fevered years may judge for himself.

2. *The Discourse on Inequality.*—The first of these was another prize Discourse.[2] Again it was the Academy of Dijon which gave Rousseau his chance. In the first *Discourse*, and subsequently in one of his *Replies*, he had referred with some warmth to the evils of inequality among men as the root of all the evils that vex society; and the Academy, which had evidently been satisfied with the distinction that had come to it through its laureate, seemed to have set its new subject to draw forth another dissertation from him. The subject proposed was : What is the source of inequality among men, and how far is it in accordance with natural law ?

---

[1] *Rousseau juge de Jean-Jacques*, ii.
[2] This time Rousseau was not awarded the prize.

If the subject was not devised for Rousseau, it was certainly one likely to suit him. During the intervening years his mind had been busy following up the train of ideas suggested but not developed in the first *Discourse*, and even his social manners bore witness to his change of view. In outward token of his contempt for all conventions, and in the endeavour to bring his practice into line with his theory, he adopted a garb that was ostentatiously simple: he ceased wearing lace and silk stockings, laid aside his sword, and sold his watch, thanking heaven that he would no longer need to know the hour. At the same time, he determined to refrain from every employment that would make him subject to the will of others, and announced himself ready to copy music at so much a page.[1] More important as an indication of the movement of his thought than this theatrical renunciation of the ways of the world was the note of revolution which began to appear in his *Replies* to his critics, all the more significant because it was accompanied by a deepening reflection with regard to the meaning of the appeal to nature made uncritically in the first *Discourse*. The *Last Reply* is specially worthy of note; for in it we see Rousseau making his way to the distinction between the goodness of man and the badness of society, which changed his problem from a sociological one with which he was not specially fitted to deal, into one of psychology in which he was a master, and so prepared the way for the second *Discourse*.

If in discussing the origin of inequality among men he had continued to follow the line of thought begun

[1] Here Rousseau's sentiment got the better of his logic. Even in copying music, a man becomes the servant of his patrons, as Rousseau soon discovered when Parisian society came calling on him to give orders for work.

in the first *Discourse*, he would probably have contented himself with an historical treatment of the subject, and attempted to show that contemporary social conditions were the result of a decline and fall from primitive grace. This indeed is what he is generally believed to have done; and the historical framework on which his ideas are arranged is partly responsible for the misinterpretation. Nevertheless, it is only a careless reading of the *Discourse*, and especially of the very explicit statements of the Preface, that makes such a misinterpretation possible. What Rousseau is really concerned to discover is not the details of life in a long-forgotten state of nature, of which he himself frankly says that it is impossible to say anything, but those ultimate facts about human nature which are the basis of society.

There is only one way to understand the differences among men that are manifest in the inequalities of social life, he points out in the Preface: that is, to know man's nature. The difficulty is that, do what we will, it is scarcely possible "to distinguish what is original and what is artificial" in man as we know him.[1] To make that distinction, we must get back to "man as nature has made him, right through all the modifications produced in his original constitution by the long succession of time and circumstances, and separate what is essential from the changes and additions made to his primitive condition by accident and by progress." The human soul is not unlike the sea-god Glaucus, which was so disfigured by wind and tide that it was more like

---

[1] As a matter of fact, it is not merely difficult but impossible. Many of the difficulties of Rousseau's social philosophy proceed from the attempt to maintain as absolute a distinction that is only relative.

a wild beast than a god.[1] In the course of the ages,
it has been so much changed in society—by the acquisition of a multitude of truths and errors, by modifications of the physical constitution, and by the jarring
of the passions — as to be well-nigh unrecognisable.
The only conclusion which the facts seem to warrant
is that we can never know what kind of a being the
primitive ancestor of man was. The human race
differs from age to age : for which reason Diogenes
failed to find a man, because he sought among his
contemporaries for the man of an age that no longer
existed. And for the same reason the quest for a
sure knowledge of the original nature of man will
always end in failure. What, then, are we to do ?
Obviously, if we are to make the distinction between inherent and acquired characters in human
nature, the materials for our investigation must be
found in the men of our own age, and our results will
always be more or less conjectural. The facts are
before us : the difficulty is in the interpretation of
them. All that any man can claim, all that Rousseau
claims for himself, is that his view of the constitution
of man makes it easier to understand humanity as we
know it.

3. *The Hypothetical Man of Nature.*—What Rousseau
says about the state of nature must be read in the light
of the explicit statement that he makes no pretension
to historical truth. "Let us begin," he says in words
open to misconstruction but nevertheless quite intelligible, "by setting aside all the facts." It is a matter
of no consequence whether the first man had long nails
like talons, as Aristotle supposed, or had a covering of
skin like that of the bear, or walked on all-fours. These

---

[1] The illustration is borrowed from Plato.

are questions of fact that have no particular bearing on the problem in hand. The picture he proposes to draw of the state of nature has nothing to do with the actual history of mankind. It is avowedly hypothetical, "intended to throw light on the nature of things rather than to show their real origin," just like those hypotheses which, as Rousseau rightly points out, physicists are constantly making in discussing the structure of the universe.[1] In short, when Rousseau refers to the state of nature, he would have us understand that he is speaking of "a state which no longer exists, which it may be never did exist, and which probably never will exist, but of which nevertheless we need to have proper ideas if we are to judge rightly concerning our present condition."

Let us see, then, what Rousseau has to say about this imaginary man of nature. Taking full advantage of the liberty he has claimed to follow the course suggested by his own speculations, he begins by assuming that from all time man's form has been much what it is to-day: that men have always walked on two feet, used their hands as they use them now, and stood erect, able to survey the whole of nature and to measure the vast expanse of heaven with their eyes. The one thing that distinguishes the primitive man from his latter-day fellow is the absence of what Rousseau calls the supranatural gifts (by which, of course, he means the special characteristics that man owes to society) and of the artificial faculties that have been acquired during his long development. "When I think of this man as he must

---

[1] Examples from modern science will readily occur to the reader: for example, the mental pictures employed by the chemist when discussing molecular structure, the physicist's hypothetical conception of the atom, the biologist's conception of the germ cell and its elements.

have been when he came forth from the hands of nature," he says, "I see an animal less strong than some of the animals, less agile than others, but, taking him all in all, better organised than any of them. I see him satisfying his hunger under an oak, quenching his thirst at the first stream, and finding his bed under the same tree that furnished his repast: and lo, all his wants are satisfied!" Constantly exposed to inclement weather and accustomed to defend himself from the attacks of wild beasts or to seek safety in flight, he needed to be sturdy and vigorous; and his children, inheriting his constitution and strengthening it by means of the same exercises that produced it, acquired all the strength of which the human frame is capable. "Nature dealt with them precisely as the law of Sparta dealt with the children of the citizens. She strengthened those with a good constitution and allowed the others to perish." In a word, the primitive man was in all essential respects an animal, sufficient unto himself. He can only be described in negative terms: "without industry, without speech, without a dwelling-place, without wars and without allies, without need of his fellows and without any desire to harm them, perhaps without ability to recognise them individually."

4. *The Original Element in Man's Nature.*—Now that we have made the acquaintance of the man-in-himself, the question which rises is how far the fiction helps us to distinguish the original man from man as society has made him. Does it help us at all? It is doubtful; for, in effect, all that Rousseau tells us by means of his fiction is that the natural man is an animal, and consequently that if we are to separate the original from the acquired in social man, we must begin by finding out the characteristics of animal man.

As a matter of fact, the *Discourse* does not depend for its value on the imaginary picture it gives of primitive times, but on the analysis made of human nature on the assumption that man was originally only an animal.

Leaving the quasi-historical conception of a state of nature out of account, let us see what Rousseau has to tell us about the characters that pertain to man considered merely as an animal. "Savage man," he tells us, "begins with purely animal functions. His first state is one of perception and feeling, in which respect he is the same as all the animals. To will and not to will, to desire and to fear, are the first and almost the only operations of his soul up to the time when new circumstances bring about further developments." The first men, then, were limited to "pure sensations":[1] they learned about the world through the senses, and their only ideas were sense-ideas formed by the concourse of several sensations.[2] With this state went certain simple emotional reactions (or, as Rousseau usually names them, "passions") which provided the appropriate response to these sense-given ideas in the form of actions, expressing either desire or fear. In later stages man desires or fears the objects of which he is apprised by his senses, in accordance with the ideas his previous experience has led him to form; but

---

[1] It must be remembered that Rousseau's psychology has the common defects of most of the pre-Kantian psychology. He constantly assumes that there can be "mere sensations" apart from concepts, and that these passive states somehow or other contrive to give us a certain limited knowledge of the presented reality that produces them in us.

[2] Compare *Rousseau juge de Jean-Jacques*, ii.: "L'homme sensuel est l'homme de la nature." With this may be connected the statement in the Preface of the *Discourse* that the obligation not to harm one's fellows rests not on the fact that they are rational, but that they are "*sensibles.*" The senses, in short, are original to man; reason is secondary.

in the beginning of things, when he was still on the animal level, he had no such experience even if he had the capacity for it, and the motion of desire or fear was due to "the simple impulse that comes from nature." Something "within him" made him reach out towards one set of things, and draw back from another. If we seek to determine further the nature of the objects connected with these "passions," we come finally to certain elementary needs, and seemingly we must stop our analysis with them. When we get to these essential needs, we have got down to bedrock in human nature. What, then, are these needs? The desires of the primitive savage, Rousseau answers, "do not go beyond his physical wants. The only good things that he knows in the universe are his food, his mate,[1] and his rest. The only evils he fears are pain and hunger."

But are these really all his needs? Is there nothing in his nature which makes him desire his fellows? At this point Rousseau hesitates somewhat. The fact that this animal does become a social being seems to suggest that even from the beginning he must have been more than an animal, and with the usual facility of the faculty psychologists in explaining such facts, Rousseau is ready on occasion to credit the primitive non-social savage with latent "social virtues." For the most part, however, he assumes that, so far as social relationship is concerned, man was really on the level of the animals. There is no reason, he says, why in the primitive state a man should have any more need of another man than a monkey or a wolf has of its fellows. In any case, self-love, the desire for self-conservation, the interest in one's own

[1] Not, be it noted, a permanent mate, or even a comparatively permanent mate, but any female (*une femelle*).

well-being—call it what you will—"is the only motive power in human action."

So far Rousseau is in the main consistent. The basal physical needs, which are the elementary constituents of man's nature, may all be regarded as particular expressions of this primary self-seeking impulse. But what are we to say with regard to the supplementary principle that Rousseau associates with self-love? The primary operations of the human soul, he says in the Preface, are due "to two principles both of them antecedent to reason: the one interests us keenly in our own well-being and preservation, the other inspires in us a natural repugnance to seeing any being that feels, and especially our own fellows, suffer or perish." This latter feeling of pity, though seemingly as much an original element in man's nature as self-love, is not to be regarded as on the same level with self-love. Rousseau even suggests (what he explicitly states in the *Emile*) that it is simply a phase of self-love, in so far as it is a feeling that puts us in the place of the sufferer and makes his suffering ours. It only moderates the activity of self-love. It never comes into conflict with it, since in the last resort the sole consideration for any man is his own good. The practical application of it is the maxim of natural goodness: "Do good to yourself with the minimum of harm to others," a much less perfect but a more useful rule of life, according to Rousseau, than the golden rule to do to others as you would have them do unto you,—for which, indeed, there is no place in his ethics of self-conservation.

5. *The Departure from the State of Nature.*—It is only when it becomes necessary to show how human society arose out of the primitive condition, that the essential weakness of the attempt to distinguish rigidly

between what man is in himself and what he becomes by social modification betrays itself. This animal man turns out to be only too perfect an animal. There is nothing in him to account for the fact that he did not remain an animal. Of this difficulty Rousseau is himself aware. When he indicates the need for language as a condition of progress, he has to admit that there is no reason why animal man, lacking all communication with others of his kind, should ever need to speak, or how, if he did, he could ever acquire the art. He cannot escape from the dilemma that either man was a social being from the beginning and in consequence developed speech, or that man was a mere unit who could never escape from his isolation to the extent required for acquiring speech and becoming social. He evades the difficulty, however, by postulating " a fortuitous concourse of various external causes, which might never have occurred and without which man would have remained for ever in his primitive condition."

But even if the possibility of evolution under such fortuitous conditions be granted, it may still be asked what there was in man's nature to make progress towards social life possible with their aid. The answer that Rousseau gives is significant. Man as an animal differs from all other animals in lacking definite instincts. An animal, he says, is only an ingenious machine, to which nature has given senses to make it self-winding. There is one difference, however, between man and beast. In the activities of the beast nature does everything, whereas man as a free agent has a share in determining his own activities. The one chooses or rejects by instinct, the other by an act of liberty. And from this difference proceeds all the rest. In the first place, it is to the absence of a complete set of instincts capable of determining all his actions mechanically that man owes his distinctively spiritual character as an agent free to will.[1] In the second place, it is to this same defect that man owes the capacity for an indefinitely continued improvement that depends ultimately on his reason. Lacking instincts, primitive man was forced to make good the lack by the development of the understanding. "Whatever the moralists may say, the human understanding owes much to the passions. It is by their activity that our reason becomes perfect. We only seek to know because we desire to enjoy; and it is not possible to conceive how any one who had neither desires nor fears should ever take the trouble to reason." And here appears the little rift within the lute; for in the outcome the animal understanding which is but the servant of the passions is transformed into the reason which is no longer content to serve, but proceeds to create new needs of its own and to rule where once it served. Through the developed understanding comes the power to act on ideas instead of on mere instinctive impulses, a power that begins by raising man above all the other animals and finally removes him from their kingdom altogether into a kingdom of his own.

The story of human progress, as Rousseau tells it, is the story of a Fall. With melancholy satisfaction he shows that it is man's intellect which is the source of all his misfortunes; and that but for his intellect he might have remained in the original animal state, dull and stupid, but good and happy. As things are, it is to the fatal power of self-perfection through the activity of reason that he owes the insight and the errors, the

---

[1] Cf. *Emile*, iv. 265, 266 (*Confession of Faith of the Savoyard Vicar*), for another expression of the same idea.

virtues and the vices, which make him in the long run the tyrant of himself and of nature. "It would be a dreadful thing to be compelled to praise the beneficence of the man who first suggested to the dwellers by the banks of the Orinoco the use of those boards they bind on the temples of their children and thus secure to them some part at least of their original imbecility and happiness." Dreadful indeed![1]

6. *The Evils of Society.*—In the First Part of the *Discourse* Rousseau has shown, as he thinks, that in a state of nature the differences that make men unequal in society are scarcely if at all appreciable. In the Second Part he goes on to show the origin and progress of inequality consequent on the successive developments of the human mind. He follows the evolution of society through its various phases: the first houses, the establishment of permanent family relations, the gradual growth of a conscious individuality leading to a conflict of interests among the different individuals, the beginnings of property, the invention of the arts of agriculture and metallurgy, the formation of a community by contract, and so on through a long series of stages up to modern government.

With the details of this "conjectural" reconstruction we have no further concern. There is, however, something to be learned from this Second Part with regard to the grounds on which Rousseau criticises social institutions, that will serve to throw further light on his conception of the opposition of nature and society. Let us consider what these grounds are.

The life of primitive man, as we have seen, like the

---

[1] Rousseau has been solemnly reproved for this passage by a hostile critic. Surely it is evident that Rousseau is poking fun at his own views by showing where they lead when carried to extremes.

life of the animal, is characterised by its simplicity and uniformity. His wants are few, and the methods of satisfying them do not vary much. Hence, as Rousseau says, the first men "all fed on the same food-stuffs, lived in the same way, and did exactly the same things." Something of the regularity that appears in all the phenomena of nature is to be seen in their lives. Now, the inevitable result of the development of speech and intelligence concurrent with the beginnings of human fellowship is to disturb this uniformity. As soon as the imagination is able to present to the mind ideas of desirable objects, man ceases to be confined to the objects to which in his primitive days instinct or habit compelled an immediate and unvarying response. One oak-tree is no longer as good to him as another; and the females of his kind begin to assume different values for him according to his preference. With the growth of the discriminating mind, individual liking—and, it may be, caprice—takes the place of law. Consider, for example, the case of the sex relationship. At first, as we have seen, there is no difference between one woman and another for the animal man. But with the establishment of abodes more or less permanent and family ties of corresponding fixity, the animal relationship gradually changes into human love. It is no longer any woman that pleases a man, but the one particular woman of his choice. "The instinctive impulse of sex is at first indeterminate: the one sex is drawn to the other. This is the movement of nature. Choice, preference, personal attachment are the work of intelligence, prejudice, and habit. For a man who had no idea of worth and beauty, every woman would be equally good, and the first comer would always be the most lovable. So far from love being a product of nature, it is the bridle of natural impulse. It is due to it that, except the beloved, the members of the one sex mean nothing for the other." [1] Another phase of the same evolution appears in the rise of private property. In the state of nature (that is, in the animal economy) there is no distinction between "mine" and "thine" of more than a temporary kind. But once man can think and hold the idea of better and worse before his mind, it is inevitable that each individual should wish to get and to hold those things that seem best to him. Property, in fact, is the most obvious external expression of morality. It bears concrete witness to the fact that once man has risen above animal immediacy, he no longer acts on casual presentations, but orders his life by relation to certain permanent ideas or ends that he keeps before himself.

But in this *Discourse* Rousseau does not choose to regard the tendency to idealise particular objects and to build up an individuality of one's own by relation to the individualised objects as in any sense good. He has certainly laid hold of the profound truth that there are no individuals in nature; and that apart from a mind which detaches and abstracts and reunites the facts of experience as units, there can be no such thing as individuality. But instead of recognising that nature thus individualised is being seen far more truly than when seen by an animal or a savage incapable of unifying thought, he attributes the changed view of things to a faculty of imagination that perverts the

---

[1] *Emile*, iv. 17. I have quoted the passage from the *Emile* in spite of the fact that there is one phrase in it foreign to this stage of Rousseau's thought: that, namely, in which love is said to be the bridle of natural impulse. There are no indications in the *Discourse* that Rousseau has yet realised the need of a bridle for any natural impulse.

facts and misleads its unhappy possessor into confusing what he thinks or imagines with what is. That is to say, his doctrine is really an inverted idealism. He admits the constructive work of mind in creating a world of its own, but discounts the worth of its creations as something spurious and unreal, because the product of an individual mind. In the *Emile*, where this view reappears with certain differences, it is expressly said that the activity of imagination forces its mental construct on the facts of sense-experience and is in this way one of the main sources of intellectual error. Here the doctrine takes a more practical form in that the evils credited to imagination are evils of conduct. But fundamentally the source of the error is regarded as the same in both cases. The understanding of man, which nature intended to direct his actions to the satisfaction of physical needs, sets up new needs of a false kind, limitless in extent, and quite incapable of satisfaction by means of the resources at man's disposal. Hence the irrecoverable loss of happiness when man left his first estate.

But how has the individualising work of the imagination brought about the evils of society? Because, Rousseau answers, it changes self-love (*amour de soi-même*) into self-assertion (*amour-propre*). The man becomes conscious of himself as an individual endowed with certain rights, and the very consciousness of his individuality brings about a complete change in his relations with his fellows. Self-love, the primary endowment of man, is the dominant motive of action in every one. In all that a man does, he must needs aim at furthering his own interests and enlarging his own life: that is the law of his being. Taken by itself, the principle of self-love is neither good nor bad. Its goodness or badness depends on the direction it takes in the course of life. Self-assertion, on the other hand, is essentially bad. It implies the thrusting forward of one's own interests regardless of those of others, and a willingness to forget the natural pity by which the promptings of self-love are held in check when they threaten harm to others. Now, so long as the mind is too undeveloped for the individual man to prefer one thing to another or to make particular things his own possessions, self-love remains innocent and harmless. It is the conflict of interests that results from the progress of mind towards individuality, and the establishment of communities for the realisation of individual ends, that pervert it into self-assertion and destroy the primitive goodness and simplicity of human life. Again, take love for an example. This sweet and tender sentiment on the least opposition "becomes an impetuous madness. Jealousy awakens with love; discord triumphs; and the gentlest of the passions receives sacrifices of human blood." In a word, in the case of the relations of the sexes, as of all other social relations, the forming of communities results in a growing sense of individual interest which inevitably provokes strife. Far better, it would seem, had man remained in the placid stupidity of his unawakened animal soul, with few wants, and with capacities ample for their satisfaction without need of help from others.

But if mankind degenerates from the first concourse of individuals, the downward movement becomes headlong once the comparative isolation of savage life is left behind, and the arts of agriculture and metallurgy tie the social bonds still tighter. In the savage state, the individual may occasionally come into relations with his fellow-men, but for the most part he leads a self-contained life. He can build his own hut, hunt for himself, fashion his own simple weapons, and provide for his various wants by the skill and strength of his own right arm. But once industrial society begins, he loses whatever worth he had as a self-sufficient individual and is forced by the division of labour to depend to an increasing extent on the aid of his fellows. In one way individuality is exaggerated to the furthest possible extent, in that the worker needs to limit himself to one particular kind of task in the fulfilment of his obligations to the community. The irony of the situation is that in the close-knit society to which he now belongs he is really less an individual than ever. Prejudices and customs press upon him on every side, and he loses completely the power of acting on his own initiative. He must do as others do, and as others want him to do. Thus it comes, as Rousseau notes, that social man, having reached the furthest point of his evolution, reverts to a condition of uniformity of action just like the uniformity that characterised the life of primitive man. But though it seems as if the wheel had come round full circle and individuality had once more been reduced to its right proportions, Rousseau is as little satisfied with the new uniformity as he had been with the individuality that first wrought confusion in human life. For it seems to him that in this final uniformity of social man, the original characters of humanity, which make man truly man, have disappeared, and thus there has been lost not merely the individuality that at one stage in development counted for so much, but the free manhood of the individual as well.

7. *The Noble Savage.*—Summing up what has been

said, we note that Rousseau distinguishes three stages in the history of humanity.[1]   The first was the state of nature, when man was but one animal among others. In this pre-social stage, Rousseau would have us believe, it was only the generic characters of mankind that were brought into play.   There was no more individuality among men than among monkeys or wolves or any other animals.   The law of human life was the law of all animal life.   The impulses of man's nature were sufficient guides for the needs of his life.   The second was a midway stage of savagery, coming after the invention of speech and the first beginnings of communal life. Family conditions had become permanent with the building of huts, but the family was still the economic and political unit, and the other social relations were only casual and temporary.   At this stage the pristine simplicity and regularity continued in large measure. The generic needs and passions still dominated life; the only difference being that the development of the understanding had brought new needs and changed some of the methods of satisfying the original ones The third stage is modern civilisation, based on the arts, and characterised, according to Rousseau, by the virtual disappearance of the primitive human characters, and their replacement by new habits having their origin in social discipline.   At this stage the development of the individual at the expense of the race is complete: "all further progress has been in appearance making for the perfection of the individual, and in reality making for the decrepitude of the species."

What are the practical applications of this whole view of the origin and growth of society?   If it be

[1] See the *Letter to M. de Beaumont* for Rousseau's own summary of the three stages of human progress.

true that all the ills that vex humanity have followed
from the departure from the state of nature, it would
seem as though the best thing to do would be to
devise some method of restoring mankind to the
primitive simplicity—for example, the method of those
Orinoco Indians which Rousseau cites with somewhat
uncertain approval. But Rousseau is not prepared to
carry his doctrine to its logical conclusion. In the
controversy that followed the publication of the first
Discourse, his reply to those critics who urged this
consequence on him was that a change such as had
been made in the course of social evolution is irrever-
sible and must be accepted with the best grace possible,
and that culture may even be justified as necessary to
prevent a lapse into a worse barbarism than had existed
in the primitive times.[1] The argument is plainly
sophistical, and makes a vain attempt to conceal the
fact that Rousseau has no real desire for a return
to animal stupidity. Even in the *Discourse on Inequality,* which begins with a laudation of animal man,
there is a quite definite abandonment of the view that
mankind was at its best before any modification of
human nature by social influences had taken place. This
is evident from the acceptance of savagery as the ideal
state. "Though men had become less patient and had
less natural pity, this period of the development of
the human faculties, keeping a just mean between the
primitive indolence and the petulant activity of modern
self-assertion, must have been the happiest and most
lasting period in the history of man. The more one
thinks of it, the more one is led to regard this state
as the best for manhood. Man would never have been
drawn from it but for some sinister accident which it

[1] See the *Reply to the King of Poland.*

would have been better for the common weal had never happened." This, he goes on to say, is the happy condition in which most savages have been found: and in the sentimental ignorance that he shared with his age, he glorifies the savage life as one that preserves the veritable youth of the human race.

It must be admitted that this new presentment of the man of nature is a more pleasing one than the unintelligent, speechless, unmoral animal which he puts in contrast with social man in the First Part of the *Discourse.* The noble savage who "is not attached to any place, has no prescribed task, obeys no one, has no law but his own will, and is compelled to reason about every action of his life," [1] in spite of his obvious defects approaches nearer to civilised man than his primitive ancestor. If his morality is undeveloped and his social nature rudimentary, in will and intelligence at least he is bone of our bone and flesh of our flesh; so much so that we begin to wonder whether, after all, this is really savage man, and not some unhappy Rousseau whose life has been put in contradiction with itself by his inability to find a place in ordinary society. The reasoning savage of Rousseau's imagination, at any rate, is an abstraction. He is neither animal man nor social man though he shares qualities with both. He is the typical Individual of Rousseau's thought, as intelligent as his civilised brother, as free as his primitive ancestor, impossible as a member of society and yet unthinkable apart from it. He is, so to speak, the embodied protest of thwarted individuality against a society that has failed to give manhood adequate scope.

We shall return to the consideration of Rousseau's

[1] *Emile,* ii. 158.

ideal savage at a later time. Meantime we note that, in this conception of what is essential to manhood, Rousseau has departed almost as far from the original type of unsocialised humanity as civilisation itself has done. After attributing the undoing of mankind to the rise of individuality, it is indeed a strange logic that makes him set up as his ideal man one who, on his own account of things, differs from the primitive man-in-himself chiefly in being an individual.

8. *The Part played by Education in Social Evolution.*—From what has been said, it will be obvious that the second *Discourse* is at the same cynical standpoint as the first. The only difference is that analysis has taken the place of invective. The cynical view is apparent in the few references made to education in the *Discourse*. Casual as these are, they show plainly enough that Rousseau realised the dependence of the whole process of social evolution on education, and consequently looked askance at it as one of the sources of the evils of civilisation.

In the primitive state, he tells us, there was no education and no progress, each generation setting out from the same point as its predecessors. It is education which makes progress possible; for education produces all those differences in *habit* which serve to differentiate civilised men from one another. " For example, a robust or a delicate physique is more often the result of a hardy or an effeminate upbringing than of the original constitution of the body. The same thing holds good with regard to the powers of the mind. Education does not merely make the difference between cultured and uncultured people, but even increases the difference among the former according to the measure of their culture." Education, then, is the ultimate cause of

those artificial inequalities in the social order which
are its condemnation.   It would almost seem as though,
on Rousseau's premises, this most characteristic and
fundamental of social institutions was the worst of
them all and furthest removed from nature.   If he has
any place for it in his scheme of life, there is nothing
in this *Discourse* to indicate what it is.

9. *The Article on Political Economy.*—Rousseau's
presentation of the cynical view of society in the two
prize *Discourses* is so single-minded and free from
qualifications that it calls for a distinct effort of
thought to realise that, even at the time of writing
these *Discourses*, that view represented only one aspect
of his political philosophy.   The Dedication of the
Discourse on Inequality to the Republic of Geneva
indeed suggests this.   "Having had the good fortune
to be born among you," he says, "I could not reflect
on the equality established among men by nature and
on the inequality they themselves have instituted,
without thinking of the profound wisdom with which
the two have been united in happy combination in
this state, for the maintenance of the public order
and the well-being of the individual citizens.   In my
search for the best and most sensible principles that
can be laid down on the constitution of a government,
I was greatly struck to see them all in operation in
yours." [1]   The further exposition of this theme shows
that these are not merely rhetorical expressions, but
that they really indicate a profound and suggestive

[1] Cf. *Letter to M. Perdriau* (Nov. 28, 1754): "I am so much
struck by the conformity which I find between the constitution of
government deducible from my principles and that which actually
exists in our republic, that I propose to dedicate my *Discourse on
Inequality* to it."

line of thought about social relations, widely different
from that followed in the *Discourse* itself (in spite of
what Rousseau says to the contrary), and no less significant for the subsequent development of his political
philosophy. For example: "If I had had the choice
of a birthplace for myself, I should have chosen a
community, limited in its extent to the capacity of
the human faculties [1] and capable of being well
governed, a community in which every one would be
fit for his allotted task and no one would need to
commit to others the functions with which he had
been charged. . . . I should have sought to live and
die a free man, so far subject to the laws that neither
I nor any one else would be able to cast off their
honourable yoke. . . . I should have sought a country
in which the right of legislating was shared by all the
citizens: for who are better judges than they of the
conditions under which it is best to live together in
the same community?"   Here we have in a new form
a statement of the problem of the *Discourse*, and indeed
of the modern problem of democracy: to find some form
of common life in which the individual man will not
sacrifice anything essential to his individuality, or (as
Rousseau would say) will remain *free*.[2] The *Discourse*
virtually denies that the problem can be solved. The
Dedication, bringing to Rousseau's mind the exceptional position of the little city state as exemplified
in Geneva,[3] suggests the possibility of an obedience

[1] Compare with this what Aristotle says about the size of the best
state (*Politics*, vii. 4): also *Social Contract*, ii. 9.
[2] *Cf.* the statement of the problem in the *Social Contract*, i. 6.
[3] Villemain draws attention to the importance of Rousseau's appreciation of the government of Geneva for his own political theory.
After pointing out that Montesquieu had preceded him in discerning
the good and the evil of the ancient republics, he adds: "Rousseau seul
et le premier en parlent avec une ardeur enthousiaste : et l'exemple

to law and a conformity to social order by no means inconsistent with personal liberty and happiness, and in this way—though Rousseau is not aware of it—puts in question the conclusion reached in the *Discourse*.

That the idea adumbrated in the Dedication was not a casual notion of doubtful sincerity is proved by the article on *Political Economy* written by Rousseau for the *Encyclopédie* about the same time as the *Discourse on Inequality* was written.[1] There we find worked out at some length the very idea of social relations which the Dedication implies.   The article, it must be remembered, was written a considerable time before Adam Smith's *Wealth of Nations*, when the exact boundaries of economics had not yet been clearly defined.   We are not surprised, then, to find that Rousseau's conception of Political Economy is very different from the modern one.[2]   Indeed, except in the sections in which he discusses taxation, his article deals with the problems of government rather than with economic problems proper.

The first principle he lays down is that government depends on the existence of the general will of the

moderne heureux qu'il invoquait sans cesse, Genève, dont il etait redevenu citoyen et co-religionnaire, donne une sorte de realité présente à ses souvenirs antiques et à ses utopies." *Dixhuitième siècle*, p. 234.

[1] The date is uncertain.   All that we know with complete certainty is that it was written before 1755, the year in which the volume of the *Encyclopédie* containing it was published.   Girardin thinks it was written before the *Discourse on Inequality*, while Beaudouin believes that it was written after it.   A comparison of the Article with the Dedication makes me incline to the former opinion.   The Article is translated in my *Minor Educational Writings of Rousseau*.

[2] M. Girardin goes further than this.   Rousseau, he says, has in him nothing of the modern publicist.   He belongs neither to the school of Grotius nor to the school of Montesquieu.   He pays no attention to history, to custom, to the state of morals, or to the age of societies.   He belongs to the school of the ancients and is wholly speculative.

state as distinguished from the individual wills of its
constituent citizens. The body politic, he says, is a
moral being with a will — this general will — which
always tends to the preservation and well-being of each
and every member, and is the source of the laws under
which the citizens live. "The first duty of the legislator
is to make the laws conform to the general will, and the
first rule of the public economy is that the administra-
tion should be in conformity with the laws." But this
view of the nature of government immediately raises
the problem of freedom. How can the citizens be free
if there is a general will capable of setting aside their
individual wills ? Rousseau's answer is that freedom
is only attainable if we can teach the citizens to be
virtuous and love their country. "A man is virtuous,"
he tells us, "when his individual will is in conformity
with the general will in all respects, and he spontaneously seeks to do what the people he loves wish
him to do."

10. *Public Education.*—By this line of argument,
Rousseau is led to insist on the necessity for a well-
directed system of public or national education, having
as its main aim the making of good citizens. He does
not think that this calls for a perfection beyond the
actual nature of mankind, or for any attempt to suppress
the passions. Indeed, he is ready to maintain that a
passionless man, if it were possible to produce him by
education, would make a very bad citizen; for the
essential work of the educator is to direct the passions
so that the children undergoing training may love the
beautiful rather than the ugly, the good rather than
the bad—and if there were no passions, what material
would he have to work on ? "If, for example, we train
them early in life never to think of their individual

interests except in relation to those of the state as a whole, and never to regard their own existence as having any meaning apart from that of the state, they would come in course of time to identify themselves in some fashion with this grand Whole, their fatherland, loving it with the exquisite sentiment that the solitary man keeps for himself, and so transforming into a sublime virtue that dangerous disposition from which all our vices flow." All this has been done repeatedly in human history ; and it can be done again whenever the state realises the necessity for shaping the dispositions of its citizens to public ends, and begins the work of education before the natural inclinations have taken their own course and become stereotyped as habits.

The consequences of accepting the view that freedom within a community presupposes a training in the loyal performance of civic duties, as Rousseau sees them, are so startling as almost to prompt the question whether freedom is not lost in the attempt to secure it. The children are to be educated for citizenship, and consequently [1] (according to Rousseau) must be taken out of their fathers' keeping. We do not permit the reason of the individual man to be the sole judge of what his duties are, he argues; still less, then, should we leave to the intelligence and the prejudice of fathers the education of their children, seeing that education for citizenship concerns the state more than it concerns the parents. The family passes, the state endures. Far better put the business of education into the charge of the best and wisest men in the state, after the

---

[1] Note the implication. The ends of the family and of the state are so far incompatible that the state must remove the child from the family. Compare with this the Platonic communism (*Republic*, v.) and Fichte's scheme of national schools (*Reden an die deutsche Nation*).

manner of Plato's *Republic*, than leave it a matter for private caprice. Moreover, if the public authority takes upon itself this important function and acquires the paternal rights by performing the paternal duties, the fathers have no real cause of complaint; for as citizens they would exercise in common the same authority over their children which they exercise separately as fathers. They will not be obeyed less readily when they speak in the name of the law than when they speak in the name of nature. A rather unconvincing argument!

"If the children are brought up in common in the bosom of equality," he goes on, "if they are imbued with the laws of the state and the maxims of the general will, if they are surrounded with objects that speak to them unceasingly of the tender mother who nourishes them,[1] of her love for them and of the return they owe her, we cannot doubt that they will learn in this way to cherish each other as brothers, and come to wish only what the community wishes, so that one day they will become the defenders and the fathers of the country of which they have so long been the children." The warrant for this hope is to be found in the fact that a system of public education like this was actually practised with the happiest results by three nations among the ancients—the Cretans, the Spartans, and the Persians. The one condition necessary for its success is the breaking up of the great nation states of the modern world into small states like these three. The modern state is too large for good government of any kind, and therefore quite incompetent to discharge duties so important as

---

[1] Rousseau means the state, of course. Does his figure not put his whole scheme in the wrong?

those involved in the direction of a national system of education.

11. *The Two Extremes in Rousseau's Political Theory.*—The *Discourse on Inequality* and the Article on *Political Economy*, written, as we have seen, about the same time, present a most interesting problem in the psychology of belief. The one is based on a thorough-going individualism : the other on a socialism no less thorough-going. In both the fundamental problem is the old problem which has forced itself upon the minds of thinking men in every age that has outlived its first faith in its social institutions —the problem of the right relation between the self-conscious individual and his society. At this stage of his thought, at any rate, Rousseau has no final solution to offer. In these two contemporaneous writings, the extremes of perfect freedom for the complete unfolding of every potency of man, and of an absolute State endowed with all wisdom and capable of fitting the whole man for its service, stand over against each other, to all appearance having nothing in common. Cynicism pushed to its furthest limit in uncompromising contempt for every form of social institution, working itself out in a mind which with all its defects is faithful to its facts, has called into being the contradictory idea of social institutions so perfect as to leave no opportunity or need for the play of individuality. In a word, extremes have met, as they ought to meet if, as Hegel has taught us, the progress of thought must needs be through contradiction into the higher truth, which includes the partial truths that contradict because they are partial. The interesting fact is not that they should meet—that is in the nature of thought—but that they should have

met so soon, and within the experience of one man. For the present it is sufficient to note the fact of the contradiction. In a later chapter we shall discuss its bearings on the educational theories, which represent one of Rousseau's mature attempts to solve the problem of the right relationship of individual and society.

CHAPTER V

THE PREPARATION FOR THE EMILE

1. *Rousseau in Montmorency.*—The *Discourse on Inequality* was published in 1755. A year later Rousseau left Paris and settled down on the borders of the Forest of Montmorency, with full intention never to reside in a city again.[1] The change from town to country was followed by the happiest results. Free from the irritation of uncongenial surroundings, he soon regained the tranquillity of mind which he had lost in the society of city people. Once at a distance from his fellows, his misanthropy steadily diminished. "The beginnings of this change," he says, "took place as soon as I quitted Paris, and the sight of the vices of that city no longer kept up the indignation it had inspired in me. No sooner had I lost sight of men than I ceased to despise them."[2] During the next six years, which were on the whole years of happiness in spite of the fact that they witnessed the beginnings of the quarrels with some of his former associates which embittered the rest of his life, he worked away steadily at various

[1] Up to the time when the *Confessions* were written, he had never been in a city for more than a day or two at a time. It was not the least of the misfortunes of his old age that the last eight years of his life were spent in Paris.

[2] "En quittant Paris, Rousseau . . . échappait au joug des entretiens à cette autorité de l'opinion de la mode, qui domine toujours un peu les esprits les plus fermes : et il se retrouvait où son génie s'était formé, aux champs et dans la solitude."—VILLEMAIN, *Dixhuitième siècle*, pp. 235-6.

literary projects and succeeded in producing the three. master-works on which his fame mainly rests: the *New Heloïse*, a romance of love and domestic life; the *Social Contract*, a section of an unfinished work on political institutions, which with the *Discourse on Inequality* furnished the leaders of the French Revolution with their main ideas on government; and the *Emile* (including the famous *Confession of Faith of the Savoyard Vicar*), a treatise on education, the greatest and most representative of all his writings.[1]

2. *The Preparation for the Emile.*—In all three cases, the substance of the book was the outcome of long years of reflection. Rousseau had a mind of unusual pertinacity; once he had got hold of an idea he did not let it go until he had made it his own by much rumination. The *Social Contract*, for example, was the final expression of the views on government which had taken shape for the first time when he acted as secretary to the French ambassador in Venice. Even at that time he seems to have planned a *magnum opus* on law and government; and as he awaited the opportunity of leisure sufficient to write it, his thought and experience gradually massed a great many new ideas round his first ideas on the subject, by a process that had in it more of accretion than of growth. This instance is quite typical of most of his literary work. Even when he seems to be indulging in mental adventure and exploring new territory, a careful study of his

---

[1] Commenting on the fact that these three works were all produced during his stay at Montmorency, Beaudouin remarks: " . . . chose remarquable qui montre qu'il avait dans l'esprit et dans le style plus de flexibilité qu'on ne serait tenté de le croire d'après son caractère, comme ces trois livres qui datent de la même époque, appartiennent à trois genres entièrement differents, l'auteur a su approprier à ces sujets divers des styles qui ne le sont pas moins." *La Vie et les Œuvres de J.-J. Rousseau*, i. 537.

earlier letters and articles will usually show that he is only turning over familiar thoughts and repeating them in a fresh form.

This is certainly true of the *Emile*. As we have seen, his thoughts were turned in the direction of education some twenty-five years before the *Emile* was written by the works of Montaigne and of Locke. The idea of writing a book on the subject seems to have first occurred to him at the time when he was wrestling vainly with the education of M. de Mably's sons, and though nothing came of the project at the time, he never quite lost sight of it afterwards. For some years the constant struggle with poverty left him little leisure for the indulgence of his literary fancies, and even after he had won a place for himself in the world of letters and had escaped from the more pressing dangers of indigence, he was too busy working out the new-found vein of criticism and denunciation to find time for more constructive thought. Yet, as appears from a Memoir presented to M. Dupin in 1749, the very year in which the first *Discourse* was written, his mind was continually busy with his educational ideas. A long time before, he declares in this Memoir, he had formed a plan of education very different from that commonly practised, but even at the time of writing he had scruples about putting it before the public. It would be presumption on the part of a young and inexperienced man to flatter himself that he had really conceived anything better than the methods which the experience of two thousand years had led the wisest men to receive with unanimity. Whether this scheme to which he refers with becoming modesty was the same as that which he had drawn up some eight years before with a view to the education of M. de Sainte-Marie, or a more revolutionary scheme on the lines of the *Emile*, it is impossible to say. More important than the details of the scheme, interesting as these would be to us, is the evidence afforded by this Memoir that Rousseau was busy thinking about education during the years when he wrote nothing on the subject.

One thing that favoured this line of thought on Rousseau's part was the remarkable increase of interest in everything relating to education during the half-century immediately preceding. The writers of Memoirs and Journals, of whom this subjective age produced a great host, all bear witness to the fact that the thoughts of serious-minded people were everywhere turning to the problems of education. Criticisms of the ordinary methods of bringing up children, and especially of the ordinary school system, were frequent, and new methods were constantly being propounded by theorists with all sorts of educational panaceas. One of the clearest indications of the widespread public interest was the steady stream of books on different phases of education which were constantly being issued. Even if we think only of the outstanding works on the subject which appeared during the years when Rousseau was coming to his own conclusions, or just before that time, the list is a considerable one. There had been Fénelon's *Éducation des Filles* and *Télémaque*, Rollin's *Traité des Études*, Locke's *Thoughts on Education* (translated into French in 1695), and the *Avis d'une mère à son fils* and the *Avis d'une mère à sa fille* of Madame de Lambert.[1] Such an

---

[1] Lemaître, *J.-J. Rousseau*, p. 213. The English reader will find an account of Rousseau's predecessors in Miss Hodgson's *Studies in French Education from Rabelais to Rousseau*. Compayré's *History of Pedagogy* should also be consulted.

output of educational works presupposes a large number of people discussing the subject and willing to read books about it.

In these circumstances Rousseau's projects for the reform of educational methods grew to maturity in a sympathetic atmosphere. Most of the ladies with whom he associated were interested in education in a more or less practical way, and the subject figured largely in their conversations. Some of them were mothers seeking the best methods for the training and instruction of their families, and (as the manner of mothers is) disposed to talk about their children whenever they found a willing listener. Rousseau, for his part, was ready to listen, partly because it gave him the opportunity of acting as adviser—a *rôle* which he was well qualified to fill,[1] partly because he was wise enough to know that he could only discuss educational problems worthily if he was acquainted with the facts about child-life which these mothers possessed. A letter to Madame de Créqui, written in 1759 at a time when he had already begun the composition of the *Emile*, may be taken as typical of his relations with his women friends. It shows him seeking for information, and evidently implies the previous discussion of educational matters with the lady : "With regard to education, I have some ideas on the subject which I should be tempted to put on paper if I had a little help, but I would need some information based on observation which I lack. You, madame, are a mother, and though a women of piety

---

[1] The common conception of Rousseau as an unpractical visionary is entirely wrong. One has but to read the advice he gave to inquiring disciples on all manner of questions to appreciate his essential sanity of judgment. See his correspondence *passim*, or such writings as his *Considérations sur le gouvernement de Pologne*.

also a philosopher. You have brought up a son. It would be an easy matter for you to think out these questions." If she would communicate her reflections to him, he goes on to say, he would be very grateful for the gift. The *Emile* itself, if the opening words of the Preface are not to be regarded as merely a little flattery for a kindly patroness, was begun as a small memoir on education "to please a good mother who was able to think." This was Madame de Chenonceaux, the daughter of Madame Dupin, one of Rousseau's first and best friends.

3. *Madame d'Epinay.*—How much Rousseau owed to his conversations on education with intelligent women is well shown in the *Memoirs* of Madame d'Epinay.[1] For a year or two about the beginning of the period with which we are now dealing, the lady was one of Rousseau's warmest admirers and a most generous patroness; and their relations reached a degree of intimacy which made it easy for him to express his opinions with the utmost freedom in her company. The record of his views on education which she made in her *Memoirs* is for the most part an admirable one, and throws some interesting side-lights on the course of his thought during the years when his doctrines were gradually forming into a systematic whole.

Before going on to discuss the more important of Rousseau's utterances which have been preserved in this way, it should be noted that Madame d'Epinay had a point of view of her own about education, not unlike Rousseau's.[2] Indeed, when we find ideas which

---

[1] *Memoires et Correspondance de Madame d'Épinay.*
[2] She wrote a book on education more than twenty years later: *Conversations d'Émilie* (1781). See Hodgson, chap. x.

we are wont to consider as characteristic of Rousseau in her *Memoirs*, our first impulse is to ascribe them to him. But it is probably a mistake to attribute ideas of this kind to either of them and say that she learned them from Rousseau or that Rousseau learned them from her. The fact would seem to be that at the time when Rousseau was discussing education with her and other ladies of like mind, certain ideas about the subject were in the air, which became more or less fixed for both of them by their discussions and conversations. It is especially important that we should realise this if we are to see the *Emile* in right perspective. Reading it as we do without its social context, we are apt to attribute to the extravagance of Rousseau's mind certain ideas which, though unfamiliar to us, were not really peculiar to him at all, but were the ordinary views held by a great number of people about the middle of the eighteenth century. There is plenty of extravagance in Rousseau's view of education, without ascribing to him the origination of ideas which were the extravagance of an age rather than of any one individual.

Occurring among the miscellaneous chronique of a diary, Madame d'Epinay's opinions are expressed in somewhat disconnected form. Nevertheless, they get a certain unity from one or two main ideas that run through them all, and the whole view, as we have noted already, is not unlike that which is familiar to us in Rousseau's treatment of education. The long discussion on the demerits of public school education which was called forth by her husband's intention to send her son to a public school, for example, might have been written by Rousseau himself. "I might compare the colleges in which children are shut up in troops for

instruction," she writes, "with the public institutions
for the care of the sick. . . . The sick people left to
the care of the hospitals have one advantage over the
children forgotten in the colleges : the doctor takes
account of the patient's constitution. In the colleges,
on the contrary, everything is done according to a
number of general maxims, sometimes true but more
often false, which are applied indiscriminately to all
the children without respect to their inclinations or
their individual characters. However great the care
paid to the children, it must always be inferior to that
which is inspired in parents by attachment and tender
interest." There are three grave disadvantages in a
public education, she goes on to point out. The first
is the impossibility of acquiring the intimate knowledge of each child's disposition which is necessary
for a right education. The second follows from the
first. The uniformity of method indispensable on this
system makes it impossible to take proper account of
the future calling of the pupils at an early age, with
the result that the soldier sometimes receives the training of the priest and the priest the training of the
soldier. The third is that the emulation produced by
competition among the pupils, which is the only real
advantage of a public education, may foster the very
undesirable traits of self-assertion (*amour-propre*) and
immoderate jealousy.

Eventually Madame d'Epinay carried her point, and
her son's education was entrusted to a tutor named
Linant. But the tutor's methods were what she called
"ordinary," and she soon had cause for thinking that
it was not only in great institutions that a boy's education might be mismanaged. One or two extracts from
her *Memoirs* will show the ground of her grievances

in the matter of "ordinary" education. Duclos on one
occasion accompanied her on a visit to the tutor. "'Sir,'
says Duclos to the tutor, 'let there be little Latin, and
above all no Greek. What good will your Greek do the
boy? You are not called upon to make him an English-
man or a Roman or a Greek or a Spartan, but a man
fit for well-nigh everything.' 'But,' objects poor Linant,
'the education you suggest is not the ordinary one. To
do what you want, one would need to refashion and
remake his character.' 'Who is speaking of that?' replied Duclos. 'It is useless to try to change a child's
character. Apart from the impossibility of it, the
greatest success one could promise you would be that
you would make a hypocrite of the boy. No, sir,
emphatically no! You must bring out every possible
phase of the character that nature has given him.
This is all you are asked to do.'"

So far Duclos. Let us take another episode into
which Madame d'Epinay herself enters. After the
tutor had been at work some time, her husband
decided to have an examination of the children in
presence of some of their friends. "'Is the boy well
prepared?' he asks the tutor. 'Splendidly,' replied
Linant. 'So much the better,' said M. d'Epinay. 'So
much the worse,' added I. 'How do you make that
out, Madame?' 'Because,' said I, 'he will answer like
a parrot.'"

Again, we find her distressed by the results of the
"ordinary" methods used in the upbringing of her
daughter. What specially displeased her was the con-
sequential airs the girl put on. According to her
overness, the girl was being made vain by the attention
paid her by her mother's friends, and especially by the
sustained and rational conversations they carried on

with her. "She is in the habit of playing a part and is puffed up with it," reports the governess. "I am afraid, madame, that that is a drawback inevitable on the plan of education we have adopted." Thereupon, adds Madame d'Epinay, "we took counsel as to the means of putting things right."

Not to multiply examples further, we may take one more instance of methods in which she anticipates the *Emile*. "I took my children to visit the poor people of our parish," she writes, "and we distributed garments to the poor children. This visit will provide us with a subject of conversation for a week; for their ideas on poverty (*misère*) and its effects are very confused."

4. *Natural Education.*—There are two important sections in Madame d'Epinay's *Memoirs* which throw special light on the evolution of Rousseau's educational theory. The one is the record of a long conversation rising out of an *obiter dictum* of his to the effect that nature did not intend children to be educated nor parents to educate. The other relates to a correspondence between Rousseau and his patroness in which he criticises adversely two letters written by her with a view to the moral culture of her son.

The first of these has already been mentioned in another connection. It is a very difficult matter to bring up a child, Madame d'Epinay said:[1] to which remark Rousseau made the startling rejoinder that education is contrary to nature both for parents and children. Asked how he reconciled this with a scheme of education he admitted he was planning, he im-

---

[1] Madame d'Epinay's letter to Grimm recording this conversation is translated in an appendix to my *Minor Educational Writings of Rousseau*.

mediately went on to explain himself. In the state of nature (meaning by that the savage state),[1] education takes place without any external interference or direction. There are certain physical needs for which the savage must make provision, under penalty of death if he fails to do so. He must be able to defend himself against his enemies, or he will be killed. He must reproduce his kind, a task to which nature invites him apart from any parental lessons. For him, all life is a learning. Left to his own resources, he must find out from experience how best to adapt himself to his surroundings. His education is practically what Rousseau calls in the *Emile* the education of things. Civilised education is quite different from this, being based not on nature but on social conventions, whiéh unfortunately are most of them at variance alike with the taste and instincts of the child, and with the opinions and interests of the fathers. To this dissertation of Rousseau's, Madame d'Epinay made the sensible reply that they themselves were no longer savages. "For good or for evil," she said, "education is a necessity. How is it to be managed?" "It is very difficult," he admitted. "I am aware of that," she said. "That was the first thing I said to you, and here I am no further on than before." Rousseau evades the practical problem by saying that it would make the task easier "to begin by reconstructing society as a whole." The crux of the matter, he goes on to point out, is in the fact that children have to be taught a great many moral principles in childhood which need to be put aside in later life. "Look at all the people who have got on in the

---

[1] In the *Discourse on Inequality*, Rousseau's natural man was either the animal man without any considerable mental powers or the savage. In this conversation, and generally in his subsequent writings, he identifies him with the savage.

world. Do you think they have won success by con-
forming to the moral maxims they learned from their
fathers? Obviously not. Though one scarcely dare
teach children to tell lies and break their word, it is
perfectly certain that they will need to do so if they
are to get on. That is the awkward thing about education." The educator is confused by the clashing of
individual and general interests which is characteristic
of all social relationships. In a well-ordered society, vice
would invariably be punished and virtue invariably rewarded, but unfortunately there is not a spot in the
world where that happens. "Not even in your native
city?" asks one of Madame d'Epinay's friends, poking
sly fun at Rousseau, whose enthusiasm for Geneva was
well known. "Perhaps things are not quite so bad there
as in other places," was his reply.

The general standpoint of Rousseau in this conversation is not different from that which appears in the two
Discourses, and yet his way of approaching the problem
shows a distinct advance. In the *Discourse on Inequality* he dismissed the subject in a few sentences
on the ground that education represents the perverting
activity of society. Here the very fact that he is
seeking a plan of education based on nature, shows
that he is willing to believe it possible to educate in
such a way as to avoid the condemnation he himself
passes on the ordinary education; though, indeed, it
does not appear that he had any clear idea as to the
method by which society and the individual were to be
reconciled in the process of educating, or whether they
were to be reconciled at all. At the same time, his
reference to the education of savage man shows plainly
the direction in which his thought was moving. Presumably in this reforming project of his, which needed

a reconstitution of society for its proper operation, he intended to take as his model for the education of the civilised child the informal education that fits the savage to survive in face of the dangers of his environment. At any rate, this idea of the educative effects of the process of self-adaptation to environment which is characteristic of lower races of men, and even more of the animals—an idea, it should be noted, first expressed by Rousseau in this conversation—is fundamental in his treatment of the education of boyhood in the *Emile*. The hypothesis of the *Emile* is that the boy, being left free to follow his own bent and not made artificial by premature training and instruction, stands on the moral and intellectual level of savage man, and develops true to his nature when kept dependent on things alone. His education, therefore, like that of the savage, is one in which the physical environment counts for much, the social environment for comparatively little.

5. *Rousseau's Criticism of Madame d'Epinay's Letters to her Son.*—Though Rousseau had not yet enunciated the parallelism between boy life and savage life, on which the method of natural education suggested in the conversation with Madame d'Epinay and worked out in the *Emile* depends, it is obvious from the criticism he passed on her letters to her son (to which reference has been made) that he had a firm grasp of the principle that every age has distinctive characteristics of its own, which make both a special matter and a special method of instruction necessary for it.

Madame d'Epinay had formed the plan of writing a series of letters on matters of conduct to her son, then a boy of twelve or thirteen. She had actually written two of these letters, but before sending them she submitted them to Rousseau for his criticism. The letters, he replied quite frankly, were good enough for grown-up people but of no use for the purpose for which they were intended. Their chief defect was their generality.[1] They put maxims in place of concrete facts. Instead of giving the boy moral principles, he suggests, she should tell him tales and fables, and leave him to draw the appropriate moral for himself. "In proportion to the development of his ideas, you should adapt the tone of your letters to his degree of progress and to the faculties of his mind. For example, what is the use of instructing him in duties which are really those of a mother? Why keep drumming into his ear the words 'submission,' 'duties,' 'watchfulness,' 'reason'? This way of speaking is repellent at his age. It is by the actions that result from these that he should be broken in." Madame d'Epinay did not altogether appreciate the criticism. "I must confess that though I am in agreement with his principles," she writes, "I do not find them applicable to my letters." All the same, she wrote no more letters, and did not send the two she had written—probably because, in spite of her protestations, she had the good sense to see that there might be something in what Rousseau had said.

Little comment is called for on Rousseau's letters. The significant fact about this and all the other details we learn from Madame d'Epinay's *Memoirs* is not that we find certain of the central ideas of the *Emile* antici-pated in them—though the fact is certainly noteworthy

---

[1] Commenting on the Second Letter, he advises her to refrain from definitions. That the warning was not unnecessary will be evident from this specimen: "La politesse est dans un cœur sensible une expression douce, vraie et volontaire, du sentiment de l'estime et de la bienveillance." For further examples, see the letters themselves at the end of the Third Volume of the *Memoirs*.

—so much as the indication which they afford of a slow growth of opinions of all kinds with reference to concrete educational problems, on Rousseau's part. The *Emile* is apt to suggest to the casual reader who takes it without its context that Rousseau is treating education in a doctrinaire spirit, starting with a theory of social life and deducing from it certain ideals and methods of education unrelated to actual experience. The view we get of him in Madame d'Epinay's *Memoirs*, busy with the discussion of the actual difficulties of educational practice, makes that mistake impossible. In her pages we get suggestive glimpses of the whole experience of life out of which his system slowly grew. We remember that she was only one out of quite a number of people who discussed their educational problems with him, and in this way we are able to form a better idea of the actual circumstances in which the ideas of the *Emile* took shape. Even if, in the study of his views, we can never quite escape from the feeling of strangeness that is inevitable when the people of one age try to penetrate to the spirit of another age separated from their own by the lapse of time and by revolutionary change, we are able by their help to realise in some small measure that these views are the outcome of real personal thought on problems of perennial interest, and not mere academic speculation.

CHAPTER VI

NATURE AND SOCIETY IN THE LATER WRITINGS

1. *The New Point of View in the Later Writings.*—
The romance of the *New Heloïse* was published in 1761,
and was followed by the *Emile* and the *Social Contract* in the following year. Though all three were
the ripe fruits of a long reflection, the actual work
of composition was done after Rousseau's settlement
in Montmorency at the end of the year 1757. The
time that elapsed between the writing of the *Discourse
on Inequality* and these three master-works was therefore quite short. It is all the more surprising to find a
complete difference in temper between them. Super-
ficially, indeed, the change is not very considerable.
The same protests against the evils of social institutions
are repeated in almost identical terms, and all the old
watchwords of the *Discourses* recur with something of
the original vehemence of statement. But behind the
sameness of the letter there is a transformation of the
whole spirit of the thought and the sentiment. An
example will make the difference evident.

"The transition from the state of nature to the
social state," he says in the First Book of the *Social
Contract*,[1] "produced a very remarkable change in man
by substituting justice for instinct as the principle of
conduct, and so imparting to his actions the moral

---

[1] Chap. viii. *De l'état civil.*

character which they originally lacked. It was only after that change, when the voice of duty took the place of physical impulse, that man, who had hitherto thought only of himself, was compelled to act on different principles and consult his reason before listening to his inclinations. Though in this state man loses many of the advantages he derives from nature, those he gains from the exercise and development of his faculties, the broadening of his ideas, the ennobling of his sentiments, and the elevation of his whole soul, are so great that, if the evils of the new condition did not often degrade him beneath that which he had left, he would have cause to bless unceasingly the happy moment that took him from it for ever, and made an intelligent being and a man out of a stupid animal beset with limitations."

This passage is typical of a great many more in the later writings. The distinction between nature and society still stands in seeming rigidity. Justice and instinct, the voice of duty and physical impulse, reason and inclination, are set up against each other as belonging to two different universes that have nothing in common. The perversion of man's nature by the abuses resulting from social institutions is still asserted. But though there is no hint of any possible reconciliation of the conflicting principles represented by nature and society, there is a distinct weakening of the assurance with which the opposition is maintained, and more than a suggestion that Rousseau had realised the defects of the animal condition as an ideal for man. Indeed, it would do no great violence to the sense of the passage to read into it the idea—quite characteristic of the later writings—of the possibility of some form of social life which would be free from the objections that led

him to set up the man of nature in flattering antithesis
to civilised man.

Speaking broadly, the difference between the two
periods, both in temper and in principles, is the difference
between Cynicism and Stoicism.[1] In the *Discourses*
we find Rousseau calling in question all the fair works
of the human spirit, and raising protest against the
authority of custom and law in the name of a sentient
individuality distressed by the limits imposed on it by
society. Like Caliban, he turns the arts that society has
taught him against society itself:—

> "You taught me language and my profit on't
> Is, I know how to curse."

In the later writings we still hear at times the cynical
note of the earlier; but as a whole they express the
broad, tolerant spirit of Stoicism rather than the
narrow, anti-social bitterness of Cynicism. The transition from denunciation prompted by personal resent-
ment to argument based on reflection, the transition
in effect from feeling to reason, the beginning of which
is to be seen in the second *Discourse,* is here carried a
stage further. It is still asserted that society is unnatural, and individual experience still seems pitted
against social institutions in such a way as to put man
in perpetual contradiction with himself; but with all
this there is a limited recognition of a possible order

---

[1] How close the parallel is will be evident as the present chapter
goes on. An example from the ethical sphere will illustrate it suffi-
ciently for the present. The sharpest difference between the Cynics and
the Stoics is in their respective views of the senses and the appetites.
The Cynics regard them as "nature" and consider their promptings
as good. For the Stoics, on the other hand, it is reason that is "nature";
the senses and the appetites, being contrary to reason, are against
nature and therefore bad. It will be seen at a later point in this
chapter (sections 14, 18) that this exactly marks the difference between the earlier and the later writings of Rousseau.

in human affairs which redeems the social outlook from sheer hopelessness, and opens up the prospect of a social state in which all those antagonisms between the individual and his society, that vex and confuse human life, will finally vanish.

What brought about so considerable a change in Rousseau's view of life we can only surmise. In one passage in the *Confessions* he himself comments on the absence of bitterness in those writings that appeared after he had broken with Diderot. In another passage he attributes the disappearance of his misanthropy more generally to his remoteness from the city conditions which had created it. But the change is more than a mere change of mood—which is all that either of these suggestions would account for. It is a fairly decisive change of principles. Perhaps we may find some explanation in the quarrels with Diderot, Grimm, and others of the Encyclopedists which disturbed the calm of these years. For a time Rousseau had identified himself with them, and the *Discourses* reflected to some extent the negative attitude characteristic of the movement they represented. But the alliance was one that could only be temporary. Rousseau, in spite of the *Discourses*, was always uncomfortable in the atmosphere of criticism and negation in which they lived, and a breach of relations was inevitable sooner or later. When it did come, it was embittered by the intense personal feeling that Rousseau's unhappy disposition imparted to all differences with his fellows. With the rights and wrongs of the quarrels there is no need to concern ourselves. The point to be noted is that, during the years when the *Emile* and the *Social Contract* were being written, Rousseau's whole mind was in revolt against the doctrines of the Encyclopedists, and that

in the *Savoyard Vicar's Confession,* which marks the
furthest advance of Rousseau's thought, a deliberate
attempt is made to combat their sensualistic philosophy.
The reaction is least marked in the earlier Books of the
Emile, which we may assume were written before his
general philosophy of life had had time to fall into line
with his new anti-sensualistic metaphysics. It is more
evident in the later Books, and most evident of all in
the *Savoyard Vicar's Confession,* which in part at least
was the latest portion of the *Emile* to be written.[1] The
Emile, in fact, was written when Rousseau's whole
thought was being recast, and the progress of the
change of view corresponds broadly with the sequence
of the Books.

2. *The Problem of the Emile and the Social Contract.*—If this explanation of the changed point of
view of the later writings is accepted, it throws some
light on the tenacity with which Rousseau holds to his
original statements about the goodness of nature and
the badness of society, after he has really abandoned
them. The fact is that he himself never realised the
fundamental change that had taken place in his thought,
and his approach to the constructive application of his
modified views was hampered by the extremeness of the
opposition between the natural and the social which
he still formally maintained. His practical ideals, the
ideal home of the *New Heloïse,* the ideal State of the
Social Contract, the ideal education of the *Emile,* only
admit of realisation to any degree if in some way or
other the individual man can be brought into social

---

[1] Information regarding the relation of the different drafts of the
Emile to Rousseau's controversy with the Encyclopedists is given in
the Introduction of Victor Cousin's *Philosophie Populaire suivie de la
Première Partie de la Profession de Foi du Vicaire Savoyard* (Paris,
1849).

relations without detriment to his nature as a man; and before even a beginning can be made with the solution of the problems involved, Rousseau has to disentangle himself from his earlier views of society.

The difficulty shows itself at the beginning both of the *Social Contract* and of the *Emile.* The problem of the *Social Contract* is "to find a form of association which protects with the whole common force the person and property of each associate, and in virtue of which every one, while uniting himself with all the others, obeys only himself and remains as free as before." [1] The very fact of stating the problem in this way shows that Rousseau has given up the idea that a man can only be free when in a position to do what he likes. The savage freedom of indifference is quite incompatible with the existence of any form of social life, and the quest for an ideal society is the implicit renunciation of the idea of such a freedom. And yet Rousseau opens his discussion of the problem of statecraft with the famous epigram that "man is born free but is everywhere in chains," [2] an epigram which means nothing if it does not claim for the individual the right to do whatever he pleases without respect to any social considerations. In the end he extricates himself from the difficulty by making a distinction between natural freedom and social freedom. "What man loses by the social contract," he says, "is his natural liberty and the unlimited right to everything he wants and is able to get. What he gains is civil liberty and the right of ownership of all that he possesses." [3] In point of fact, the distinction is largely one of words, and would not have been needed at all if Rousseau had not made a false start on a line of thought that made advance completely impossible.

[1] I. 6.   [2] I. 1.   [3] I. 8.

The same *impasse* is reached quite explicitly in the
Emile, where Rousseau finds himself confronted with
the problem of individual and society as it presents
itself in the work of education. He notes that three
main factors determine the development of the child to
maturity : (*a*) "the education of nature"—the native
impulse to growth of body and mind, which is the central
fact in the process of education ; (*b*) "the education of
men"—the guidance by means of which the developing
faculties due to this impulse are made to assume socially
valuable forms, that enable the child to take his place in
society ; and (*c*) "the education of things"—the effect
produced on the child by the reaction of the physical
environment during the years of growth, that makes
him at home in the world of nature.[1] So long as the
three factors co-operate, Rousseau goes on to point out,
education results in the harmonious development of the
child's nature. The unfortunate thing is that such co-
operation is very rare in actual experience. Society
being what it is, the education of nature and the education of men seem inevitably to make in different directions. The child is impelled by the inner promptings
of nature to seek his own advantage; social education
seeks to curb this self-regarding tendency and to fashion
him for the service of others. In these circumstances
agreement is obviously impossible. "Being compelled
to combat nature or social institutions, we have to
choose between making a man or a citizen. We cannot
make both at once."[2] Having come to this conclusion,
Rousseau ought surely to have brought the *Emile* to an
abrupt close. What meaning can he possibly attach to
a natural education "that does not corrupt the man of
nature in making him a member of society"? On the

[1] I. 6.   [2] I. 13.

one hand, he refuses to regard as natural any education which merely makes citizens. That would be "an education of man" but assuredly not "an education of nature." Equally, on the other hand, he refuses to consider the alternative of an education for life independent of society. "What would be the use to other people," he asks, "of a man who had been educated entirely for himself?" But though by this dilemma Rousseau succeeds in proving the impossibility of a natural education under present conditions, he is not willing to abandon his own plan for a natural education. If by any means the double end of education could be attained in one system, he goes on to suggest in a hesitating way, the removal of the contradiction between the demands of nature and of society that would be achieved by the combination would take away one of the main obstacles to human happiness. Such a consummation, he thinks, is at least worth a serious effort to obtain; and in spite of his own overt expression of disbelief in the possibility, he sets out on the search for the man of nature living in society, that "extraordinary man" who does not cease to be natural in becoming social.

In both the *Social Contract* and the *Emile*, then, we see Rousseau confronted with what seems to be the same insuperable difficulty. Beginning on the one hand with the abstract individual who has "no more need of another man than a monkey or a wolf has of its fellows," [1] and who finds himself less free the moment he requires to depend on the services of another, and on the other hand with the abstract society which is the product of "a fortuitous concourse of external causes" and does not answer to any real need of man's nature,

[1] *Discourse on Inequality*, Part I.

he cannot logically work out a system of natural education or establish a state compatible with natural freedom. If all social institutions are of necessity unnatural, as Rousseau had in effect argued in his criticisms of them, the processes of education and of government must be included in the general condemnation. But the very fact that he should ask whether it is possible to have a system of education or government in accord with nature is a tacit disavowal of the fixed antithesis, an implicit expression of the faith in a possible reconciliation of the opposing claims of nature and institution. The obvious course for him, once he had raised the question, would have been to abandon, or at least to modify, the initial abstractions to which the difficulty was due, as a more systematic thinker would have done. But Rousseau's principles were too deeply imbedded in personal experience to be readily moved. He is certainly compelled to shift his ground considerably : otherwise it would have been impossible for him to make any attempt at the solution of the problems he had set himself to solve. But he does so with reluctance, and only so much as is absolutely necessary. The consequence is that even after he has embarked on a line of argument that is meaningless if the absolute opposition of the natural and the social is maintained, he is continually harking back to it; and however much he may modify his views under the pressure that comes from the necessities of his thought, he never succeeds in freeing himself altogether from the abstract ideas of the man-in-himself and of the artificial non-natural community, with which he began.

3. *The Two Opposing Ideals.*—The effect of this is apparent in the development of the argument in both the *Emile* and the *Social Contract*. Different as their

subjects seem to be, these works are really complementary treatments of the same practical problem. In
both cases we see Rousseau bent on showing how the
discords of human existence may be removed by making
social life more natural. His diagnosis of the cause of
man's unhappiness is that it proceeds from his nature
as a "double man," [1] who is in part natural and in
part educated, and therefore being continually drawn
in opposite directions by the calls of duty and of inclination. For the cure of the ills that result from this
discord, his prescription is that by some means or
other the natural and the social should be brought into
harmony in individual experience. How this is to be
done he is by no means clear. But his argument forces
two alternatives upon him. Either society should be
reconstructed in such fashion that the natural man can
find in it a congenial environment for the development
and exercise of his native capacities; or, if such a reconstruction of society is not feasible, the child should
be so educated that he can live under unsatisfactory
social conditions and yet remain true to himself as a
creature of nature. In the one case it is assumed that
the original dispositions of the individual are to remain
unchanged, and that the state and all the other institutions of civilisation are to be remade so as not to
interfere with his natural liberty. In the other case it
is assumed that nothing substantial can be done to im-
prove society, and that the reconciliation of interests
can only be effected by modifying the man-in-himself
so as to adapt him to society without making him
unnatural. The former is the solution of the problem
offered in the *Social Contract*, the other the solution
suggested in the *Emile*.

[1] *Emile*, i. 24.

It will be evident at once that these two lines of thought follow widely diverging courses. Whatever else is implied in the ideal social order that is in harmony with the fundamental impulses of man, there can be no place in it for capricious individuality any more than there is in the natural order which presumably it resembles. Idiosyncrasy and law are incompatible, and a natural society (if there could be such a society) would satisfy the generic needs of men without regard to their individuality. This way, then, lies the most absolute socialism. On the other hand, to train a child to remain natural in the midst of an artificial environment is only possible if the individual can be "in the world but not of it." It implies the possibility of a man withdrawing into himself and there finding capacities to enable him to remain true to his nature as a man, in spite of the social pressure that would substitute prejudice and convention for a personal faith. This complete self-sufficiency presupposes an individualism almost as absolute as the socialism of the other course.

If, in view of this, it be asked whether Rousseau is a socialist or an individualist, the answer must be that he is both. The consequence of trying to find common ground between nature and institution without re-thinking his premises is that he goes to the one extreme or the other, according as his emphasis is laid on the immutability of man's nature, or on the difficulties of reforming the existing society. But once his line of thought is chosen, he is ready to follow it out to the end with a remorseless logic, regardless of the fact that there is another line of thought quite inconsistent with it but equally open to him on his own premises. We have already seen this exemplified in the sharp contrast between the doctrine of the *Discourse on Inequality* and the contemporaneous Article on *Political Economy;* and now again it appears in the simultaneously issued *Social Contract* and *Emile.* In the later writings the contrast is in some ways more striking than in the earlier. Not only do they represent a maturer phase of thought, but they bring ideas which at first were only enunciated abstractly into closer relation to the actualities of life—and seemingly without making Rousseau any more conscious than before of the fundamental incompatibility of the two lines of thought, or leading him to call in question the convictions with which he set out on his quest for the truth about man and society.

Here we are only concerned with the consequences of this cleavage in Rousseau's thought so far as it affects his educational doctrine. It is obvious that the social-istic method of education must be profoundly different from the individualistic, and we turn with some degree of curiosity to his discussion of the subject to see which line he will elect to follow. As a matter of fact, we find the same impartiality as before. The *Emile* is the exposition of education from the point of view of the individual child; and its complement appears in the *Considerations on the Government of Poland* (written in 1772, ten years after the publication of the *Emile*), in which it is advocated that the state should determine the character of the education given to its citizens in its own interests. Before entering on the discussion of these opposing ideals of education, we must examine carefully the respective sociological concepts underlying them. The one is the idea of the Natural Man in Ordinary Society. The other is that of the Ideal Society of Natural Men.

A. THE NATURAL MAN IN ORDINARY SOCIETY

(*a*) *Considered from the Sociological Point of View*

4. *The Natural Man in Society.*—The student of Rousseau who passes directly from the *Discourse on Inequality* to the *Emile* finds some difficulty in understanding the idea on which the whole treatment of education in that book is based. After being led to think of the natural man as essentially non-social, as man "despoiled of all the supranatural gifts he may have received, and of all the artificial faculties he may have acquired, in the course of long ages of progress," he is invited to think of natural man as no longer wandering in the woods a solitary savage, but as being educated to take his place among civilised men, " the natural man living in the social state." The question immediately rises whether this new man of nature is the same person as the dull clod whose nearest kinsman in modern days is the dweller by the Orinoco whose brain has been kept from growing by timely pressure in infancy.

To outward seeming, at any rate, they are very different beings. The primitive man was a sense-bounded animal, living without foresight and needing " to educate himself *up* to the level of the brutes." There was nothing individual about any of his actions. Every situation that might arise for him could be met unintelligently by the aid of certain instinctive impulses that were common to him with the rest of his race. He had no permanent family and no social relations. A woman was but a female to him, and he could not recognise his own offspring, much less others of his kin. Emile, the latter-day man of nature, does

not appear to have anything in common with this
ancestor of his. Whatever he is, he is not stupid.
After his senses have been developed to a perfection at
least as great as that of primitive man, he learns to
judge and to think about all that concerns him with a
wisdom which most civilised men might envy. Moreover, while a complete and perfect *man*, he is none the
less an individual. All the training and instruction he
receives are adapted to his particular bent, and the
attempt is made to bring about the fullest development
of those distinctive powers that qualify him to fill a
place of his own in society.

Why, then, call Emile the man of nature at all, since,
both by his intelligence and by his individualised capacities, he belongs to society rather than to nature?
The real difficulty would seem to be, not to distinguish
him from the primitive man, but from the ordinary
respectable citizen whom no one, least of all Rousseau,
would regard as a man of nature.

5. *Two Views of the Man of Nature.*—Rousseau himself is quite aware of the difficulty, and makes an
attempt to dispose of it by what is really a change of
ground. He admits that in learning to judge and
reason Emile is apparently departing from the direct
contact with reality which is the essential feature of
a natural life, and making himself liable to all the
intellectual and moral errors from which the primitive
man is happily free. But he contends that the danger
is averted by the special education Emile receives. Unlike the education of the schools, which leads the pupil
into abstractions remote from the facts of nature and of
human life, Emile's education leads him by slow steps
from sense-experience to thought, and never loses touch
of the sense-given facts that are the ultimate court of

appeal in the matter of truth. In this way he is able to remain true to himself even in thinking, and avoid all the snares into which thought unchecked by experience is apt to lead man. So, again, it is his education which makes Emile a real individual and yet saves him from the common defects of individuality. As a rule, the specialised ability that fits a man for a particular social position is acquired at the expense of the fundamental human nature.[1] The soldier or lawyer or carpenter, for example, generally receives too special a training. He gains the necessary proficiency in his own profession or craft by an undue narrowing of his interests as a man and by the sacrifice of capacity in all save one or two lines of activity. Emile's education is his safeguard against the evils attendant on social specialisation. Under the guidance of the philosophical tutor, who never forgets that the boy's life is bound up with the great life of humanity, he learns to fulfil the duties of his own station without losing the power to adapt himself to all situations, and thus remains the master of his fate whatever his external conditions.

These are indeed significant admissions on Rousseau's part. But a certain ambiguity attaches to them. They ought to mean that those characters of body and mind which man acquires through his social relationships have their origin within himself, and are as natural as the appetites or the primitive dispositions. But they may also be taken to imply that in adapting himself to society man adds to his original nature certain new capacities by a kind of external accretion. In which of these senses are we to read Rousseau? On this depends the view we take of the relation of Emile, the man of nature living in society, to

[1] *Emile,* i. 29.

the dull, brutish man of nature who wandered lonely in the primeval woods. If society has grown out of nature, if social man is not a perversion of a simpler pre-social person but a higher being better equipped for living in every way, it would be altogether wrong to attempt to identify the two. On that view, life in society is not merely an accident which has resulted in certain advantageous additions to human faculty. It is a fact on a different level from all other facts, an experience that transforms all other experiences. If, on the other hand, civilisation is only a veneer, a separable accident of man's existence, then, great as the difference between the two types may be in outward seeming, it is not a real difference. Get beneath the surface of things and Emile will be found to be just the same savage animal as his primitive forbear, disguised in a covering of social manners. As a matter of fact, we find both of these views in the *Emile*.

(a) *The Atomistic View.*—Let us turn in the first instance to a striking passage in the Third Book where Rousseau, rebutting the charge that in making Emile capable of judgment he is rendering him less natural, gives an atomistic view of social man. "It will be said that I am making him less natural. Personally I do not think so. Nature chooses her instruments and makes use of them not according to opinion but according to need. Now, the needs of men change with their situation, and there is a great difference between the natural man living in nature and the natural man living in the social condition. Emile is not a savage to be banished to a desert, but a savage made to dwell in cities. He must be able to get the necessities of exist-ence there and profit by their inhabitants, and must at

least live with them, even if he does not live like them." [1]
Now, there can be no doubt about Rousseau's meaning
here. He finds the element common to Emile and the
primitive man in the fact of *need*, and especially in
the deepest need of all, the need to preserve life.
Seemingly the law of self-preservation is the supreme
law of human action. Whether it be savage man,
contending with wild beasts and wild men, or man
with all the culture of civilisation, depending on the
co-operation of others and rendering them service
in return for the services rendered to him, there is
the same basal impulse to self-preservation and self-
expansion, which justifies any course of action taken
in obedience to it.

But if we have learned the lesson that Rousseau is
constantly teaching, we immediately ask at this point
whether the man who has acquired characters foreign to
his original nature, even for the sake of self-preservation,
can any longer be said to be natural. Rousseau generally evades the difficulty when it arises, but the suggestion of the passage that has just been quoted is clearly
that the power of judging and thinking—which has raised
the question for him here—is a capacity that may be
acquired without changing man's nature in any fundamental way. In a word, judgment is a social trick
which Emile the savage needs to master if he is to live
among men. If, like the Mowgli of Kipling's *Jungle
Book*, he had found himself among wolves instead of
men, then the same law of self-preservation that led him
to master the tricks and manners of the men-folk would
have led him to acquire the wolfish arts. Wolf tricks
and men tricks are equally indifferent to the real man of
nature.

[1] III. 177.

In this connection may be noted the frequency
with which Rousseau presents the savage as a model
for civilised man, especially in the first three Books
of the *Emile*. It is true that he does not regard
the savage as properly natural any more than his
civilised compeer. As he points out in the *Discourse
on Inequality* and again in the *Emile*,[1] the savage
life is marred by defects of its own, such as cruelty,
which show that it too represents a departure from
the natural goodness of the primitive man. Still, even
with these defects, the savage exhibits the operation
of the native impulses comparatively free from the
modifications that result from social influences. He
is not bound to any one place or forced to labour at
a prescribed task, and his own will is his only law.
Moreover, he is *free*, not only from external interference
with his actions, but also from the tyranny of desires
which his powers are too limited to meet : free, therefore,
within and without, and so far superior to civilised man,
who lives in constant dependence on others for the satisfaction of his simplest wants, and is vexed by a diseased
imagination which makes him long for countless things
that no human power can obtain for him. Withal, he
is intelligent. His very independence forces him to be
so. Since he must rely on himself for everything, "he
is compelled to reason about every act of his life.
He does not move one step without having called up
the picture of the consequences beforehand. In this
way, the more his body is exercised, the greater his intelligence becomes. His strength and his reason grow
together."[2]

The same ideas are repeated in another and higher

[1] *Discourse on Inequality*, Part II. ; *Emile*, ii. 289.
[2] *Emile*, ii. 158.

form when Rousseau comes to deal with the education
of the lad just out of his boyhood and not yet into his
adolescence. Here the model held up is no longer the
savage, but Robinson Crusoe living alone on his desert
island.[1] There are differences between the two types,
notably the difference represented by the irresponsible
freedom of the wandering savage and the more human
freedom of the self-dependent tiller of the ground. But
at bottom the point of the comparison is the same. Both
give concrete expression to the idea that the man who
lives out of social relations is nearer nature than the
civilised man, and that the relations into which society
forces a man have always in them a foreign element
which is absent from the life of the man who stands
face to face with the elemental realities, and prospers
or fails according to the attention he pays to natural
laws.

(b) *The Social View.*—The cynical conception of the
man of nature which we have just considered is specially
characteristic of the earlier Books of the *Emile.* In
the last two Books there is another conception, very
different in import, which represents more adequately
Rousseau's general attitude to society during the later
period of his thought.

We find this latter view expressed definitely in a
passage of the Fourth Book which, in spite of the
complete difference of principle, is curiously like the
one already quoted. " If we want to form the man of
nature, there need be no thought of making him a
savage and banishing him to the heart of the woods.
Assuming him to be shut up in the whirl of social life,
it is enough that he should not allow himself to be
drawn into it either by his own passions or by the

[1] *Emile,* iii. 98 *seq.*

opinions of men; that he should see with his own eyes and feel with his own heart; and that he should be governed by no authority but that of his own reason. It is clear that in this situation the multitude of objects which impinge on him, the frequent sentiments by which he is affected, the diverse means of providing for his actual needs, are bound to give him many ideas which he would never have had or which would have come to him more slowly. The natural progress of the mind is accelerated but not changed in direction. The very man who would remain stupid in the forests is sure to become rational and acute in the cities, even if he is only a spectator of what goes on." [1]

In this passage, as in the corresponding passage already quoted, Rousseau is thinking of the possible objection to the course of education which he proposes, that the man of nature can only be brought up true to himself if he be kept out of society altogether, and here again he insists that there is no need for isolation. Note, however, the difference in the reason given. In the first passage it is assumed that, whatever happens, Emile remains a savage, and that what he learns does not affect his nature, since his relationship to society is only casual. Here a sounder line of thought is followed. Without entirely abandoning the hostile attitude to social institutions, Rousseau recognises that man can be a member of a community without losing himself as a man. Let him see with his own eyes and feel with his own heart, he says: let him be governed by no authority save that of his own reason, and the development of body and mind that takes place under social conditions will be the direct continuation of the natural growth that preceded the social stimulus, involving no such breach of con-

[1] IV. 162.

tinuity with the past as there would be if nature and society were really antagonistic in their demands.

This must not be taken to mean that all the forms of civilisation and culture are natural; for many of them (according to Rousseau) are not. All it implies is that some of these social forms may possibly be compatible with a natural life and are to that extent natural themselves.[1] This view is confirmed by the fact that Rousseau himself makes the distinction between conventions that are in accord with nature and those that are not.[2] He even urges that the only sound basis for any social relationship is some natural impulse. For example, in a wise discussion of the function of women in the Platonic Republic, he condemns the promiscuous employment of the two sexes at the same tasks because it involves a sacrifice of the sweetest sentiments of nature to an artificial arrangement which depends on these very sentiments for its existence—" as if," he goes on, " a natural tie were not needed to form the bonds of convention ! as if the love of a man for his neighbours were not the basis of that which he owes to the State ! as if it were not through the small fatherland of the family that the heart is attached to the great fatherland ! as if it were not the good son, the good husband, the good father who makes the good citizen !"[3] The outstanding example of this development of institution out of a natural relationship appears in marriage and all the

---

[1] Cf. *Social Contract*, ii. 6 : " That which is good and in conformity with order is so in the nature of things, independent of human convention. All justice comes from God. He alone is the source of it."

[2] Cf. *Emile*, v. 19 : " The inequality of the sexes is not a human institution, or at least it is not the work of prejudice but of reason." This implies clearly that the institutions created by reason are natural, whatever the others may be.

[3] *Emile*, v. 24.

social functions of the two sexes, to which we shall have occasion to refer at a later stage.[1]

The practical applications of this half-hearted acceptance of social conditions on Rousseau's part are interesting. He cannot shut his eyes to the fact that, in the world as it is, the preparation for adult duties involves in most cases living the unnatural life of the city, where men so easily lose their birthright of freedom and spontaneity; and he accepts the challenge that this makes to his principles by attempting to show how Emile can take his place *in partibus infidelium* without any surrender of the essentials of natural living. But he never conceals his opinion that the city is no fit dwelling-place for the man of nature;[2] and though he admits that it is necessary to educate the boy so that he may be able to live under all possible conditions, the admission is made under protest, and qualified by the assertion of a working ideal in sharp contrast with the life of the city-dweller. Not in savage life, and not in a future society incapable of present attainment, but in the actual life of country people, he finds the nearest approach to the best life for civilised men. "The natural condition of man," he says, "is to cultivate the earth and to live on its fruits. The peaceful country dweller only needs to feel his happiness to be aware of it. All the real pleasures of mankind lie to his hand· The only pains he suffers are those which are inseparable from humanity, the pains that men seek to escape only to find that they have exchanged them for others more cruel." [3] In one respect the countryman is like the natural man of the second *Discourse:* his faculties are all undeveloped and his individual talents lie hid. Is

---

[1] *Emile*, v. 150, 172.   [2] *Ibid.*, i. 120, 121.
[3] *New Heloïse*, v. 2.

this not a defect in the ideal? Rousseau will not admit
it. He grants that nature has conferred diverse abilities
on men, and that these seem to find proper outlet in a
society where the tasks of the community are portioned
out among its members in accordance with their talents.
But, he says, there are two things of more consequence
than talent, namely, goodness and happiness. " Man is
too noble a being to be obliged to serve as a merè instrument for others, and should not be employed at what he
is fit for without also taking into account what is fit for
him; for men are not made for their stations, but their
stations for men. In the right distribution of things,
therefore, we should not seek the employment for which
each man is best suited so much as the employment
most suitable for making each man as good and as happy
as possible." [1] This is indeed a noble ideal, and one
which Rousseau thinks can only be realised in a rural
life, where a man lives for the race rather than for
individual ends. In the country, according to him,
men are free and independent. The arrest of individual development has the happy consequence that
the true countryman is never distraught with over-
weening ambitions and inordinate desires. All the
needs of his life are capable of being satisfied either by
himself or within his family circle. " This brown bread,"
says Emile's tutor to him, in comparing a tiresome
dinner at a rich man's table with the simple repast they
have enjoyed in a peasant's cottage, " which you find
so good, comes from wheat picked by the peasant
himself. His wine, black and coarse but healthsome
and refreshing, is from the vine he grew himself. The
linen comes from his own hemp and was spun during
the winter by his wife, his daughters, and his servant.

[1] *New Heloïse*, v. 2.

No other hands than those of his family have prepared the articles on his table. The nearest mill and the neighbouring market are the limits of the universe for him." [1]

Compared with the savage ideal, this conception of the best life represents a real advance in almost every respect. The critic, probably forgetful of the fact that modern industrialism has still to solve most of the problems which Rousseau with some degree of truth finds solved in country life, may object that the highest type of goodness and happiness is not got by keeping the mind dull and unintelligent, and that the real problem for the social reformer is that very reconciliation of individual and social interests which Rousseau avoids by taking as his ideals men who lack individuality of mind and character. But, so far as Rousseau's own doctrine is concerned, the significant thing about the ideal is that it brings together the natural and the social; for the countryman, despite his rudeness and "inhumanity," is a member of society, and fulfils the duties of a station that includes the family life and the life of a neighbourhood extending at least as far as "the nearest mill and the adjoining market." And though it is still maintained that a man may live the best life even if his mind is scarcely open to any ideas beyond the immediate facts of experience, and even if he is only one man among others with no opportunity for the exercise of his distinctive powers, the assertion that reflection or individuality is unnatural is no longer made. On the contrary, it is even suggested that they are a provision made by nature herself against the possibility of a life complex beyond the wildest dreams of primitive man. Doubtless it

[1] *Emile*, iii. 125.

would have been better if the need for them had
never arisen, but once it has arisen it is recognised
that it is good that man should possess the capacity
to meet it. "Each man comes into the world with
character, genius, and talents peculiar to himself.
Those who are destined to live in rustic simplicity
do not need their faculties developed to make them
happy. Their buried talents are like the gold mines
of the Valais which the public good does not allow to
be exploited. But under the conditions of city life,
where the head is of more use than the hands, and
every man has to depend on himself and his fellows
for the reward of his labours, it is important to be able
to get out of men all that nature has given them, by
directing them on the side whence they can go furthest,
and above all by encouraging their special inclinations in every way that can make them of use. In
the first case, only the species needs to be considered.
Every one acts alike. Example is the only rule,
habit the only talent, and only that part of the soul
which is common to all is brought into play. But in
the second case, we are dealing with the individual,
with man in general, and our endeavour is to develop
every capacity in which he excels his fellows, and to
go as far as nature will take us. We are prepared to
make him the greatest man on earth if only he has
the necessary ability." [1]

6. *The Criterion of what is Natural.*—In seeking to
determine the meaning to be attached to the idea of the
natural man living in society which underlies the whole
treatment of the educational problem in the *Emile*, we
have found that Rousseau has two quite different views
on the subject. The one is the view that occurs for the

[1] *New Heloïse*, v. 3.

most part in the first three Books. We have called it
the atomistic view, because it implies that the individual
man is complete in himself apart from his fellows, and,
consequently, that society is only an accidental condition to which man has been compelled to accommodate
himself, to the detriment of his original nature.[1] The
ideal state on this view is most fitly illustrated by the
savage, the forceful, intelligent embodiment of an individuality free from all social restraints, which knows no
law but self-will and the necessity that is in things.
The second is the view which occurs most definitely in
the two last Books of the *Emile*. We have called it
the social view, because it rests on the idea that social
institutions are but the elaboration of some natural
impulse or disposition in the sphere of communal
action. On this view there is no difficulty about the
man of nature being found in society, since it is out
of those characters which are fundamental in his constitution that society itself has sprung. It is an
indication of the hesitation with which Rousseau advanced to the reconciliation of the natural and the
social that the man who illustrates this point of
view is the countryman with his comparatively simple
social life. His predominant characters are almost
at the opposite pole from those of the savage. Intelligence and individuality, so conspicuous in the
savage, occupy quite a subordinate place in his personality. In him the great basal impulses of humanity
find expression, free from intermixture with merely
individual traits and comparatively unchanged by social
influences.

---

[1] " The natural man is complete in himself : he is the numerical unit,
the absolute whole, related only to nimself or to his fellow. Social
man is but a fraction of unity dependent on its denominator, whose
value is in its relation to the whole, which is society."—*Emile*, i. 15.

Postponing for a brief space the inevitable question as to which of the two views is the more fundamental in Rousseau's thought, we cannot but note that neither of the two is identical with the conception of the natural man in the *Discourse on Inequality*. The savage resembles him in being free from social obligations: the countryman, in being dominated by the racial impulses rather than by personal reason. But in both cases the differences are quite as striking as the similarities, a fact that leads us to suspect that the natural man in society is not the same person as the antesocial man of nature. This is confirmed by a remark made by Rousseau in the course of an attempt to distinguish between the natural and the conventional elements in a particular social relationship: "What is natural in the savage state," he says, "must not be confused with what is natural in the social state."[1] This is a definite abandonment of the distinction made in the *Discourse on Inequality* between a primitive natural part in man that is prior to society, and the artificial modifications and additions that society itself has produced.

This shifting of ground is just what we might have expected. The practice of education and politics forces us to deal with man as he is to-day, and the definition of his "nature" by reference to a prehistoric condition about which, in the nature of the case, it is impossible to know anything, is quite useless. We want to know the nature of the being with which we are actually dealing, and to say that he was or is an animal is obviously a very inadequate account of him. As a matter of fact, Rousseau's criterion of what is natural is quite different in the later writings

[1] *Emile*, v. 172. *Cf.* iii. 177.

from what it was in the earlier. The question he asks is no longer what characters of humanity were first in order of historical development, but what characters are the permanent unchanging features of human life under all the vicissitudes of social condition. His quest is for the highest common factor of actual human nature, for human nature stripped of all its social variants. "Man," he declares in one passage, "is the same in all states. . . . For a thinking man, all the ordinary social distinctions disappear. He sees the same passions and sentiments in the rogue as in the man of renown." [1] "After comparing as many ranks and peoples as I have been able to see in the course of a life spent in observing men, I have marked off as artificial whatever was characteristic of one people or class and not of another, and have regarded as characters indubitably pertaining to mankind only those that are common to every age, rank, and nation." [2]

Compared with the pseudo-historical method of the *Discourses*, this attempt at defining man's nature in terms of its common elements represents a considerable advance. It corrects at once the fundamental error of the *Discourses*, of limiting the real nature of man to animality. Certainly man is an animal, and no conception of society that omits to take that into account can be regarded as satisfactory. So far Rousseau's view is of value, in that it reminds us, by its over-emphasis, of the physical basis of the mental and moral life. But though man is an animal, the animal characters are not the only or even the most important elements in his nature; and the method of the common factors serves to bring the omitted elements of his nature into view. If

[1] *Emile*, iv. 62.   [2] *Ibid.*, iv. 159.

the natural is that which is found everywhere among men, then society, being a universal fact of human life as we know it, must be regarded as natural. Some of its institutions may be the products of man's artifice, but all the more important—the family, the church, the state, education—have their origin in some fundamental human need and have an unquestionable right to be viewed as essential facts of human life. So too, if we turn from society and its institutions to those characters of man which have come into existence under social conditions, faculties such as reason and conscience, which in the *Discourses* were treated as suspect because they were involved in the general progress that withdrew man from his first simplicity, need to be recognised as natural on the same terms as society itself.

So far, the new criterion is much superior to the old. By its adoption, the conception of society as in some sense natural ceases to present an insuperable difficulty, and it becomes possible to seek a meeting ground common to the natural and the social. But if it has great merits, it has also great defects. It is a mistake to think that we can know any class of objects aright so long as our acquaintance with them is limited to the characters that are common to all the members of the class. The higher the order of existence to which an object belongs, the more necessary it becomes to know not merely the common features but also those that are peculiar to individuals and groups of individuals. The differences between the individuals making up a group are often as characteristic of the group as their resemblances, and in any case we can never know the group without knowing them. The result of seeking only the common factors in the characterisation of

humanity is that we lose sight of the relations in
which the supposed common characters stand to each
other. We see, for example, the operation of all the
functions that pertain to man as an animal, and on
the strength of them we write down animality as a
human character. What we fail to see is the relation
between this fact and the other facts of man's nature.
There is nothing in the method of the common factors
to show that animality in man is quite different from
animality in the animal. The transformation that the
merely animal characters inevitably undergo in becoming elements in the higher life of a spiritual being
is certain to be overlooked by a method which simply
shows us that man is an animal *and* a spiritual being.
In the same way, the application of the test of uni-
versality gives quite a wrong view of the relation of
individual and society. It shows on the one hand that
every man comes into the world with a distinctive
nature of his own which determines more or less profoundly the manner of his reaction on the facts of
physical and social experience; and on the other hand,
that every man is a member of a community which
impresses on him certain forms of conduct which are
common to him with the other members of the community. What it·does not show is the connection
between the two sets of facts. So far as is indicated
by the cataloguing process that takes into account all
that is common and nothing but what is common,
individuality and socially determined habit are distinct
and unrelated phenomena. The individual nature *and*
the social nature appear side by side in seeming
unconnectedness. The picture we get of humanity
by stripping off all but the common characters,
accordingly, is that of an aggregate of separate

qualities. One might almost compare it with the mis-leading view of plant or animal structure that is got on looking at a single microscopic section. The different organs are represented there, but all those inter-relations that can only be appreciated when we see the single section as part of the whole organism are wanting. Rousseau's view of human nature is a cross-section view.

7. *The Relation of the Two Views of the Man of Nature in Society.*—What has just been said has an obvious bearing on the two views that Rousseau gives of the man of nature in society in the *Emile.* Though contradictory, both are necessary, because either in itself is incomplete. We can always dis-tinguish two phases in the life of an individual man. On one view of him, he is the man that his social environment makes him; apart from the social forms in which his nature finds expression, he would have no nature to express. But there is another view of him, complementary to this, on which it can be asserted with equal truth that for him there can be no self-expression through these forms, except in so far as they come into being in response to the felt needs of his nature—by being individualised in his experience and becoming *his* forms.[1] In truth, the two aspects are aspects of the same fact. A man's nature, whether we mean by that the nature he shares with all mankind or that which is distinctive and individual, cannot exist *in vacuo :* by itself, it is nothing but mere formless impulses. Nor is

[1] " Except thine own eye have got to see it, except thine own soul have victoriously struggled to clear vision and belief of it, what is the thing seen or the thing believed by another, or by never so many others ? Alas, it is not thine . . . but only a windy echo and tradition of it bedded in hypocrisy, ending sure enough in tragical futility, is thine."—FROUDE: *Carlyle,* ii. p. 10.

society separable from individual experience. It only exists and continues to exist by continually reproducing itself in the personal ideals of its members. But there are times when institutions wax old, and the best men find themselves craving in vain for adequate means of realising themselves. Then there opens up a gulf between man and society which impatient souls deem impassable. *Either* man is set up against society as though he had a nature of his own independent of it and had no need of his fellows for the realization of himself—an exaggeration of individuality which involves a misapprehension of the nature of social institutions as something external to the real man and incapable of doing justice to him. *Or* organised society is set up in contrast with the individual as endowed with all the attributes of strength, permanence, wisdom, and goodness which the individual lacks. On this view, the man is only what his society makes him. Either individualism or socialism : these are the extremes between which thought fluctuates in an age uncertain of itself. Sometimes, in minds more open to every wind of doctrine than the ordinary, individualism and socialism appear in compensatory alternation.

This was the world of half-truths in which Rousseau lived. His alienation from all the great institutions of humanity, his failure to find a worthy place for himself among his fellows, threw him back on himself. The blame of his failure, he was well convinced, did not lie with himself but with society ; and generalising this conviction, he reached the conclusion that the individual as such is essentially good, and that if he becomes bad or fails to realise all his potentialities the fault is with society rather than with himself. " According to M. de

Wolmar,[1] the different characters that men have are all good and sound in themselves. There are no blunders in nature. All the vices we impute to natural disposition are the result of the bad forms it has assumed. There is not a scoundrel living whose natural propensities would not have produced great virtues if they had been better directed."[2]   It is this faith in the inherent goodness of the individual man and the consequent distrust of every form of social interference that is the dominant motive of his earlier thought about society, and even though much of the exaggeration that attached to the first statement of it disappears in the *Emile* and the later writings, the cynical view to which it led him is never completely abandoned.   It is recognised, as we have seen, that man is by nature a social being, and the various problems of education and government are discussed on the explicit assumption that the individual can only realise his nature as a man by becoming a worker and a citizen.   All the while, however, there is a cynical under-current which manifests itself in the recurrence of certain of the earlier criticisms of civilisation, and even more perhaps in the hesitation to recognise any but a few of the simpler of the institutions of society as based on natural relationships.   In brief, we have an individualism, formally repudiated but never entirely abandoned; and alongside of it a much qualified and restricted acceptance of social conditions as not altogether contrary to nature.[3]

---

[1] One of the characters of the romance of the *New Heloïse*—clearly enough Rousseau himself, in this passage.

[2] *New Heloïse*, v. 3.

[3] In this connection, the two types of natural man to which reference has already been made are worthy of note. The savage typifies an aggressive individualism, while the husbandman is significant of the narrow limits within which Rousseau is willing to recognise social institutions as in accord with nature.

8 *The Social Doctrine of the Emile.*—The relation between the two views of society in the *Emile* will be best understood by considering the argument of the book as a whole. It has already been pointed out that the one view is found chiefly in the earlier part of the book, the other chiefly in the later part. The meaning of this will be evident if we remember that the *Emile* presents in succession the various stages of human growth from birth to manhood. In Book I. we see the infant "without feelings or ideas, scarcely even with sensations, and not conscious of his own existence." [1] This is the genuine animal man. In Book II. we reach the second stage of human life, boyhood from two to twelve. The boy is still a creature of sense and incapable of thought about anything except the immediate facts of his experience. Consequently he is not to be regarded as either a rational or a moral being. He acts on impulses checked only by an ever-increasing knowledge of their physical consequences, and he understands nothing of the adult world around him ; duty and obedience and all the words that imply motives other than those of self-interest are meaningless for him. In his experience of life he reproduces many of the traits of savage existence, and the comparison of him with the savage is peculiarly appropriate. Book III. deals with the intermediate period between boyhood and adolescence, extending from twelve tr fifteen. According to Rousseau, this stage is characterised by a certain development of reasoning power which lifts the boy out of the present and makes him capable of ordering his life with reference to future well-being. On this side of his being the lad reaches forward. On the moral side, however, he has still the limitations of boyhood. As yet con-

I. 193.

science is asleep, self-interest is his one consideration,
and he is outside the ordinary relationships of the adult.
His social analogue is the self-sufficient worker, whose
individual strength and intelligence enable him to face
the world without any help from his fellows—Robinson
Crusoe, for example, or the old-time farmer. Book IV.,
dealing with the last stage of immature life, shows how
the adolescent gradually becomes a member of society.
The coming of puberty marks the beginning of the most
profound changes in every department of life. " We are
twice born, so to speak : the first time for mere existence,
the second time for real living ; the first time for the
species, the second time for sex." [1] Henceforward, the
boy no longer lives to himself, for with the wakening
of conscience his life has become bound up with the life
of his fellows. At this stage, with the nascent glow of sex
making him realise that it is not good for a man to be
alone, the comparisons with savages and Crusoes are no
longer in place. He becomes in every essential respect a
social being, and apart from society in some form it is
not possible for him to satisfy himself. Book V., dealing
with the education of the girl, stands by itself ; but in
social attitude it is allied with Book IV. rather than with
the earlier Books. The need of preparation for the right
discharge of the various duties of wife and mother,
which on Rousseau's view should determine the character of the girl's education from her earliest days,
has a direct reference to social ends. It is only in
civilised society that any preparation is needed for
the special functions of womanhood. Such an education as Rousseau proposes, therefore, implies the most
intimate relation between nature and convention.

It will be evident, on consideration of this survey of

[1] IV. 2.

the moral and intellectual development of the child, that, quite apart from the progressive modification of Rousseau's doctrine of society as the writing of the *Emile* went on,[1] it is not an accident that the social doctrine of the first three Books differs from that of the fourth and fifth. The subject-matter of the first three Books is man in what Rousseau rightly or wrongly regards as the pre-social stage of his life. As the child passes from birth to adolescence in the course of his growth, he goes through stages which correspond broadly with those traversed in the evolution of the race : he is first an animal, then a savage, then a solitary like Crusoe, and only at adolescence is he a human being in the full sense of the word. That being so, Rousseau maintains that there is no use pretending that the boy is a social being. By all means develop the capacities proper to his years, he would say, and appeal to the motives that his immature mind can appreciate, but do not think to make him understand anything of moral or social obligations. The infant is an animal : treat him as an animal. The ten-year-old boy is a savage : expect no more from him than from a savage. Even from twelve to fifteen, be satisfied to see the boy play the game of Crusoe, since in social outlook he is still a solitary. The only natural life, and therefore the only natural education, is one that takes into account the motive interests proper to the actual stage of development reached by the child, and ignores all reference to stages beyond the scope of his present vision.

Here, then, is the key to the individualism of these Books. According to Rousseau, the child in his development is living over again the great epochs through

[1] See the first section of this chapter.

which humanity has passed on its upward movement
to civilisation; and to do justice to childhood, we must
get at its peculiar point of view, or what is the same
thing, at the point of view of undeveloped humanity
in the childhood of the race. As far as possible, we
must unlearn all that society has taught man, and try
to see life with the eyes of pre-social man, whether that
be the boy or the savage. Not that Rousseau puts
the matter in this way. He is only vaguely aware
of the significance of that suggestive parallelism between the development of the race and the growth
of the individual which he himself was the first to use
as a principle of guidance in educational practice, and
he never attempts to enunciate it in so many words.
Nevertheless the idea of the parallel is implicit in all
his discussion of the characteristics of boyhood. In the
endeavour to get at the point of view of the boy, he
makes constant use of his conceptions of savage or
solitary life, and constitutes himself the spokesman of
boyhood, whether of the individual or of the race. One
might almost say that in the first three Books of the
Emile Rousseau does not speak *in propria persona*,
but makes himself the advocate of humanity on its
lower pre-social level.

It is not intended to suggest that the crude individualism of the *Discourses* is entirely absent from
these Books. The fact is that it reappears occasionally
even in the later Books, where there is less reason for
its recurrence. But when it does occur, it runs counter
to the spirit of the *Emile* as a whole, and is to be
regarded as an unfortunate reversion to an earlier
strain of thought rather than as a fundamental idea
really relevant to the discussion of the problems of
education. If proof of this be needed, it is to be

found as clearly in the first three Books as in the last two.

The doctrine that the natural man is a social being and dependent on a social environment for his right development is, as might be expected, most definitely stated in Books IV. and V. There it is expressly asserted that man is not truly man without those sentiments and notions of good and evil that come into existence in society,[1] and that, so far from being naturally a solitary, he "is sociable by nature or intended to become so."[2] In accordance with this view, education is looked on as an art that "seconds nature"[3] and enables "a man to become all that he has the capacity to become"[4] by carrying nature's work still further; and the teacher, so far from being an intruder on natural process, does his work "in co-operation with nature,"[5] deriving from nature herself "the instruments wherewith to rule her."[6]

But though the conception of the relation of nature and society conveyed by these illustrative references is most consistently maintained in the Books where the social implications of education are necessarily made explicit, it is no less definite throughout the Books that treat of the child in his pre-social stages. The express declarations with regard to the final end of education which occur in various forms in the First Book clearly establish this. "A father only performs a third part of his task when he feeds the children he has brought into the world," he says in the well-known passage in which he confesses his own sins in abandoning his children. "To the race he owes men: to society

---

[1] IV. 39.   [2] IV. 293.
[3] V. 52. *Cf.* v. 109, iii. 56.   [4] *New Heloïse*, v. 3.
[5] IV. 357.   [6] IV. 402.

he owes sociable beings: to the state he owes citizens."[1]
Again, when discussing the work of the tutor, he insists
that he must be a "*gouverneur*" and not merely a
"*précepteur*," guiding and directing the boy's life and
not merely giving lessons. "There is really only one
form of knowledge to be taught to children," he goes
on to say: "it is the knowledge of a man's duties."[2]

If, then, it be asked what Rousseau means by the
man of nature living in society, we may consider ourselves warranted in answering that he is quite a different being from the primitive man of the *Discourse
on Inequality* who does not need society in any form.
The natural man whose career is set forth in the *Emile*
is only a non-social being in his immature years. The
time inevitably comes when he must take his part in
social life in order to complete his own nature as a man,
and then it becomes manifest that, so far from his
nature being necessarily at variance with the form
which it takes under social education, a social form of
some kind is indispensable for its right development
and exercise. It is only by travelling the common
highway of reason and living the life of the good
neighbour and the honest citizen that man is able to
realise all or any of the potentialities of his original
endowment. Apart from society, he would not be man.

A. The Natural Man in Ordinary Society

(b) Considered from the Psychological Point of View

9. *The Nature of Man.*—After so much talk about
the natural man, it is necessary to remind ourselves
that he is only a symbolic personage. The comparison

---

[1] I. 64.   [2] I. 81.

between the natural man and the social man which
bulks so largely in all Rousseau's sociological discussions
is simply a convenient means of expressing the fundamental contrast between what man is by nature and
what he owes to nurture—a contrast of elements within
the individual man, and not a contrast between one type
of man and another. In other words, Rousseau's socio-
logy rests on his psychology, his doctrine of society
on his doctrine of man. Consequently, for the understanding of the significance of those views of social
relationships which have been under discussion, we
must now go on to seek more definite ideas with
regard to the nature of man.

What is this "nature" to which Rousseau is constantly
referring ? This is the question which he sets himself
to answer in the discussion of general educational principles at the beginning of the *Emile*.[1] He leads up to
his answer through a characteristic passage in which he
compares education with plant culture. " Man changes
and disfigures everything," he complains : " he is not
satisfied with anything as nature has made it, not even
with mankind. . . . He must needs shape man to his
fancy as he does the tree in his garden." Yet he has
no sooner brought this charge against the evil works of
social man than he proceeds to qualify his statements
by admitting that, apart from this interference with
nature, there are conditions under which neither man
nor plant could survive, and indeed that, so far as man
is concerned, these conditions actually prevail at the
present time. As things now are, he goes on to say,
with mankind living everywhere in communities, a man
left to himself from birth would fare even worse than
the man whom society has fashioned for its own ends.

[1] I. 1–31.

He would be like the shrub that by some chance had
sprung up beside the roadway and that would soon be
destroyed by those who passed by if it were not for the
gardener's care. We may take it for granted, then, that
under the only conditions that we know, education is
necessary if man is to live at all. "We are born weak
and need strength. We are born devoid of everything
and need help. We are born stupid and need judgment." [1] For all these reasons, education which sup-
plements our initial deficiencies is as much needed
as the culture given to the plant. But the illustration indicates clearly the narrow limits within which
this help is legitimate. Man certainly resembles the
cultivated plant in some important respects. Just as
the plant has its own tendencies and habits, its own
ways of reacting to its environment, its own laws of
growth, all of which may be modified and set aside for
a time by the skill of the gardener, so, too, man has a
distinctive nature of his own which forms the raw
material for the educator. And in both cases the
original nature imposes limits beyond which the work
of cultivation cannot be permanently carried. "Are
there not some habits which are only acquired under
compulsion and which never stifle nature? Such, for
example, is the habit of those plants which the gardener
bends over from the vertical position. When set at
liberty, they retain the inclination they have been forced
to take; but, for all that, the sap has not changed its
primitive direction, and if the plant continues to grow
the new shoot returns to the vertical. It is the same
with the inclinations of men. So long as their condition remains unchanged, those that result from habit
and are least natural may be kept, but immediately the

[1] I. 5.

situation changes, the habit disappears and the natural tendency returns." [1]

Obviously, these inclinations, tendencies, habits in conformity with nature, or whatever they are to be called,[2] are the constituent elements in man's nature which have to be given their social forms (or shapes) by the educator. Can they be defined more exactly? Rousseau thinks they can, and attempts to do so in a noteworthy passage in which the idea of man's essential nature, that is suggested by the analogy of the plant, is further expanded and developed. "We are born capable of feeling (*sensibles*), and from our birth are affected in various ways by the objects around us. As soon as we have what may be called a consciousness of our own sensations, we are disposed to seek or to avoid the objects that produce them: in the first instance, according as they are agreeable or disagreeable to us; at a later time, according to the congruity or incongruity

---

[1] I. 11.

[2] I am tempted to call them instincts, to bring Rousseau's doctrine into line with modern biological thought. The following passage from an able exponent of this thought on its psychological side expresses Rousseau's view with great exactness: "We may say, then, that directly or indirectly the instincts are the prime movers of all human activity; by the conative or impulsive force of some instinct (or of some habit derived from an instinct), every train of thought, however cold and passionless it may seem, is borne along towards its end, and every bodily activity is initiated and sustained. The instinctive impulses determine the ends of all activities and supply the driving power by which all mental activities are sustained; and all the complex intellectual apparatus of the most highly developed mind is but a means towards these ends, is but the instrument by which these impulses seek their satisfactions, while pleasure and pain do but serve to guide them in their choice of the means. . . . These impulses are the mental forces that maintain and shape all the life of individuals and societies, and in them we are confronted with the central mystery of life and mind and will."—MACDOUGALL, *An Introduction to Social Psychology*, p. 44. Again: "The fundamental problem of social psychology is the moralisation of the individual by the society into which he is born as a creature in which the non-moral and purely egoistic tendencies are so much stronger than any altruistic tendencies." *Ibid.*, p. 18.

between ourselves and them;[1] and ultimately according to the judgments we form about them by reference to the idea of happiness or perfection given us by reason. These dispositions extend and strengthen with every increase in our sensibility and intelligence, but under pressure from our habits they change more or less with our opinions. The dispositions before this change are what I call our nature."[2]

In this striking account of the mind of civilised man we have an epitome of the conception of man's nature which underlies the whole argument of the *Emile*. We shall find in a careful analysis of its terms the clearest indication of Rousseau's view of human nature. By way of preparation for this analysis, the leading ideas of the passage and their immediate implications may be summarily stated.

1. The two ultimate elements of mind are sense-experience and will.
2. The nature of man is shown by what he wills or is "disposed" to do.
3. Man's nature does not consist of a set of characters fixed once for all, but is capable of development.
4. That development depends on the development of his mind as a whole.
5. Three stages of mental progress are distinguishable, characterised by—

   (*a*) the simple feeling of pleasure and pain, a state of mind unrelated, so far as the feeling individual is concerned, to the causes of the state;

---

[1] What this means is brought out clearly by iv. 292, where the same phrase is used.
[2] I. 12.

> (b) sentiments of attraction or repulsion—that
> is, determinate feelings giving an immediate
> knowledge of objects in their bearing on
> one's well-being;
>
> (c) personal ideals, by which the worth of
> affecting objects is judged.
>
> 6. The "dispositions" to act of which man's nature
> consists are not specific activities, but impulses
> to action that derive their specific character from
> the environment in which they are realised, and
> from the whole context of the mind of which they
> form a part.

10. *The Primitive Dispositions.* — It is worthy of
note that the problem with which Rousseau is dealing
in these sections at the beginning of the *Emile* is
exactly the same as that which occupied him in the
preliminary discussions in the *Discourse on Inequality*.
In both cases he sets himself to define what is original
in the nature of man as we know him. But the solu-
tions proposed are different. In the *Discourse*, it will
be remembered, he tried to mark off certain faculties or
mind elements as primary constituents, and so was able
to represent man's nature as complete once for all in the
person of the natural man. On this statement of the
distinction between what is native and what is acquired,
every character added to the original faculties in the
course of human progress is regarded as an addition to
man's primitive endowments, about which the best that
can be said is that it is not contrary to nature. Natural
man, in short, is man at a certain early stage in his
development. In the *Emile*, Rousseau escapes from the
difficulties that beset the attempt to think of man's

nature as something complete in itself, by stating the essential human characters as *dispositions*. Now, a disposition is nothing actual. It is a mere tendency awaiting a suitable material for its embodiment, a potentiality which depends on environing circumstances not only for the opportunity to realise itself but also for the manner in which it will realise itself. Consequently, if man's nature be simply certain dispositions or inclinations, it is not something unchanging and incapable of change. Rather it represents an infinite number of possibilities, any one of which can only be regarded as a more or less inadequate expression of potencies whose complete fulfilment it is beyond our power to conceive.[1]

This, it will be noted, alters the whole point of view with regard to the story of human evolution. When the state of nature is considered even hypothetically as having had its existence sometime about the beginning of history or before it, it is necessary to think of what man once was, rather than of what he has become, in order to interpret his evolution. With human nature viewed as disposition, on the contrary, the stress is laid on what man has become rather than on what he has been. The significance of his evolution is found at the top, and not at the bottom, of the series of life stages through which he has passed. An important consequence is that, on the new conception of man, it is no longer necessary to regard society as essentially antagonistic to human nature. There is even a strong presumption, if not more, that since man is a social being and owes to society all his developed powers, society itself must be in some sense natural. To this point we shall have to return after examining the various stages

[1] I. 132.

through which man's nature has passed in the course of its evolution.

11. *The First Stage of Human Development: Animal Feeling.*—According to Rousseau, the beginnings of mind, both in the race and in the individual, are to be found in a purely subjective state of individual feeling. Children are born endowed with senses and capable of feeling (*sensibles*),[1] and the first impact of external things "affects" them only to the extent of engendering feelings of pleasure and pain : their "first sensations are purely affective, there is only the perception of pleasure and pain."[2] The consequence of this engrossment in sense appears in the indeterminate response they are "disposed" to make. It is a mere vague striving to repel the cause of pain, which spends itself in movements and cries of a "mechanical kind, without anything of knowledge or will in them."[3] When they have pleasurable feelings, they enjoy them in silence. When they are in pain, they make it known in their own language,[4] which is always the same, because for them the different pains are merely pain without differentiation.[5]

With this infantile condition may be compared that of the primitive man before enlightenment came to him from a developed understanding. "We may assume," Rousseau says in a passage in the *Discourse on Inequality* which forms an interesting parallel to those we are now studying, "that savage man begins with purely animal functions. His first state is that of per-

---

[1] *Emile*, i. 12.   [2] I. 135.   [3] I. 128.   [4] I. 145.
[5] I. 148. "If the child is hungry or thirsty, he cries. If he is too warm or too cold, he cries. If he wants to be moved and he is held quiet, he cries. If he wants to sleep and is being disturbed, he cries. He has only one language, because (so to speak) he has only one kind of ill-being. Owing to the imperfection of his organs, he does not distinguish their different impressions. All his ills produce only a sensation of pain."

ception and feeling, in which respect he is at one with all the animals. To will and not to will, to desire and to fear, are the first and almost the only operations of his soul up to the time when new conditions bring about further developments." [1] The one advantage he has over the child is in the possession of animal instincts—"the simple impulses of nature"—which direct him as to things to be desired or to be feared, and enable him to take the right line of action in any particular case, without the exercise of intelligence on his part. In all other respects he is on the mental level of the child. The only personal element in his actions is the striving to retain what pleases and to repel what hurts.

12. *The Second Stage of Human Development: The Self-regarding Sentiments.*—The child passes out of the condition of unintelligent feeling at a very early age. In the course of time, the regular recurrence of certain sensations produces habits of mind and gives the sensations a more or less definite association with the objects causing them, which makes them "representative sensations." [2] Once he begins to move about freely, his learning proceeds apace. He discovers the existence of foreign bodies, senses their physical qualities by touching and handling them, and gets some idea of space from his movements. In these ways his feelings gradually cease to be mere states of his individual consciousness and acquire meaning with reference to the external world. They become not merely sensations but perceptions, or, to make one word of it, sense-perceptions. [3]

---

[1] Part I.   [2] I. 135.

[3] It is important that the reader should note that what the modern psychologist calls sense-perceptions Rousseau usually calls "sensations," a most unfortunate usage that leads to the confusion of two things so different as sensation and perception.

All through boyhood he continues to make progress in the direction of mental definiteness, but never wholly escapes from his first dependence on the senses. So far as ideas imply the reflective activities of comparison, judgment, and reasoning, which bring the different sense-experiences into relation to each other, he is wholly devoid of ideas. He has "simple ideas," however, which are produced in him by the regular concourse of sensations without any directive activity of mind on his part. His daily life is rich in the materials from which such ideas are derived, and he has constant opportunities for adding to his stock of them. He can even judge and reason on the level of the senses. That is to say, from what happens when a particular sense-presentation comes within his ken, he learns to modify his conduct on any subsequent occasion when that presentation recurs, the modification not being a general modification but one that is only effective in a single situation. On the intellectual side, therefore, his knowledge consists of so many isolated individual percepts or images.[1]

But though this progress is important in view of the fact that "all that enters into the human understanding comes through the senses," [2] it is not the central fact of childhood. It is not what comes from without, but what issues from within, that is fundamental in man's development. Consequently the rise of self-consciousness is a fact of deeper significance than the increase of sense-experience. It is the first consciousness of self, extending over all the moments of his existence and imparting unity to his life, that really marks the departure of the child from animal feeling. Only then is it

[1] II. 116 *seq.*, 303.
[2] II. 186. *Cf.* iv. 292. "We necessarily feel before we know."

possible to consider him as "a moral being" with the potentialities of social life in him.[1]

With the growth of self-consciousness from childhood onward, new elements make their appearance in mind, to which Rousseau gives the name of "sentiments."[2] What these sentiments are, and whence they come, he nowhere states; but in his incidental references to them, we note that he attributes to them both cognitive and conative functions. They are innate feelings or passions which come to us with the same immediacy and the same convincing directness of appeal as the sense-presentations, and enable us to pass judgments of value on certain orders of facts. The sentiments of conscience, for example, are called up instantly at the sight of a good or a bad deed, and take the form of definite feelings of love or of hate, of approval or of disapproval. Evidently thinking of this immediacy of pronouncement, Rousseau speaks of them at times as though they implied the existence of an "inner sense,"[3] to which they are related as the sensations are to the five senses; but in so far as they involve powers of discernment, they are plainly more nearly akin to ideas, the products of judgment and comparison, and he recognises this when he says somewhat loosely and inaccurately that sentiments and ideas are the same in kind, the idea being an explicit senti-

---

[1] II. 8.

[2] *Cf.* Ch. Bonnet, *Essai de psychologie* (to which Rousseau's psychology owes much), chap. 53 : "But why does the soul experience certain sentiments in presence of certain objects? It is its nature to do so. . . . The soul has its sentiments just as it has the sensation of heat."

[3] The idea of an "inner" experience comparable with that mediated by the senses is repeated by Rousseau in many different forms, especially in the *Confession of Faith of the Savoyard Vicar*, in which he speaks of the inner voice, the inner light, the inner assent, the inner feeling, the inner witness, &c., not once but many times.

ment and the sentiment an implicit idea.[1] But though involving cognitive elements, the sentiments differ fundamentally (on Rousseau's view) from both sense-percepts and ideas, in their power to lead to action and to determine conduct. Conscience, for example, does not merely discriminate between good conduct and bad, but impels to an appropriate course of action. This impelling power, indeed, is the characteristic feature of all the sentiments, and it indicates their real character. They are evidently nothing more nor less than the primitive impulses or dispositions to action, on a higher mental level. In the beginnings of human experience, the will which prompts to a responsive activity when external objects affect the mind through the senses, finds expression in blind strivings. But with the progress of the mind towards a clear knowledge of the world and of itself, the impulses become more and more definite, and are gradually transformed into sentiments. The sentiments, in short, are the determinate impulses in which selfhood finds expression once mind rises above the level of animal instinct.

It is an obvious corollary of what has been said that each age of life has its own sentiments, and in particular that the sentiments of the boy are different from those of the man. The sentiments are specific states of feeling, having their origin within the soul, which evaluate those other experiences that come in from without through the senses;[2] and they cannot make their appearance until the experiences on which they give judgment are definitely discerned.[3] Consequently, in

---

[1] *Emile*, iv. 292 (note).   [2] IV. 292.
[3] IV. 293. " To know the good is not to love it. Man has no innate knowledge of the good. But as soon as his reason makes it known to him, his conscience makes him love it. It is this sentiment that is

boyhood (with which we are here specially concerned), when the passive non-relating mind makes the existence of any proper idea of social relationship impossible, none of the social sentiments—such as those due to the operations of conscience—can be present. The only sentiments possible at this age are those which relate to the actual state of the boy as an individual person. These Rousseau enunciates as " self-love (*l'amour de soi*), the fear of pain, the dread of death, the desire for comfort "; [1] and, he might have added, the greatest of these is self-love. It is the greatest for the sufficient reason that it includes all the others. " The only passion [2] natural to man is self-love." [3] " The source of our passions, the origin and fount of all the others, the only one that is born with man and that never leaves him as long as he lives, is self-love. It is a primitive innate passion prior to all the others, which are all in a sense but modifications of it. . . . It is always good, and conformable to law." [4] It is self-love that makes a man seek his own good in everything he does. In itself, however, it is not a selfish impulse, since primarily it refers only to the individual well-being and is not concerned with a man's relations to others.[5] Only at a later period than boyhood, when the man comes to associate with his fellows in society, does it change its character and become self-assertion (*amour-propre*) through the conflict which results from the selfish in-

---

innate." *Cf.* i. 56 : " Reason alone teaches us to distinguish the good and the bad. On that account, conscience, which makes us love the one and hate the other, though independent of reason, cannot develop without it."

[1] IV. 293.

[2] "Passion" is used by Rousseau either in reference to the sex passions or, more generally (as here), to mean " sentiment," a feeling that prompts to action.

[3] II. 62.   [4] IV. 10, 11.   [5] II. 62.

terests of different individuals.[1] On the physical side,
it is the "disposition" or impulse which leads a man to
seek the means for the satisfaction of his wants, and
therefore it takes up into itself the instinctive striving
after physical satisfaction which was the main characteristic of the lower stage of mind immediately preceding. But even in boyhood it is never merely
physical. It is to it that the boy owes an intuitive
sense of his rights. "Our first duties," says Rousseau,
"are towards ourselves. Our primitive sentiments are
concentrated selfward, and all our natural movements
are related in the first instance to our own conservation
and our own well-being. For this reason, the first
sentiment of justice does not come to us from what we
owe to others, but from what others owe to us."[2] It is
one of the stupid blunders of the ordinary educator,
Rousseau goes on to point out, that he teaches the boy
his duties to others before teaching him his rights. In
the natural order of things, self always comes before
others, rights before duties.

The corresponding epoch in the history of the human
family is that of the first savagery, when men emerged
into intelligent individuality out of the crass stupidity
of animal instinct. The savage is the racial boy, living
without thought of others, knowing no law but his own
will, actuated in everything by self-love, which in his
case means simply the desire for his own preservation.
Rousseau speaks of his actions as good in the same
sense as he speaks of the spontaneous activities of

[1] II. 14. Cf. *Rousseau juge de Jean-Jacques*, ii.: "Self-assertion
and the movements derived from it, being only secondary passions produced by reflection. . . ." See the *Discourse on Inequality*, Note (o) on the distinction between *amour de soi* and
amour-propre.
[2] II. 82. *Cf.* i. 56.

the boy as good:[1] not in any moral sense, since the
relationship to others in which moral badness or goodness becomes possible does not yet exist, but in the sense
that it is impossible for him to aim at anything but his
own weal.[2] In the simple non-social conditions of his
life, the actions he performs at the prompting of the
self-preserving impulse are amply sufficient to ensure
his safety and well-being. Rousseau does not mean to
suggest that either in boy or savage the basal instincts
of his nature lead to good conduct under all circumstances. All he says is that if the savage is left to live his
own life in natural isolation, and if the boy is not forced
prematurely into social relations, the instinctive actions
done at the behest of self-love will in both cases lead to
the right result. But, he expressly says, "distrust
instinct as soon as you are no longer confined to it.
It is good as long as it acts alone, but becomes open
to suspicion whenever it is mixed up with human
institutions."[3]

13. *The Third Stage of Human Development: The
Other-regarding Sentiments.*—In the last years of the
second stage of development a change comes over the
whole character of the boy's mind. During the first
twelve years of life the mind is largely shaped by its
environment; for the senses, which are the dominant
faculty, are essentially passive and non-selective. But
some time about the thirteenth year the mind awakens
and becomes active. "Attention, meditation, reflection,
call it what you will,"[4] begins to show itself as an active

---

[1] II. 62.
[2] Rousseau sometimes expresses this by saying that the boy is good
but not virtuous. Virtue implies the conquest of the passions. The
boy has (or should have) no passions, and therefore has no need to
conquer them.
[3] IV. 422.   [4] IV. 231.

principle that combines the separate "sensations" and compares them with a view to bringing them into relation. In a word, the boy begins to *think*. "Formerly our pupil had only sensations," says Rousseau, speaking of the lad just into his teens; "now he has ideas. He used only to feel: now he judges. For, as a result of several sensations, whether successive or simultaneous, and of the judgment passed on them, there comes into being a kind of mixed or complex sensation which I call an idea."[1]

This new power of comparing experiences and apprehending their relations, which is implied in having ideas, opens up a new world to the boy. Not only is the future made conceivable and brought into ideal touch with the present, but, more important still, he begins to understand something of his relations to his fellows and of their relations to each other. Not that he becomes a social being in the full sense of the word even yet. Knowledge in itself, as we have seen, never determines conduct in the absence of the inner impulse; and the social sentiments which would give this impulse are still lacking when boyhood ends. It is not till the nascence of the sex impulses at puberty that the sentiments which give the boy a personal interest in social activities come into being and make him a real member of society.

In the primitive state, when man was a solitary wanderer, the sex impulse was purely physical and had but one end. But in the course of social evolution the impulse has undergone a complete transformation and become the mainspring of the varied forms in which man's aspirations after a more complete life have expressed themselves.[2] This does not mean that there is

[1] III. 167.   [2] IV. 16.

nothing in common between its first form and its last.
The truth is that behind all its forms, the most spiritual
as well as the most physical, the highest as well as the
lowest, is the one common element of self-love.   In
the last resort, the sex impulse, like all the fundamental
impulses that constitute the "nature" of man, makes
for the fuller life of the individual man.   But the
special feature of the fuller personal life to which sex
points is that it is essentially social.   When sex awakens
in the body and the soul of the boy, he begins to feel
that he is no longer sufficient to himself.   Somehow or
other, there is borne in on him that he needs others
even to be himself.   What this consciousness of loneliness means, he does not and should not know at first.
The heart hunger should find temporary satisfaction
for itself in friendship and in love for humanity.[1]   In
this way the self is carried far beyond the limits of its
childish individuality and enters on a broad expanse of
life before undreamed of.   Its interests broaden out in
every direction until the well-being of others becomes
identified with its own.   "When the force of an expansive soul identifies me with my fellow, and I feel
myself in him, so to speak, it is to avoid suffering myself
that I do not wish him to suffer.   It is self-love that
interests me in him. . . . The love of mankind based on
self-love is the foundation of justice."[2]

It is this fellow-feeling with others that makes the
youth a moral being.   It is only when his sensibility
extends itself beyond his individual interests in generous
concern for others " that he acquires first the sentiments
and afterwards the notions of good and evil which make
him truly man and an integral part of his species."[3]
Conscience, in fact, is bound up with self-love, and is as

[1] IV. 43.   [2] IV. 93 (note).   [3] IV. 39.

natural as self-love. " Just as we do not *learn* to seek our own good and avoid what threatens us with evil, but get the inclination to do so from nature, so love of goodness and hatred of evil are as natural as self-love. The acts of conscience are not judgments but sentiments." [1]

But the tree of the knowledge of good and evil has bitter fruits as well as sweet. Unhappily for human weal, the ethical sentiments are not the only ones that quicken into life under the inspiration of sex. There are also the sentiments which Rousseau calls sentiments of preference, the self-assertive impulses that manifest themselves in emulation, rivalry, and jealousy.[2] In these as in the others, self-love is the dominant principle, but it is a self-love perverted and changed for the worse by the comparison of one's lot with the lot of others. " Self-love, which is concerned only with ourselves, is content when our real needs are satisfied ; but self-assertion, which makes comparisons, is never satisfied and never can be satisfied, because it is a sentiment that does not merely lead us to prefer ourselves to others, but makes the impossible demand that others should also give us preference. This is why the gentle, kindly passions spring from self-love, while the spiteful, irascible ones spring from self-assertion." [3]

It is indeed strange that out of the same love of self there should proceed two tendencies so diverse as the altruism of an expansive self-love and the egotism of an aggressive self-assertion. We may well ask how these things can be. Rousseau, with a deep faith in the essential goodness of man's nature and a distrust of society no less deep, finds the explanation of the one in the original goodness of man, and of the other in the

[1] IV. 292.   [2] IV. 18.   [3] IV. 14.

evil influence of society—an explanation not altogether convincing, seeing that the basal impulse in both cases is the same, and that society is needed for the genesis of the altruistic sentiments as much as of the egotistic. However that be, the result of the twofold development of the original self-seeking impulses is to bring contradiction into human life and make man a dual being with centrifugal and centripetal forces warring within his soul.[1]

The social condition parallel in development with this stage of human evolution is obviously the society that now exists. The conflict between altruism and egotism which is continually going on in the individual soul is writ large over society as a whole in the opposition of individual and common interest. To be a member of society a man must be a citizen, and yet to be a citizen he must do some violence to his individual nature: for "the individual will acts unceasingly in opposition to the general will," [2] even though it is only by identifying itself with the general will that it can attain its ultimate satisfaction.

14. *The Fourth Stage of Human Development: The Idea of Happiness and of Perfection.*—It might seem as though the obvious way to remove the contradiction in the nature of social man would be to eliminate, or even to prevent the formation of, those passions which have their origin in self-assertion, and thus leave self-love as the sole determinant of conduct. As a matter of fact, this method works well enough up to a certain point. It is the method which Rousseau advocates for the training of the adolescent during the susceptible years when the sentiments are being formed. But it has

---

[1] IV. 258. *Cf.* Ch. Bonnet: *Essai de Psychologie*, p. 3.
[2] *Social Contract*, iii. 10.

a serious drawback in actual practice, when questions of personal conduct are at issue. So long as we are only playing the part of spectators, it provides us with a sure criterion of moral judgment. We naturally take delight in the happiness of others rather than in their misery, and our hearts always applaud good deeds and condemn bad ones. " If there be nothing moral in the heart of man, whence come these transports of admiration for heroic actions, that rare delight in noble souls? Why would I rather be Cato rending his entrails than Cæsar triumphant? " [1] But whenever the decrees of conscience come into operation in a case when personal interest is involved, they immediately cease to be of any use as a guide for our conduct; for no sentiment can ever lead us to put the interest of another person before our own.[2] If the choice must be made between our good and the good of others, we invariably prefer our own. After all, the other person is only one individual among others, and there is no reason in the nature of things for his individuality being promoted rather than ours. Preference for another person's weal may even be a wrong thing, if (as in a case of misplaced pity) it is given at the expense of the greatest common happiness. The happiness of all, says Rousseau, should be "the first interest of the wise man after his own private interest; for each man is part of his species, and not of another individual." [3]

The fact is that so long as Rousseau is engaged with

---

[1] IV. 284.

[2] *Cf.* v. 72. " When a man pretends to prefer my interests to his own, I am sure he is telling me a lie, however he may try to disguise it."

[3] IV. 151-2. The implication of this argument seems to be that Humanity has a kind of personal unity comparable with that which leads Rousseau to ascribe a general will to the state. For a worthier statement of the doctrine see the *Lettres sur la vertu et le bonheur* in Streckeisen-Moultou, *Œuvres inédites*, p. 137.

the problem of the *Emile*—the problem of training an individual to be faithful of his nature under the ordinary conditions of social life—there is no possibility of reconciling self-interest with the common good. There is, indeed, more than a suggestion of a possible solution in the idea of a self that is able to feel itself in the interests of others, so as to be hurt by any evil befalling them and to be made happy when things go well with them. If only the people comprehended in this expansiveness of soul represented a cause much greater than one's own personal interests, it is not inconceivable even on Rousseau's premises that self-sacrifice might be justified as a losing of the individual self in a greater self. If, for example, a man were a member of a state in whose service he was able to find complete satisfaction, the sentiment of self-love might approve of his dying for his country.[1] But it must be remembered that Rousseau is here considering the case of the ordinary state, which, on his view, is so far from being natural, that even as a member of it the man of nature must perforce regard himself as a pilgrim and a stranger on the earth with a desire ever unsatisfied, for a better country.

The difficulty of making the peace between our own good and the good of others when there is conflict of interest is twofold. In the first place, a personality based on feeling is essentially an exclusive personality. Even when the feeling is an expansive one which takes in others, it always remains an individual state, as is evident from the fact that the suffering of another hurts us, not because it is the suffering of another, but because somehow it has become an element in our own feeling.[2]

[1] Cf. *Social Contract*, ii. 4. "When the citizens risk their lives in defence of the state, they are only giving back what they have received from her."

[2] IV. 93 (note).

Fellow-feeling in itself is not really a bond of social union, since feeling is never anything but an individual experience. In the second place, it is a defect inherent in action based on sentiments, that when the sentiments impel in diverse directions—as the self-regarding and the other-regarding sentiments must sometimes do—there is no way of escape from the contradiction involved. As a sentiment, the one is no better than the other, and without going beyond sentiment, there is no reason for preferring either to the other.

So far as morality is a social matter then, Rousseau really gives up trying to solve the problem; and seeks for the escape from contradiction *within* the soul which he has failed to find in its external relations. At first sight the new problem appears quite as unpromising as the old. "On contemplating the nature of man," says the Savoyard Vicar, "it seemed to me that I could discern two distinct principles, one of which raises him to the study of eternal truths, to the love of justice and of moral beauty, to the regions of the intellectual world on which the wise man delights to meditate, while the other thrusts him back on his own pettiness, subjects him to the dominion of the senses and to the passions which serve them, and by means of them frustrates all that the sentiment of the first principle inspires in him. I wish and yet I do not wish. . . . I feel myself at once a slave and a freeman. I see the good and love it, and yet I do evil. I am active when I listen to reason, passive when my passions lead me astray; and my worst torment when I succumb is to feel that it was in my power to resist."[1] Man, as the Vicar points out, is really a dual being, and the two parts in him, indicated

[1] IV. 258.

by the self-seeking instinct and the sense of justice, are elements in one personality. As before, the difficulty of finding a satisfactory *modus vivendi* lies in the fact that both elements have the sanction of sentiment. The "inner voice" of conscience comes into conflict with the prompting of the senses; and if the two are to be regarded simply as forms of feeling, there is no reason whatever for calling the one higher and the other lower. In the feelings themselves there are no such gradations of worth.

Rousseau finds a way out of the contradiction by tacitly introducing a standard other than that based on feeling. By a restatement of the opposition inherent in man's nature, he turns the distinction between the two orders of sentiments into a distinction between body and soul,[1] basing that again on the distinction between the senses (which he identifies with the passions) and the reason;[2] and in this way he introduces reason as an arbiter between the claims of the opposing sentiments.[3] But in doing so, he is compelled to make what seems a complete reversal of all his previous judgments with

---

[1] IV. 283. "Conscience is the voice of the soul, the passions are the voice of the body. Too often the reason deceives us. Conscience never deceives us, but is the true guide of man. Conscience is to the soul what instinct is to the body. The man who follows it follows nature, and is in no danger of going astray."

[2] See, for example, iv., 300, 302, 357, 360, 396, 402.

[3] Rousseau is by no means clear as to the relation of reason and conscience. Sometimes he speaks as though conscience were primary, and reason a mere auxiliary of it. IV. 93 and 93 (note). At other times he regards them as on a footing of equality : *e.g.* v. 326. "The virtuous man is the man who follows his reason, his conscience" (*Cf.* with this a passage in *Rousseau juge de Jean-Jacques*, iii. "The voice of conscience can no more be stifled in the human heart than the voice of reason in the understanding "). At other times, again, he admits the defect of conscience and makes reason the supreme authority. See v. 92, where reason is spoken of as the arbiter between conscience and opinion in the case of women : it "does not allow conscience to go astray, and it redresses the errors of prejudice."

regard both to the senses and to reason. On the earlier view—which is repeated with little change in the first Books of the *Emile*—the senses are the part of man's mind which is primitive and natural. Without ceasing to consider them as natural, he now treats them as a source of lawlessness in the life of social man, needing to be combated and reduced to order in the interest of the best life.[1] The change of view is even more striking with regard to the reason. In the *Discourse on Inequality*, the understanding is represented as a secondary faculty subsidiary to the passions, which has brought confusion into human life by departing from its original function and creating imaginary needs foreign to man's real nature. Even in the *Emile* itself this conception of the "meddling intellect" recurs in various forms. It appears, for example, in the view that mental passivity both in the regions of intellect and of morals is the natural, and therefore the best condition for man. Thus: "I only know that the truth is in things and not in the mind that makes judgments about them, and that the less of my own mind I put into my judgments, the surer I am of getting to the truth. In this way, my rule of trusting to feeling rather than to reason is confirmed by reason itself."[2] But now that the need is felt for the recovery of the lost unity of human life, this distrust of reason is set aside so far as conduct is concerned. Reason, freed from suspicion, is recognised as a principle of organisation, by means of which man's random passions are brought into a system comformable with the order of nature, and con-

---

[1] Cf. *Rousseau juge de Jean-Jacques*, i. "Virtue often obliges us to combat and to conquer nature." Here the natural is no longer identified with the good. At this point Rousseau has explicitly ceased to be a Cynic and has become a Stoic.

[2] IV. 232. *Cf.* iii. 169.

duct based on reasoned principle is recognised to be the expression of man's nature at its best.

But further consideration will show that though undoubtedly this new view of the opposition between reason and the senses implies a considerable change in point of view, the change is less than appears. To begin with, it is to be noted that while Rousseau speaks of reason as curbing passion, he has not really abandoned his original doctrine that it is only passion which can control passion;[1] for, as he is careful to insist, reason by itself can never make men virtuous, not merely because reason lacks the driving power which sentiment has, and is incapable of leading to action of any kind, whether good or bad, but because reason taken by itself, if not essentially self-seeking, is at any rate morally neutral.[2] Virtue is ordered or rational conduct; but more than ordered conduct is needed to constitute virtue. It is useless, says the philosophical Vicar, to attempt to establish virtue by reason alone. "Virtue, it is said, is the love of order. But is this love of order able to prevail over that of my own well-being? And even if it could do so, is it right that it should? Let those who say so give me a clear and sufficient reason for the preference. At bottom their pretended principle is a pure play of words. For my part, I assert that vice is also a love of order, taken in a different sense. There is some moral order wherever there is feeling and intelligence. The difference is that the good man organises his life with relation to the whole, whereas the

[1] IV. 402. "It is only by means of the passions that we get any hold over the passions. It is always from nature herself that the instruments for ruling her have to be got." *Cf.* iii. 94. "In vain the tranquil reason leads us to approve or blame. It is only passion that makes us act."
[2] IV. 93.

wicked man organises the whole with relation to himself."[1] In other words, intelligence alone does not make a man either good or bad. It is possible to organise life either for selfish or for unselfish ends. The ground of difference is not the presence or the absence of rational organisation, but something beyond reason altogether.

But why, in that case, bring reason into morality at all? If it be true that "whatever I *feel* to be right is right, and whatever I *feel* to be wrong is wrong,"[2] there does not seem to be any sufficient cause for summoning reason to the aid of conscience, even if reason were able to define goodness and badness more precisely than it can. But just here, in spite of Rousseau's reassertion of the ability of sentiment to judge of good or evil by a spontaneous act, comes in the difficulty. There is a stage in human history when the life of man is comparatively simple, at which conscience is able to make intuitive judgment concerning the course of action that should be pursued in any given case. But when in the course of social evolution life has become more complex, feeling begins to speak with uncertain sound and to leave man halting between right and wrong. Hence for civilised man conscience apart from reason is no more adequate as a guide in matters of conduct than reason apart from conscience. It is therefore in the direct line of moral progress that conscience should be fortified by reason and get from it clear and definite principles wherewith to strengthen the higher passions in their struggle with the lower.

[1] IV. 298. In this section, Rousseau is referring to Ch. Bonnet, *Essai de psychologie*, chap. 53, *De l'ordre:* "The ideas of justice and injustice, . . . of virtue and vice, of good and evil, reduce themselves to ideas of order and of disorder."

[2] IV. 283.

The significance of this alliance of conscience and reason in the right ordering of conduct will be best realised if it be kept in mind that in the lower stages of mental and moral evolution, before reason and deliberation play the large part in human affairs which they subsequently do, the sentiments belong to both the cognitive and the conative spheres. Conscience, at the pre-rational stage, for example, not merely discerns between good and evil, but provides the motive power for the appropriate action to follow on its discernment. Consequently, when at a later time reason and conscience co-operate in determining conduct, the clarifying activity of reason does not involve the intrusion of a new faculty into the sphere of practice, nor even a fundamental change in the character of reason itself. The work that reason performs in the right ordering of life is rather to be regarded as the fuller development of the cognitive function of conscience. The distinction of the good and the evil, which in the pre-rational period was made in the seeming immediacy of feeling and without conscious reference to principle, becomes a matter for deliberate judgment with more or less explicit criteria. In one aspect of it, the change seems to involve the displacement and negation of sentiment. It should rather be considered as an evolution from action based on sentiment into action based on ideals,[1] which take up into themselves the dynamic power of the sentiments and set them free from their limitations as individual feelings.

When, therefore, in the important passage on the primitive dispositions from which we set out in this part of our discussion,[2] Rousseau makes conduct which

---

[1] IV. 292. The note deserves special attention.
[2] I. 12. See section 9 of this chapter.

has in view the idea of happiness and perfection the final stage in the evolution of human morality, he recognises clearly the need of a rational life for the most complete development of man's nature. But the conception of a rational life thus understood is not an abstract universal which excludes from its scope the self-seeking of the previous stages. On the contrary, it takes up into itself all the elements of worth in both the feelings and the sentiments in which that self-seeking first made itself manifest. The very fact that the organising idea should be one of happiness and perfection implies that the ideal is a personal one. The good which a man seeks is necessarily a good for self at whatever level of development he be.[1] But the further fact that this good on the highest level takes the form of an ideal rather than of a feeling or of a sentiment imparts quite a new character to the good that is sought. The exclusiveness that attaches to the striving after self-realisation even on the plane of sentiment disappears in greater or less measure when it is made subject to an ideal. For an ideal is essentially an expression of reason, and it is the function of reason to bring individuality into relation to the ordered scheme of things as a whole, to see the individual, not as an isolated unit, but as a member of greater wholes and ultimately of the one greatest whole in whom all things move and have their being. To speak, then, of an idea of happiness and perfection implies that the individual no longer seeks his happiness merely as an individual, but seeks it by fulfilling his functions as a member of a rational universe in greater or less consciousness of his relation to the whole. In a word, when rightly understood, an idea

[1] "Quidquid petitur, petitur sub specie boni."

of happiness or perfection, as Rousseau vaguely appre-
hends,[1] is only capable of realisation when morality
comes to perfection in religion, and man rises above
the contradictions of his nature and enters into relation
to God.[2]

15. *Man and Society.*—Throughout the discussion
which has just been completed the assumption has
been made that on Rousseau's view of human nature
there is an intimate connection of some kind between
the individual development and the social *milieu* in
which the later stages of that development take place.
To bring this discussion into relation to the previous
discussion of man's nature from the sociological point
of view, we must now try to define more precisely
the character of the interdependence of man and
society.

That the relationship, whatever it is, is an intimate
one, is evident from the statement Rousseau makes with
regard to the primitive dispositions that are the essentials of human nature. A man's nature, he tells us,[3]
shows itself in certain dispositions to seek or to avoid
objects : in the first instance because they bring pleasure
or pain, at a later time because self-love or pity or some
other sentiment impels him, and finally because they
seem likely to make for or against what he thinks is his
happiness or perfection. If we leave out of account
actions due to mere feelings of pleasure and pain, as
belonging to a stage which has been outgrown by the

---

[1] IV. 358.
[2] There is no social analogue of this fourth stage in individual
development. The contradictions of life cannot on Rousseau's view
be completely resolved in any form of society. Seemingly it is only
by turning away from the conflict of interests in all actual states, and
seeing man's life *sub specie quadam aeternitatis* that Rousseau can find
prospect of peace for the human soul.
[3] I. 12.

civilised man whose "nature" we are considering, we find as the motives of human action certain sentiments and ideas, all of social origin—with the important exception of the self-regarding sentiments [1]—and all assuming the forms under which we know them in a social context.

Does the fact that the altruistic impulses are meaningless apart from society, and that it is only in society that we rise to the conception of a rationally determined life, justify us in saying that man is by nature a social being? The answer would not seem at all doubtful were it not for the contradiction that cleaves man's life in two, both in the sphere of conduct and of thought, and seems to penetrate to the springs of action in the opposition of the self-regarding and the other-regarding sentiments. If the existence of an inner law compelling us to altruistic courses leads us to regard man as essentially a social being, does a self-love that is not merely the most powerful but ultimately "the only motive that makes man act," [2] not point to the opposite conclusion? Or, to do justice to both sets of facts, must we not say that man is only in part a social being, and that there are elements in his nature which social life does not merely fail to satisfy but to which it may even be inimical? This indeed would seem to be the final

---

[1] Rousseau is wrong in making the exception. We are not conscious of self before we are conscious of the world and of other selves. Rousseau recognises this quite clearly when he points out that the little girl first finds herself through the external self of the doll. *Emile*, v. 44. Nevertheless, he usually speaks as if self-consciousness were independent of experience. See *Emile*, i. 29, where he assumes that the fictitious child-man whom he uses to illustrate his exposition of the mental state of the child begins with but one idea, that of the self. It is only on this wrong assumption that it is possible to speak of *self*-love as existing prior to the general development of intelligence that takes place in society.

[2] *Correspondance:* A. M. l'Abbé de . . . le 4 Mars, 1764.

verdict that Rousseau passes in the *Emile*.[1]   After Emile has wandered over the world during the last two years of his training, seeking for a fitting place of abode for the man of nature living in society, he is compelled in the end to return to the land from which he set out without discovering anywhere a state founded on justice.   Everywhere he goes he finds private interest and passion masquerading as law, and government being carried on in the interest of the stronger.   From this he draws the conclusion that the satisfaction which cannot be found in the external world must be found within the soul, and that though it is impossible to find individual and common interest reconciled in any actual state, the wise man who orders his life on the principles of reason is able to effect the reconciliation for himself.   The eternal laws of the natural order are inscribed in his heart " by conscience and by reason," and in willing obedience to them he can find true freedom.   " Freedom is not in any form of government.   It is in the heart of the free man.   He carries it with him everywhere.   The vile man, on the contrary, is everywhere in bondage.   The one man would be a slave in Geneva.   The other would be free in Paris." [2]

It is not quite clear what the practical implications of this old-world doctrine of the self-sufficient wise man are.   On one reading of it, it may be taken to imply that in order to be natural a man should hold himself aloof from the world of men and work out his own salvation in Stoic *ataraxia*.   The idea undoubtedly had some charm for Rousseau, and it is one which he was wont to preach in the modified form of a recommendation to abandon the conventionalities of city life for the

---

[1] V. 467 *seq*.   [2] V. 472.

free life of the country.[1] But in the *Emile* he takes the
bolder line of preparing the man of nature for life in
any society. He recognises that for the fullest development of his nature man needs the company of his
fellows. That makes it necessary that the natural man
should be a social being, but leaves it a matter of indifference whether he is a member of any one society.
What is more important for him than membership of a
particular community is the ability to keep himself free
from the limitations of the community to which he
chances to belong. If only he can avoid conformity
with those passing fashions that run counter to nature,
he will be safe: and since that depends largely on himself, it should be a simple enough matter to educate
him for freedom. To remain natural, it is sufficient
that the customs and prejudices of other people should
never take the place of personal experience for him—
"that he should see with his own eyes and feel with his
own heart, and be governed by no authority save that
of his own reason."[2] So long as he puts personal conviction before social convention, the motives for his
actions will be found in his own sentiments and his
own ideas, and he will remain true to his nature as
a man.

But whichever of the two versions we accept, whether
we think of the self-sufficient wise man as a recluse
shunning the common life of men, or as a dweller in
cities who lives in society without belonging to it, it is
evident that the bond that links individual and society
on Rousseau's view of social obligations is somewhat

---

[1] It was on this recommendation that Pestalozzi gave up his thought
of a professional career and became a farmer. De Guimps, *Life of
Pestalozzi*, p. 20.

[2] IV. 162.

slight when it comes to the practice of life. Like the
Stoics who professed an unbounded love for humanity
but fought shy of actual political duties, Emile, the
typical man of nature living in society, has no well-
defined status in any community, either as worker or
as citizen. Apart from the over-development of his
individuality, his fitness for membership of any state
does not qualify him for the duties of any particular
state. Altogether, his training prepares him better for
picturesque carpentry [1] or the life of a knight-errant [2]
than for the more substantial social virtues that enable
a man to go through the daily round and the common
task in the spirit of good citizenship.

In reality, Rousseau never wholly escapes from the
hyper-individualism which marred his first views about
society; and to the end his treatment of the problems of social relationship shows its influence in the
tacit assumption that man can never find himself completely at home in any actual society. This strain of
thought finds illustration on the psychological side
in the doctrine (already discussed) that "nature" is
essentially disposition. To become actual, a disposition
must find expression in some concrete experience: it is
an empty form which needs to materialise itself before
it can exist. Now this implication of the externality
of the medium of expression which the categories of
"disposition" and "form" convey is characteristic of
Rousseau's view of society as a whole, and reveals its
central weakness. For society, as Rousseau himself
came to see, is not an indifferent environment in
which man chances to find himself able to realise
his "dispositions" more or less imperfectly. On the
contrary, all its institutions, the bad as well as the

[1] V. 293 seq.   [2] IV. 144-5.

good,[1] are the outcome of just such dispositions as those with which the individual man is endowed. The problems of life that rise up in his narrow experience have been the common problems of untold generations of men; and the varied institutions which constitute society represent the accumulated experience of the race in dealing with these very problems. In the illuminating phrase of Hegel's,[2] these social contrivances are "mind objective," mind taking external form in institutions. By approaching society too exclusively from the individual or psychological point of view, Rousseau appreciates this very inadequately when he appreciates it at all. The consequence is apparent in his condemnation of all but the simplest phases of social life as artifices alien to the fundamental nature of man, and in the failure to see that social man even at the worst is not less but more natural than his animal and his savage progenitors. The truth indeed is in him—witness the Fourth and Fifth Books of the *Emile*—but it never gets out into perfectly clear consciousness because of the subjective pre-occupation that "sicklied o'er" his thought about man to the end of his life, and made him suspicious of society in practice even after he had accepted it in theory.

B. The Ideal Society of Natural Men

16. *The Ideal of a Natural Society.*—The educational method adopted in the *Emile* avowedly represents a policy of compromise. If Rousseau had been free to choose the

---

[1] Rousseau never got the length of admitting this with respect to the bad institutions. It was only to nature that he cared to apply the maxim that "whatever is, is right."

[2] In his *Philosophy of Mind.*

conditions under which to give an education according
to nature, he would certainly have preferred a better
environment than that provided by contemporary
civilisation. But in the *Emile* he is not attempting
to describe an ideal system of education. He is merely
seeking for a method of keeping men as near nature as
is possible under existing social conditions; and looking
at the facts of the case as a practical man, he recognises
clearly that a method of education which does not prepare a child for life in an ordinary community is worthless when judged by the standards of natural living.
The fundamental law for every living being is the law of
self-preservation; and that law justifies all courses of
action that enable the individual to adapt himself to
his environment. Once it is clear that even a natural
education must fit the child for social life, the only
question is whether it is possible to educate him for
society without making him wholly unnatural. The
answer of the *Emile*, reached only after considerable
hesitation and doubt, is that it is possible. Emile, the
man of nature living in society, is the concrete solution
of the problem of natural education.

But the solution offered in the *Emile* has very obvious
drawbacks. The reconciliation of nature and society is
certainly effected in the person of Emile, but it is a
reconciliation made on the assumption that the social
evils which call for it are permanent evils. Emile's case,
therefore, is wholly exceptional and is only possible in
special circumstances. The brand is plucked from the
burning, but the burning still goes on. The more
fundamental way, the way which if it were practicable
would give a real solution not only of the educational
problem but of all social problems, would be to re-
construct society, beginning as it were *de novo* and

building up a perfect society in accordance with natural law. The difficulties that attach to all schemes which attempt to make a social being natural in spite of his society, would then disappear, and the education that made good citizens would also make good men.

The idea of drastic social reconstruction was one that presented fewer difficulties to most eighteenth-century thinkers than it does to an age like ours that appreciates keenly the worth of continuity in social evolution; and it is not at all surprising that Rousseau, whose historical sense was never very strong, should have allowed his thoughts to follow this line of speculation with some degree of persistence. For a mind constituted like his, with a genuine intolerance of criticism for the mere sake of criticism,[1] continuance in a purely negative attitude was not possible for any length of time. Others might find in the denunciations of social evils in the *Discourses* reasons for the undoing of society. He himself refused to follow out the argument to its conclusion, and set himself to show men how a better society could be created. It was characteristic of Rousseau that the Second *Discourse*, with its political nihilism, should be followed by the *Social Contract*, in which the ideal of a government not inconsistent with individual freedom was presented; and that the *Social Contract* in turn should have as its corollary the more practical *Considerations on the Government of Poland*, demonstrating the possibility of realising the ideal under the actual conditions of modern life.

---

[1] A very instructive incident is recorded in the *Memoirs* of Madame d'Epinay. After a "philosophical" conversation on religion, which had been brought to an end by Rousseau threatening to leave the company if it went on, he remarked to Madame d'Epinay: "I cannot endure this eagerness to destroy without rebuilding." It was this difference in mental attitude which led him to detach himself from the Encyclopedists.

To the possible criticism that speculation about the reconstruction of society is idle, because it is impossible to start afresh in the making of nations at this stage in the history of the world, Rousseau replies in these *Considerations* by quoting the precedent of the ancient lawgivers, and especially of Moses, Lycurgus and Numa Pompilius.[1] All three of these great men, he says, devoted their lives to causes at which our wise men would smile, and achieved successes that would have been thought impossible if they had not been well attested. Moses conceived and executed the astonishing enterprise of creating a nation out of a swarm of wretched fugitives devoid of all the qualities required for political stability. Lycurgus performed a similar feat by raising to greatness a nation degraded by slavery. Numa was the man who really founded Rome by welding together into a people the brigands gathered by Romulus.

But even if there were no precedents, or if the precedents cited were to be set aside as irrelevant when modern social conditions are under discussion, it would still be open to Rousseau to maintain that the worth of his social idealism did not wholly depend on its practicability. In every kind of project, he reminds us in the Preface to the *Emile*, there are two things that have to be taken into account: the one is the absolute goodness of the project, the other is the ease with which it can be executed. A plan is not necessarily bad, because it is difficult to carry it out. It may be a good plan in spite of that. Even if this distinction be admitted and the

---

[1] *Government of Poland:* chap. ii. This reference to the ancient lawgivers must not be regarded as mere rhetoric. As we have noted already, it was on the model of the city-states of the ancient world and of Geneva, his native city, that Rousseau framed his ideal of social life.

question of practicability be waived, however, the difficulty involved in Rousseau's projects for an ideal society is not wholly removed. An ideal society, as Rousseau thinks of it, is a society in which men can live natural lives: in other words, it is a natural society. But after all that Rousseau has said about the incompatibility of nature and society, is the conjunction of nature and society in a natural society thinkable? Surely not.

Yet it would be a mistake to lay too much stress on consistency here. The attempt to plan out an ideal society really raises the whole question of the relation of nature and society in a fresh and suggestive way; and it will throw new light on the tendencies of Rousseau's thought to examine it at length. Meanwhile, an important difference in point of view consequent on the change of problem is worthy of note. In the *Emile*, as we have seen, the utmost that is attempted in the direction of reconciling nature and society is to find means of keeping the individual natural in spite of his social environment. With the widening of the problem from education to politics, the aim comes to be to make society itself natural. In neither case is it admitted that society is in accord with nature; but while in the one case it is taken for granted that the opposition between them is a permanent one, in the other there is hope held out of a final reconciliation.

17. *The Ideal State based on Feeling.*—It must not be thought, however, that the idea of a natural society necessarily implies such a reconciliation. The hypothesis of a conjunction of nature and society in a natural society is only of value when it implies the abandonment of the individualistic doctrine of society in its extreme form. If by a natural society all that is meant is that so many individuals are somehow enabled to live a

natural life in common, the emphasis is laid on the individuals, and society is still regarded atomistically as a group of independent units.

Such a conception of a natural society is strikingly illustrated in a curious representation of what Rousseau calls an ideal world, in the first of the hyper-subjective *Dialogues, Rousseau juge de Jean-Jacques.* " Picture to yourself," he says, "an ideal world that is like our own and yet different. Nature there is the same as on our earth, but the arrangement of things is finer, and there is a more obvious order in them. The view is more admirable, the contours are more elegant, the colours more vivid, the odours more fragrant, and everything is more interesting. Nature is all so beautiful that even to look on it inspires men's souls with the desire to be in concord with the beautiful system and makes them fear to disturb its harmony." Truly a paradise of the senses, a lotos-eaters' island! And the inhabitants are fit denizens of this favoured spot. Nature keeps them in a beatific state of mind, and they never lose their original natures. None of the troubles that vex the souls of other mortals come near them. Even the unsatisfied yearning for happiness, which as creatures of the senses they share with the rest of mankind,[1] does not break through the steady calm of their souls. Instead of indulging in vain repinings and useless strivings they remain in a state of placid inaction, content with such measure of voluptuous joy as falls to their lot, and free from all the vexations that ordinary men bring on themselves by unappeased desires or by deference to opinion.

It is somewhat surprising to meet this gross con-

---

[1] Cf. *Emile*, v. 316. " It is necessary to be happy. That is the end of life for every creature of sense."

ception of human bliss in one of the latest of Rousseau's
writings. To understand it we have to unthink all the
advance made in the *Emile* and the *Social Contract*,
and fall back on the cruder conceptions of the early
writings; for this ideal world in which men avoid
unhappiness by doing nothing and entering into no relationships is the logical outcome of the psychological doctrine which we have already met in the *Discourses*, that
it is feeling and not reason which unites men in society.
" If I am under obligation to do no harm to a fellow-
creature," Rousseau said in the second *Discourse*, " it is
not because he is a rational being but because he is a
being who feels." What he fails to see in the *Discourse*
and in this strange passage is, that as a creature of
sense man is fellow not only of other men but also of
the brutes, and that the only kind of society that could
be based on feeling would be a brute society, which
would indeed be no society. In feeling by itself there
is no social bond. What is sometimes called fellow-
feeling is only possible for beings who do more than
feel. It is not feeling, but feeling differentiated into
common action and common thoughts, which unites
men as social beings. Men who do nothing but feel in
company, like the men of Rousseau's ideal world, would
therefore not be social beings at all. The question is:
would they even be men ?[1]

18. *The Ideal State based on the General Will.—*

---

[1] The criticism which I have suggested on a particular phase of
Rousseau's thought, representing in my opinion a lapse from the
comparative sanity of his later position, is applied without reservation
to his whole view of human nature by Davidson: *Rousseau and Education according to Nature:* p. 103. It is one of Rousseau's cardinal
errors, according to him, that " he makes life consist in feeling but
forgets that all the distinctness, variety and wealth of feeling are due
to intellectual categories. Without these, feeling if it were anything
would be at best but a vague meaningless striving."

While this picture of a natural society, with feeling as its basis, is an interesting commentary on the individualistic psychology that makes feeling fundamental in human experience, it would be a mistake to attach too much importance to it in the discussion of Rousseau's later social philosophy. For as a matter of fact, the virtue of the idea of a natural society, which is suggested both in the *Emile* and in the *Social Contract*, is that it carries with it the implicit recognition that society has not been constituted by the chance congress of a number of individuals (as the passage referred to suggests), but is a real spiritual unity with a rational personality and a general will different from the individual personalities and wills of its constituent members.

This view of society receives most definite statement and exposition in the discussion of the theory of government in the *Social Contract*, of which indeed it forms the philosophical core.[1] In the *Emile*, it only occurs in casual references; but as it happens, it is in these that its significance is most evident. We may begin our examination of the view by considering an important passage in the Second Book of the *Emile* relating to the contrast between man's relations with his physical and with his human environment. "Dependence on things," Rousseau tells us, "having nothing moral in it, does not destroy liberty and engenders no vices. Dependence on men, involving the absence of orderly relations, engenders them all." "This social evil," he goes on to say, "can only be remedied, if at all, by substituting the law for the man, and arming the General Wills[2] with a real power superior to the action

---

[1] See Books I and II, especially i. 6, 7, ii. 1–4.

[2] Why the plural? In the *Social Contract*, he always speaks of the General Will. Perhaps the difference is to be explained by the fact

of every individual will. If only the laws of nations could be like those of nature and have an inflexibility which no human power could overcome, dependence on men would then come to be like dependence on things. The body politic would combine all the advantages of the natural and the social states. The liberty that keeps man free from vice would then go along with the morality that raises him to virtue." [1]

The noteworthy feature of this passage is the new form assumed by the familiar contrast between nature and society. Venturing for once into the region of metaphysics, Rousseau makes a comparison between the laws of nature and the laws of society, which serves to give the idea of nature a definite positive content. He is never very fond of definition at any time. In the earlier writings, and even in the *Émile* itself, " nature " is generally spoken about without any precise indication of the meaning of the word. Social institutions are declared to be contrary to nature, and the method of nature is held up as the sure guide for man in the practice of life. " Observe nature," Rousseau urges, " and follow the path that she marks out for you." [2] But all the while no attempt is made to analyse or define the explicit idea. Seemingly Rousseau employed the word with the meaning it had in current talk, to suggest a condition with none of the defects of society. At any rate, this negative reference is most prominent in what he says about nature. When he needs greater definiteness, his practice is to convert the

that in the *Social Contract* he is speaking of the state, while here he is speaking of society, which is composed of a number of subordinate communities, each presumably with its own law and its own will.

[1] II. 35. In a footnote, he points out that in the *Social Contract* he has shown the individual will to be a source of disorder in the social system.

[2] I. 56.

opposition between nature and society into one between
the man of nature and social man, and thus divert the
analysis on to psychological lines. The injunction to
follow nature then becomes an injunction to respect
human nature—the nature of the child, or of the man,
or of the individual as the case may be. For practical
purposes, the change is of supreme importance, especially
when human nature is interpreted in biological terms,
but on the side of theory it leaves us still in doubt as
to what this "nature" may be that is so much superior
to society and the works of man.

With the general advance of his thought in a constructive direction, the negative use of the word
"nature" as a category of denunciation became less
frequent. And, as we have already noted, sometime
during the years when the *Emile* and the *Social
Contract* were being written, there began a process
of mental change which affected his philosophy of life
at many points, and issued in the deeper and more
adequate conception of nature that finds expression in
passages like the one to which attention has just been
called. These were the years just after his breach with
the Encyclopedists, when his mind was in active revolt
against the philosophical sensualism that was the
dominant creed of the party. To combat philosophers
like Condillac and Helvetius, he himself turned philosopher, and attempted to meet them on their own
ground and fight them with their own weapons. The
result of his philosophical studies appears in the interesting pages of the *Savoyard Vicar's Confession of
Faith*, written for the most part after the rest of
the *Emile* had been completed, and representing the
furthest point reached by Rousseau's thought. With
the argument of the *Confession* as a whole, there is no

need to concern ourselves; but its outline must be
given for the sake of the view of nature and society
it contains.

The *Savoyard Vicar's Confession of Faith* is an
attempt to attain the assurance with respect to those
fundamental truths about God, man, and the world
which is necessary for the conduct of life. The Vicar,
who is no other than Rousseau himself,[1] begins by protesting that he is no philosopher and disclaiming any
intention to use the arguments of philosophy. But
despite his depreciation of all philosophy, he is soon deep
in metaphysics. Starting with a pseudo-Cartesianism
that infers the reality of the self from the fact of feeling,[2] and then passes to a belief in material things
because of the distinction that is *felt* to exist between
self and matter, he finds himself led to believe in God
by a twofold argument. In the first place, the experience we have of will-originated movements in our own
case makes it necessary to regard the movements of
the universe as due to will. In the second place, every
part of the universe of which we have knowledge bears
witness to the intelligence of this prime will or cause.[3]
But beyond the fact that there is a God, a supreme
intelligent will, the Vicar (that is, Rousseau) cannot go
in the way of belief. He refuses to admit that there
can be any real *knowledge* of God. Everything we
know must come to us through the medium of the
senses, and God cannot be so known.[4]

But, he goes on to ask, if we do not know God,
what do we know? Our own existence, of course.

---

[1] *Correspondance :* À. M. Moultou, Dec. 23, 1761.

[2] It may be well to point out that, in Rousseau's use of the word,
" feeling " has a cognitive element in it. For Rousseau, as for Hegel,
feeling has in it the promise and the potency of thought.

[3] IV. 219-252.   [4] IV. 163, 213.

We feel: therefore we are. And likewise the existence of the universe other than ourselves, that bears
witness to this intelligent first cause : in other words,
nature. Let us consider what this knowledge of ours amounts
to. I know myself, and I know nature. First, then,
what am I ? Undoubtedly a feeling being, since it is to
feeling that I owe the consciousness of myself: and a
being different from the objects which cause feeling in
me. Nay more, I am not merely a feeling being. I am
conscious of the ability to compare and arrange my sensations and establish relations among the objects that
cause them. I am therefore a thinking being, an intelligence. Further, since I am able to move my body,
and through the movements of my body to determine
the movements of things external to me, I am also a
will, endowed with the power of spontaneously originat-
ing movement. Like God, then, I am a will and an
intelligence.[1]

In both respects, I am different from the natural
universe which is known to me by the same direct intuition that gives me self-knowledge. Looking abroad
on the world, I see evidence on every hand of the reign
of law, and note that in the great system of things every
being has its fixed place and function. I behold the

---

[1] IV. 219-232. The difference between the divine and the human
intelligence must not be forgotten. IV. 280. "God is intelligent, but
in what sense ? Man is intelligent when he reasons, but the supreme
intelligence has no need to reason. For him, there are neither
premises nor conclusions, and not even propositions. His intelligence
is purely intuitive, seeing equally all that is and all that can be. For
him, all truths are but one idea, just as all places are a single point
and all times a single moment." (Compare with this what Kant says
about God as intuitive understanding. Critique of Pure Reason, First
Ed., 72, 311, 312. Critique of Judgment, 421.) There is a like difference between God and man in the moral sphere. "God is good,
not virtuous." V. 324.

whole universe in connected movement, showing perfect regularity and uniformity in its various parts.[1] All this leads me to think of nature as the ordered whole of things, marshalled according to a supreme law. But in it all there is no indication of intelligent activity or of spontaneous movement. It is neither intelligence nor will. It is only a vast world system, which bears witness by its orderly evolution to its origin in, and its maintenance by, the creative activity of some great intelligent will.

From all this, it is obvious that man and nature are akin: the one being an intelligent will, the other a product of the supreme intelligent will. Man's place in the universe indeed is not doubtful. Alike by his will and the possession of instruments to give it effect, and by an intelligence that comprehends all things in its scope, he is quite unique among created beings. He is truly king of the earth he inhabits. All the animals are subject to him, and the very elements are under his control. If we consider him with the whole world in subjection to him, we cannot but think his position an enviable one, which ought to make him bless the hand that put him in it every day of his life. But when we turn to consider him as a member of society, what a different spectacle meets our eyes. "Where is now the order I beheld ? The picture of nature showed nothing but harmony and proportion : that of the human race shows only confusion and disorder. Concord reigns among the elements, and human affairs are in chaos. Oh wisdom, where are thy laws ? Is this the way in which thou rulest the world, oh Providence ? " [2]

---

[1] IV. 246, 247. See also *Morceau allégorique sur la révélation* in Streckeisen-Moultou, *Œuvres inédites*, p. 173 *seq.*
[2] IV. 253-257.

Why this disorder and confusion, this seeming absence of reason in the affairs of men? It cannot surely be because man is not a rational being! And yet, if man is a rational being, it seems strange that there should be so little reason manifest in his mode of life. Can it be that the root of the evil is misdirected reason? That is the suggestion which comes from the conception of the cognitive faculties given in the *Discourse on Inequality*. There Rousseau works out the view that a man's intelligence is only at his service for purely personal ends, and regards the thought for others which is a necessary condition for the existence of social institutions, as a contradiction of the basal sentiment of self-love, and consequently the source of disorder in human existence. In the *Savoyard Vicar's Confession* he modifies this view to the extent of recognising the altruistic motives which conflict with the self-seeking motives to be as much a part of man's nature as they. But whether the contradiction in human nature is imported from without by external conditions or is innate and present from the beginning, the essential fact is that there is contradiction and that it manifests itself in an incessant conflict between the self-seeking of individual members of society and the general will of the community. Society consisting of beings like man with natures so contradictory cannot well escape lawlessness and disorder.

Sooner or later the question is bound to arise as to the possibility of avoiding or preventing this lawlessness. The answer of the Savoyard Vicar we know. It is the Stoic answer. Let man resign himself to living in whatever community his lot may be cast, since apart from society it is impossible for him to develop all his powers; but let him keep the social ties as loose as possible, and seek within himself for the freedom that is impossible of attainment in the world without.[1] As a rational being, it is the duty and the privilege of a man to rule his own spirit by bringing the flesh into subjection to the law of the mind. In this way reason which has failed to realise itself in social relationships may find opportunity for its legislative work in the regulation of the senses and appetites.

But there is another answer—the bolder answer that we see Rousseau feeling after in the passage of the Second Book of the *Emile* which has already been quoted. Put the law in place of the man, he there suggests, and find a General Will which can dominate all the individual wills and convert their warring interests into a common interest. In a word, create a natural society, a society unified and ordered like nature herself by the activity of a supreme intelligent will, which appoints each man his station and makes sure that he duly performs its duties.[2]

The *Social Contract* treats of such a society in one of its aspects.[3] In that work Rousseau tries to show how an individual may become a member of a state without forfeiting his freedom or suffering any essential loss. So far as the discussion relates to the details of government, it does not concern us here. What is really important is to know how the idea of the dominant General

---

[1] V. 468 *seq.*

[2] It is a suggestive fact that the same two phases of thought occur in Stoicism, the problems of which are very much like Rousseau's. On the one hand, there is the personal solution appearing in the idea that in subjecting himself to the law of his own reason the individual comes into harmony with the law of the whole universe : on the other hand, there is the political solution in terms of which the wise man, though failing to reconcile himself to actual society as a citizen, claimed to be the citizen of an ideal world-state, of a πολιτεία τοῦ κόσμου.

[3] Rousseau points out this limitation of his work himself. II. 12.

Will, which is the presupposition of a natural society, can be reconciled with the view of human nature we have already got from Rousseau. How does it come about, for example, that a great many individual wills, each of them antagonistic to any other and every other, become united into a single General Will? We seek in vain for an answer, because in point of fact no answer is possible on Rousseau's premises. Out of merely individual wills, it is impossible that anything but individual wills can come. Before there can be a contract or agreement of any kind, there must be a meeting ground other than in the fact that each of the contracting individuals seeks to further his own interests as an individual. The truth is that will *per se* can no more provide a basis for social life than can feeling *per se*. Feeling and will in the abstract are simply phenomena of an individual soul and nothing more. If individuals by coming together have, by any means whatever, succeeded in creating or in discovering in themselves as a body a common rule of action, it can only have been because their aggressive individualities concealed a deeper principle of agreement. In other words, it is because will is never mere will but always the outgoing activity of an individuality that is more than individual, because (to express the matter in Kantian phraseology) the will is the practical reason and essentially universal, that there can be a General Will. The General Will is not composed of the wills of all.[1] It is the expression of a new personality that is created by the reason common to all coming to ever fuller realisation of itself in the common life which it produces and inspires.[2] As mere will, it would be one

[1] *Cf.* ii. 3.

[2] *Cf.* i 6. The moment the contract is made, "the act of association produces a moral and collective body which receives from this

more will to join battle with the other wills. As the General Will grounded on principles common to all, it is (or may be) the unity in which all the individual differences are at an end.

But here the difficulty emerges in a new form. Can there be an effective General Will which does not absorb in itself all the individual wills? Rousseau does not pretend that even in the ideal state the citizens will in every case agree with the laws in which the General Will finds expression, or that they will always obey them even when they do. What is to happen then? The state will evidently be forced to make use of the powers of coercion with which it has been endowed by the social contract,[1] and it would seem as though freedom must inevitably disappear with this exercise of compulsion. Rousseau, however, will not admit the conclusion. "In order that the social contract may not be a mere formulary, it tacitly includes the understanding which alone can give force to all the other understandings implied in it, that any one who refuses to obey the General Will will be compelled to do so by the whole body politic—which only means that the culprit will be forced to be free."[2] Clearly, freedom has a very different meaning here from what it had when Rousseau praised the freedom of the noble savage whose impulse was his only law. In the ideal state the man who allows his impulse to prompt him to a course of action contrary to the General Will finds impulse immediately curbed, not only for the good of the state but for his own good. It is in the social condition, Rousseau explains in the following chapter, that moral freedom

very act its unity, its collective self (son *moi* commun), its life, and its will. The public person formed in this way was formerly called a City, and is now called a Republic or a Body Politic."

[1] II. 4.   [2] I. 7.

"which alone makes man truly his own master" is acquired: for, he adds, "to be impelled by mere appetite is slavery, and obedience to self-prescribed laws is freedom."[1] The principle involved is the same as that which explains the existence of a General Will: that the essential nature of man does not appear in his individuality but in his reason. If the real man were the creature of the senses that Rousseau represented him to be in the earlier writings, then this repression of impulse and appetite would be a sin against humanity. It is because the real man is a rational being, and, as such, conscious in himself of a law of reason to which the senses must be subject if he is to live his proper life, that the greater reason of humanity operative in the General Will of the state makes him free in compelling his obedience. For a season he may be blinded by his passions, but when he comes to reflect he will see that the coercion he resents at its first exercise is not the act of an arbitrary external power but the expression of a law to which his reason gives assent and which it recognises as its own law.

[1] I. 8. *Cf.* Emile's request to his tutor (IV. 396): "Make me free by protecting me against my passions. Force me to be my own master by making me obey my reason and not my senses."

CHAPTER VII

THE TWO EDUCATIONAL IDEALS

1. *The End of Education.*—In the Preface to the *Emile,* Rousseau speaks of education as "the art of forming men" (*l'art de former des hommes*). The phrase is full of significance. It declares the work of the educator to be the forming of men: that is, giving them some particular form. In the light of the conception of human nature as essentially constituted by "dispositions" to action, which Rousseau gives in the opening sections of the *Emile,* this idea of education as a process of "forming" is quite intelligible. Following up the implications of his view of human nature, we have to think of man as beginning life with certain indeterminate impulses or strivings, and needing the help of the educator to give these impulses and strivings definite form in particular modes of life which are likely to satisfy the vague needs behind them. "Everything we do not possess at birth that we need when grown up is given us by education." [1] This applies as much to the simplest as to the most complex needs. Take the need of food, for example. If the child is hungry, he is "disposed" to seek food. But the new-born child, unlike the young of many of the animals, has no definite instinct that enables him to find his food for himself. The disposition is there, but all unformed. Even the

---

[1] *Emile,* i. 5.

sucking instinct, one of the few definite instincts of the infant, is so aimless that without the maternal direction to give it "form" it would not serve its purpose, and the child would speedily perish. And the older the child grows, the greater the difficulty of self-sustenance becomes. Later in life he has either no instincts at all, or those that he possesses are useless for the acquisition of food in the conventional world in which social man lives. It is plain that apart from some kind of education to teach him the arts and artifices necessary for self-sustenance, he would be completely helpless and would find it impossible to exist. To escape that fate, he needs to have his first incoherent impulses gradually transformed into definite methods of action suited to the requirements of the life he is called upon to live in society. Impulse, in Rousseau's phrase, must receive the necessary "form."

But the complementary truth which must not be forgotten when speaking about the individual's need of education is that there is equal need for society to educate. To this extent, it is true that man is not by nature a social being, and that there is not a single action done by social man which does not call for some kind of education. Society is based on education, and without education could not exist at all. The child requires to be educated, because the crude untrained dispositions of his nature do not fit him for living as a social being: society requires to give this education in order to win from nature social men to carry on her affairs.

It is evident, then, that on the definition of education as a process of forming men there are always two factors in education. On the one hand, there are the primary dispositions to action which constitute the nature of the

child and which provide the driving power in all forms
of human activity. On the other hand, there are the
permanent social institutions which educate by calling
forth adaptive responses from the child, and through
the mediation of the educator produce definite forms of
thought and action out of the raw materials of impulse.
Combine the two aright—interpret and satisfy the deep
yearnings of the human soul, and create out of them the
equipment of a social being—and you have a natural
education.

But what is the right combination of the two factors ?
Is there a right combination ? Perhaps we will get at
Rousseau's answer to these questions best, if we leave
for the moment the narrower sphere of education, and
consider his view of the right relations of the natural
and the conventional elements in a relationship like
that of marriage, in which the original basis has not
wholly disappeared behind the conventions. "What is
natural in the savage state must not be confused with
what is natural in society," he says, opening a somewhat
lengthy discussion on marriage. "In the first case, all
women suit all men, because as yet both of them have
only the common primitive form. But in the second,
each character has been developed by social institutions,
and each mind has received its own determinate form,
not from education merely but from the combination,
well or ill ordered, of natural disposition and education;
and consequently it is no longer possible to mate them,
except by presenting them to each other to see whether
they suit." [1] In another passage in which these principles
are worked out, he declares that a good marriage calls
for three kinds of conformity : first, natural compatibility,
compatibility of "tastes, humours, sentiments, and char-

[1] *Emile*, v. 176.

acters"; second, conformity with institution, based, for example, on consideration of rank and wealth; and third, the proprieties that pertain to opinion. All three, Rousseau points out, must be taken into account, and none of them is unimportant. At the same time, the really fundamental relations are these of nature, and it is a mistake to unite people in marriage who would not suit each other in any situation, in any country, in any rank of life. That being so, "the parents are the best judges of the two last conformities, the children the only judges of the first."[1]

Now, it must be borne in mind that Rousseau considers preparation for marriage an exceedingly important phase of natural education; and what he says about marriage, being said in direct view of this preparation, admits of a wider application. It is not merely in regard to marriage that those responsible for the development of mind and character in the young have to take into account nature and institution, and even opinion. In every aspect of knowledge or skill it is possible to distinguish between the individual impulses and the social "forms" given to these impulses as a result of education; and so long as we keep clearly in mind on the one hand, that apart from culture the dispositions of the child's nature are altogether formless, and on the other hand, that the institutions of society are only dead tradition until the individual by personal sentiment and thought has brought them into relation to his primary dispositions —in a word, avoiding the errors to which Rousseau is prone with regard to both individual and society—the distinction is one of great value for the educator. It is his special work to bring nature and society together in

[1] *Emile*, v. 154.

the experience of the individual child, and in doing so, it is of the utmost importance that he should do full justice to both factors. Unless the balance is held even, the education he gives cannot be perfectly natural. At the same time, if he must incline to one side or the other, it should be to nature's side. Necessary as it is to make the child a social being by directing his natural tendencies with reference to the appropriate institutions, nature is always more to be considered than institution. It is not merely in marriage that the possibility of realising the best life depends on taking account of the individual. The same is no less true of every social institution. Institutions were made for man, not man for institutions.

2. *National and Individual Education.*—The end of education, then, as Rousseau understands it, may be summarily stated to be the "forming" of men as social beings in such wise that the "forms" imposed on them are in conformity with their "natures": or less precisely, but still in Rousseau's own words, to make them both men and citizens.[1]

It is obvious that the attempt to educate with the double end in view must proceed on the assumption that there is no essential opposition in the nature of things between the natural impulses and the social forms given to them by the educator. If there was really anything in the qualities of manhood incompatible with those of citizenship, or *vice versa*, it would be foolish to propose to combine them in the same person by education or by any other method. And yet it is just at this point that Rousseau hesitates. His difficulty is not due to any doubt about the possibility of making man social and keeping him natural the

[1] *Emile,* i. 26–7.

while : he sees too clearly the need for the completion
of nature by society to have any real doubt on that
score. His difficulty is entirely concerned with contemporary civilisation. On the view he takes of society,
it seems to him quite impossible for any one to be
true to his essential manhood and yet be the citizen
of a modern state. Many of the ends that society sets
before its members (he maintains) are not merely unconnected with anything in their nature as men, but
involve demands on them incompatible with it. Whether
he will it or not, the modern man has continually to be
making choice between his duty to himself and his duty
to society, or (to put it in another way) between his own
interests and the interests of others. In these circumstances, the conception of the man who is at once man
and citizen represents an ideal that is incapable of
realisation until, as Rousseau said to Madame d'Epinay,
society has been reconstructed and brought into harmony with nature.

Does this mean, then, that under existing conditions,
it is useless to educate ? That is a possible conclusion
from the premises, but it is not the one that Rousseau
draws. Failing the absolute best, he is willing to get
as near it as conditions permit; and for that reason he
recognises the divergence of interests as a fact of the
situation in seeking this approximation. Not being
able to make a man and a citizen, he is content if he
can make a man or a citizen.

But note this important point. When Rousseau
asserts the necessity to make choice between forming
a man or a citizen, it is not to approve of it. He is
stating a fact, not passing a judgment; and he states
the fact, because it is one which must be taken into
account in devising a scheme of natural education that

aims at being practicable in the modern world. His point is that so long as the conflict of interests between an individual and his society goes on, the practical educator cannot ignore it. If he could be sure that in training the child to seek his own good, he was also making him a good member of society, or that in making him a good member of society he was promoting his welfare as an individual, it would not be necessary to raise the question of the educational end in this form at all. But it is only shutting one's eyes to the plain facts of the case to pretend that the good man will certainly be an efficient member of society, or that the efficient member of society will certainly be a good man. If we are to educate at all under present social conditions, it is impossible to avoid asking whether the primary aim of education is to make a good man or a good citizen.

Usually the question is not explicitly raised, because it is settled in the individual case by the aim of the agent who undertakes responsibility for the work of education. If it is the father, then the good of the child is the main concern : if the state, then the common good counts for most. " From the two aims, necessarily opposed to each other, come two contrary systems of education, the one public and common, the other individual and domestic." [1] When the child's education is undertaken by his parents, or by a tutor acting on their behalf, we have a system that may be called "individual" or "domestic" indifferently : individual, because its first object is the advantage of the child as an individual ; domestic, because this development of individuality takes place in the home. Where, on the other hand, education is the care of the

[1] *Emile*, i. 20.

state, the advantage of the individual children is only an incidental consideration. The immediate end is the welfare of the community, so far as that is served by the training of good workers or soldiers or statesmen. From Rousseau's point of view both of these systems are open to criticism. In spite of the fact that the family stands midway between nature and society in constitution,[1] and that it is the form of society nearest nature, the ordinary tuition which takes place under its auspices (as Rousseau is well aware) has many defects that make it compare unfavourably with the education commonly given in schools and colleges. Perhaps its chief defect is that it tends to make the child over-rate his own consequence. In school, a boy speedily finds his level, but the child on whose lips nurses and tutors hang, never gets a proper chance to realise his own unimportance in the scheme of things. If it is contrary to nature to neglect individuality, it is no less contrary to nature to exaggerate it, as is often done in the home.

About the weaknesses of national education Rousseau has nothing to say. His admiration for Sparta, in which national education assumed what he regarded as its most perfect form, was undiscriminating. That fact, and also perhaps the fact that there was no opportunity for him to see this kind of state training in actual operation, is sufficient to explain his silence. Nevertheless, whether he was conscious of it or not, a rigid system like that of Sparta, which had no place in it for individuality, was quite as much opposed to his principles as the indulgence of the home training. If the indulgent family over-rates the individual, the

[1] Social Contract, i. 2.

Spartan state goes to the other extreme, and under-rates him.[1]

But though Rousseau does not regard any of the contemporary methods of education as satisfactory, he recognises that so long as society is not what it should be, his own problem can only be solved by recognising the opposition between individual and society and making his plans accordingly. His aim in the *Emile* and in the other writings that deal with education, it should be noted, is not to construct an ideal scheme of education. His ideal, as he quite explicitly states, is only possible of attainment in a reconstructed society, and in order to be practical, he deliberately sets aside that ideal and seeks a second best that admits of achievement without any drastic change of social relations, or even it may be without any change at all. For this purpose, it is immaterial to him whether he starts from the individual or from the national point of view. What he is concerned to urge is that it should be from one of them, and not from both of them at the same time. To try to educate a child both for himself and for others in a society where the interests of self and others are so often in conflict would in his opinion inevitably lead to confusion and to the loss of that singleness of purpose without which a man cannot be natural. It is possible to organise life with a view either to the individual or to the common good. Except in an ideal community that is free from the clashing of interests which characterises every actual community, it is impossible to organise it for both at once.

But does this not mean that Rousseau himself intends

[1] *Cf.* Rousseau's condemnation of the two extremes of excessive severity and over-indulgence. *Emile*, ii. 40. The same ideas underlie the whole discussion of maternal duty in the First Book of the *Emile* (32–59).

to perpetuate that very division of interests for which he condemns society? Is he not attempting to keep the individual in an artificial simplicity of life by making him merely a self-centred man, or merely a social unit? This is the common interpretation of his educational position,[1] but quite a wrong one. It is true that in the *Emile* we have what may be called an individualistic method of education. The boy and his tutor withdraw to a little country village as though to escape all contact with humanity, and the boy's education proceeds for the most part on the assumption that like the savage he lives only to himself and has no need of his fellows. But an individualistic method, such as this is, does not necessarily imply an individualistic end. The crucial question after all is not how the boy is trained, but for what he is being trained; and in Emile's case, there does not seem to be any real cause for doubt. In spite of all that Rousseau has to say about the virtues of solitary and savage life, he never regards the self-sufficiency that is characteristic of boyhood as an end in itself, but only a means to an end. The clear proof of this is that under the direction of the tutor the self-regarding nature of the boy broadens out, and without altogether ceasing to be self-regarding, finds a larger and worthier self by assimilating the interests of humanity. The individual developed to the full as an individual becomes a social being who finds his own good (within limits) in the good of others. In those parts of Rousseau's discussion of education, on the other hand, which start from the national point of view, we appear to be presented with an education as absolutely socialistic in character as that

---

[1] To be more precise, the common view of Rousseau's doctrine, based on a mis-reading of the *Emile*, is that he wishes to prepare the child to live solely for himself. It is rare indeed, that Rousseau's critics are aware that the complementary view is also held by him.

of the *Emile* is individualistic. In this case also the working out of the method results in the end making good to a certain extent the deficiencies of the beginning. The education for life in society, when brought into accord with nature by Rousseau, is found to be in the long run the best education for personal life. In both cases, the extremes tend to meet. The complete individual must be a good member of society: the good member of society must be a complete individual.

In effect, then, Rousseau accepts the division of interests that marks the life of social man as a fundamental fact for the educator. He recognises that some forms of human action make more directly for individual good, and others more directly for common good; and starting from the one end or the other, as the opportunity presents itself, he works out in both cases a better method, in which the reconciliation of individual and common good which he himself had denied to be possible is on the way to being effected. We shall appreciate the value of this reconciliation better by studying in some detail his two complementary working ideals for educational reform.

A. NATIONAL EDUCATION

3. *The National Ideal.*—"If you want to get an idea of what public education really is," says Rousseau at the beginning of the *Emile*, "read the *Republic* of Plato. It is not a work on politics, as people who only judge of books by their titles think. It is the finest treatise on education ever written. Plato's scheme is generally regarded as chimerical; but if Lycurgus had only put his in writing, I should have thought it even more

chimerical. Plato only improved the heart of man. Lycurgus made it unnatural." [1]

"The system of public education," he adds, "no longer exists and can no longer exist, because there cannot be citizens now that there are no longer any fatherlands. The words 'fatherland' and 'citizen' ought to be expunged from modern languages." [2]

Though this is all that Rousseau says about the ideal and method of national education in the *Emile*, the general principles underlying his conception of it are quite evident. In the first place, it is an education that prepares every member of the state for the duties of the special station which his character and abilities fit him to occupy. It implies therefore a highly organised state, like Plato's, which is capable of dealing with its citizens as individuals and of making sure that every man is spending his life to the best advantage of the community, neither higher nor lower in the hierarchy of public offices and functions than his capacity warrants. In the second place, it is an education that cultivates a patriotic devotion on the part of every citizen, so that each man finds his own deepest satisfaction in the service of the state. The ideal state in which it is conceivable is not a despotism that coerces its members into obedience, but a paternal power that inspires their affections and makes them willing to devote their lives to its service. In short, this system of national education is a system which would find fitting habitation in the ideal state contemplated in the *Social Contract*. It presupposes a community in which the general will prevails in the making and in the execution of the laws, and would be out of place in any other. In a state where the individual wills of the citizens conflict with the general will, it is impossible for

[1] *Emile*, i. 21, 22.   [2] *Ibid.*, i. 23.

the citizen to find his personal good in the good of all, and education for social service would probably put a man as much at variance with himself as the "public education" of the colleges so vigorously condemned by Rousseau.[1]

The need for a special type of state for its realisation is the cardinal weakness of the system. Like the education given to Emile, it is only practicable under exceptional circumstances. It worked in Sparta, as it might have worked in Athens, or in any of the other city-states of the ancient world, or as it might work in an independent city like Geneva. In a word, it calls for a very small community. In the large nation states of the modern world, the governing body and the ordinary citizens stand far apart, and the different sections of the people have little chance of understanding each other. The result is that patriotism has no real place in them. There is no mutual knowledge, no general will, no common interests and sympathies: all that really constitutes nationality is wanting. "Whatever may be said, there are no longer Frenchmen, Germans, Spaniards, or even Englishmen[2] nowadays, but only Europeans. They have all the same tastes, the same passions, the same moral standards, because none of them has received the stamp of nationality (*formes nationales*) from a distinctive education. In the same circumstances, they all do precisely the same things."[3]

---

[1] *Emile*, i. 24.

[2] Note—"even Englishmen." Rousseau had a great admiration for the violent patriotism of the English. "The only nation of men," he says of them, "which remain among the various herds that are scattered over the face of the earth." *Nouvelle Heloïse. Cf.* Texte: Book II., chap. i. p. 105.

[3] *Government of Poland :* chap. iii. Taine (*L'Ancien Régime*—18me. *Siècle*, pp. 259, 260), points out as characteristic of the French writers in the eighteenth century, that, "la différence prodigieuse qui sépare les hommes de deux siècles ou de deux races leur échappe."

4. *Polish Education.*—Curiously enough, there came to Rousseau even in the unpromising circumstances of the modern world, an opportunity to formulate a method of national education according to nature. About ten years after the publication of the *Emile*, at the time when Poland was in the last throes of her death-struggle with Russia, a Polish patriot appealed to Rousseau for his views on the situation. Rousseau, always ready to give advice, responded to the appeal by setting forth *Considerations on the Government of Poland and on the Reformation of it projected in April 1772*."[1] He began wisely enough by pointing out that only the Poles themselves could create, or re-create, the institutions needed for the preservation and maintenance of their national life, and that all an outsider like himself could do was to lay down general principles that might help them in the task. Then he proceeded to emphasise the necessity for a distinctive national life as the first condition of Polish regeneration. "It is the national institutions," he said, "that form the genius, the character, the tastes, and the morals of a people, and make them different from every other people. It is the national institutions that inspire them with an ardent love of country based on ineradicable habits, and make them perish of heart-weariness in foreign climes, even when surrounded by luxuries altogether lacking in their own land." "Make it impossible for a Pole ever to become a Russian, and I will guarantee that Russia will never subjugate Poland."[2]

To bring about this result far-reaching changes

---

[1] The sections dealing with education are translated in my *Minor Educational Writings of Rousseau.*
[2] Chap. iii.

would need to be made in the life of the people.
Customs should be modified, and antiquated methods
of government adapted to modern conditions. And
above all, attention should be paid to the education
of the young, since the future of the state depends
on that. "It is education that should give men's souls
the national stamp, and so shape their opinions and
tastes as to make them patriots by inclination, by passion, by necessity."[1] Then without going into any great
detail, he outlines what seems to him a feasible scheme
for setting up and carrying out a system of national
education likely to have the desired effect. Like Plato,
he entrusts the direction of the educational system to
a board of magistrates of the highest rank. To them
he gives power to appoint or to dismiss teachers, and
to administer the special laws relating to the courses
of study.[2]

In his scheme the instruments of education assume
two forms. In the first place it would be the business
of the colleges and academies to give the young Poles[3]
all the knowledge about their own country that good
patriots ought to possess. "I would have the boy who
is learning to read, read about what concerns his own

---

[1] For this and all that follows, see chap. iv. of the *Considerations*.

[2] The direction of education by a board of magistrates of the
highest rank recalls the *Republic* of Plato. The idea of national
education was one that was much in men's minds at the time when
this tractate was written, on account of the struggle between state
and church that culminated in the expulsion of the Jesuits from
France in 1764. It had found expressions in works like the *Essai
d'éducation nationále*, published by La Chalotais in 1763 just after
the *Emile*, but Rousseau seems to owe more to Plato than to contemporary thought. On the development of the idea of national education
in France, see Compayré's *History of Pedagogy*, chap. xv.

[3] Rousseau does not refer to *all* the young Poles, but only to the
young Polish nobles. The limitation of education to the upper classes
is also suggested in *Emile*, i. 86. (*Cf.* section 12 of this chapter);
but the reasons for the limitation are different in the two cases.

country. At ten he should be familiar with all its productions, and at twelve with all its provinces, highways, and towns. At fifteen he should know its whole history, and at sixteen, all its laws. There should not have been a noble deed or a great man in all Poland whose fame does not possess heart and memory so that he can give instant account of them." These national studies are so fundamental that the law should regulate "their matter, their order, and their form," and only Poles should be allowed to teach them, "all of them, if possible, married men, distinguished for character and probity as well as for good sense and intelligence, and destined for other occupations, not more important or more honourable (for that is not possible) but less exacting and of greater repute, after they have fulfilled the duties of teacher for a certain term of years."

In the second place, there ought to be established in all the colleges a gymnasium, or place of physical exercise, for the children. This, in Rousseau's opinion, is the most important part of the work of education, not only because it makes for vigorous bodily health, but still more because of its moral influence. "I can never repeat often enough that good education should be negative. If you keep the vices from springing up, you have done enough for virtue."[1] Happily, it is not difficult to do this in a system of public education

---

[1] This is a somewhat guarded statement of objection to clerical teachers. La Chalotais expresses his mind more openly. "I do not presume to exclude ecclesiastics, but I protest against the exclusion of laymen. I dare claim for a nation an education which depends only on the state, because it belongs essentially to the state ; because every state has an inalienable and indefeasible right to instruct its members ; because, finally, the children of the state ought to be educated by the members of the state." Compayré, *History of Pedagogy* (translated by Payne), p. 345.

such as that which Rousseau contemplates. All that is required is to make the children join in the exercises of the gymnasium and take part in the common games, instead of spending their time poring over lessons which compel them to sit still and learn when their growing bodies are calling for movement. The games in particular he considers of the greatest consequence. It is the children's games, regarded by superficial people as a waste of time, "which make the hearts glow, and create deep love for the fatherland and its laws." [1] Consequently, the regulation of the games is a very important matter. "The children should not be permitted to play separately according to their fancy, but encouraged to play all together in public; and the games should be conducted in such a way that there is always some common end to which all aspire, to accustom them to common action and to stir up emulation. The parents who would rather have domestic education, and want their children brought up under their own supervision, ought nevertheless to send them to these exercises. Their instruction may be got at home and be adapted to individual need, but their games should always be played in public and shared by all. It is not merely a question of keeping them busy, or of cultivating a sound constitution and making them alert and graceful. The important thing is to get them accustomed from

[1] Chap. ii. *Cf.* a passage from the same chapter: "All the ancient legislators sought to attach the citizens to the state and to each other; and they found bonds of attachment in distinctive usages—in religious ceremonies which by their nature were always exclusive and national; in games which kept the citizens much together; in exercises which increased their vigour as well as their pride and their self-esteem; in plays, which by recalling the history of their ancestors won their hearts, inflamed them with a lively emulation, and attached them closely to the fatherland that unceasingly filled their thoughts."

an early age to discipline, to equality and fraternity, to living under the eyes of their fellow-citizens and seeking public approbation."

5. *The Individual under a National System of Education.*—Even with the concrete illustration of what Rousseau means by a national education in accordance with nature, which is provided by this tractate on Polish Government, we are left in doubt about many points on which information would be desirable. We want, for example, to know the relation of the system of education expounded and illustrated in the *Émile* to this new system. There is, of course, common ground in the principle that early education should be negative and aim at the exclusion of vice rather than at the inculcation of virtue, and, again, in the recognition of the value of play for the moral culture of children. But on the most fundamental considerations there seems to be complete divergence, in that the sole purpose of the national institution is to make good citizens, while the outstanding, if not the sole, purpose of individual education is to make good men. What place has the individual in this national system? Has he a place at all? Plato, it will be remembered, had to answer this very question with reference to the guardian class, to whom, in the interests of the state, he had denied home life and private possessions.[1] The critic not unreasonably raises the objection that, under these conditions of privation, the guardians will not be particularly happy. To this Plato's answer is that the prime consideration is not the happiness of any one class, but the happiness of the whole community; but that in all likelihood the guardians would be happy, since happiness comes in the performance of one's proper functions as a citizen. If

[1] *Republic*, iv. 420, 421.

the question had been raised, Rousseau would probably have followed the same line of defence; and up to a certain point the answer is sound enough. If the individual man can only realise himself as a social being, then an educational system that enables him to play his part in society cannot be regarded as altogether indifferent to individual well-being; and if it be true that Plato "believed that neither a state nor an individual can undertake to educate in a systematic way unless they start with some idea, not only of what they wish to teach, but also of the living being to whom the matter to be taught is relative,"[1] much more is it true of Rousseau.[2] Even in the very scanty outline of the scheme for Polish education, we note his solicitude to adapt the instruction to the child in the recognition of the differing capacities of children at different ages, as well as in the preference for those lessons which can be learned in the playing field to the tasks that have to be mastered at the desk.

But even after we have granted the soundness of the principle that it is the duty imposed on the child by his nature that should determine the course of the instruction given to him, and have admitted that happiness comes through obedience to recognised laws and in the service of the community, there remains a certain misgiving. Before we can allow that the education for citizenship is really satisfactory, we require to be convinced not merely that the individual man can be happy in doing his duties as a citizen—that may be taken for granted—but also that his whole nature finds adequate expression for itself within the round of civic tasks.

[1] Nettleship: *The Theory of Education in Plato's Republic*, in *Hellenica*, p. 87.
[2] Cf. *Émile*, v. 24, for an interesting criticism of Plato.

This, indeed, is the crux of the whole situation. If the individual man is not only a citizen, but more than a citizen, if in love of the beautiful, the good and the true, he transcends the limits imposed on him by membership of any one community, then it is possible that a narrowly national education by producing in him a partisan devotion to a single state may prevent him entering into that ideal *Civitas deorum et hominum* in which alone his selfhood can find perfect realisation. Nothing that Rousseau says about natural education does anything to remove this misgiving.

B. INDIVIDUAL EDUCATION

6. *The Individual Ideal.*—The most obvious drawback, from the practical point of view, of Rousseau's ideal of a national education capable of forming both citizens and men, is that it demands for its realisation conditions which are rarely ever met in actual political life. His scheme for Poland presupposed the complete reconstruction of her government on the model of the ideal state of the *Social Contract*.[1] If Poland had followed his advice about education to the letter, and reorganised her system on a national basis without this change in her methods of government, the result would have satisfied him as little as the system superseded. For in that case Poland would still have come under the category of "ordinary" nations; and in ordinary nations, where custom and law (according to Rousseau) are not in any proper sense the expression of a general will but the resultant of a number of conflicting individual wills, a civic education that inculcates

---

[1] As a matter of fact, the greater part of the *Considerations on the Government of Poland* is taken up with the problem of political reconstruction.

devotion to the public weal and respect for the established order, inevitably puts the child in contradiction with himself as a rational being by making him subject to an irrational authority. The truth is that, as things are, national education is open to the very same objections that Rousseau brings against all contemporary education. Without more fundamental changes the change of authority does not remove the defects inherent in the ordinary education. If education merely means the imposition *ab extra* of certain habits and opinions unrelated to the child's "dispositions," it matters little whether it is the father or the state that directs and controls it. So long as the law to which the child is made subject is not the law of his own being, domestic education and national education are alike contrary to nature.

So great did the practical difficulties attaching to the national ideal appear to Rousseau at the time when the *Emile* was written, that in that work he begins by assuming the impossibility of educating for citizenship consistently with the demands of nature. In doing so he does not assert that a national education is necessarily unnatural: only that it is bound to be unnatural without a very thorough transformation of society. And since he saw it was vain to hope for that without revolution,[1] he attempted to approach the problem on the individual side to see whether it might not be possible to form the individual man for society without departing from nature in the process.

What makes the problem simpler in this case is the

---

[1] Rousseau rather looked forward to revolution. In the *Emile*, he refers to the possibility of revolution to justify the course of education through which Emile passed. See iii. 136, for the famous prophecy: "We are approaching a state of crisis and an age of revolutions." *Cf.* i. 31.

reduction of its extent.   For the national system there
was need to make the whole social environment natural.
When only a single individual is in question it suffices
to modify his immediate environment.   Of course, if the
difficulty in the case of national education were due to
an absolute incompatibility in the claims of nature and
society, it would be no more possible to educate one
child naturally than the children of a nation.   But
if Rousseau ever held that position, he had entirely
abandoned it at the time when he wrote the *Emile*.
The fault he finds with social institutions in the *Emile*
is not so much that they are contrary to the natural
order of the universe as that they are inadequate to
meet the needs that arise out of man's nature.   His
condemnation in fact is not a condemnation of social
institutions as such, but of imperfect social institutions.
So far from saying that man suffers loss in becoming a
social being, he states quite explicitly that the end of
education is to enable the individual child to enter
whole-heartedly into the great basal relationships or
civilised humanity, without which ·he would not be
truly man.   The real difficulty is that this social life
which man needs for the completion of his being is a
very imperfect expression of human nature, and consequently is apt to exercise a harmful influence on the
developing individual.   Among the different institutions
that constitute it, there are some which are "in the nature
of things and independent of human conventions." [1]
These may rightly be said to be natural.   But there
are others which are mere artifices that do not answer
to any real need of man's nature.   It is these that tend
to pervert man and make him unnatural.   But for
them the educator's task would be the comparatively

[1] *Social Contract*, ii. 6.

simple one of acting as mediator between the rich and
varied life of social man and the immature mind of the
child, and his only difficulties would be those due to the
limitations of an undeveloped heart and intellect. As
things are, it is as important (perhaps for one period of
life more important) for him to exclude error and vice
as to teach truth and goodness.[1] For this reason, in
attempting to approach the ideal as nearly as circumstances permit, he withdraws his pupil from the main
course of human activity, not indeed into a desert where
there is no society at all, but into some quiet spot where
he is able to control in large measure the social environment by excluding the malign influences of the merely
conventional and preventing a dangerous prematurity
of experience. Failing to find an ideal society in the
ordinary world of men, he is compelled to create one
on a small scale for his pupil.

7. *The Forming of a Man.*—It must be admitted
that Rousseau's account of natural education of the
individual type is marred at times by unmistakable
reversions to the earlier doctrine that man is only
natural when out of society altogether. And quite
apart from these lapses, his exposition of the idea of a
natural education as the forming of the individual man,
is couched in language that makes misunderstanding
easy. The very fact that he should regard the forming
of the man as alternative to the forming of the citizen[2]
seems *prima facie* to carry with it the implication that
the one process excludes the other. So, too, the striking
passage in the First Book of the *Emile*, in which he
contrasts the training for manhood with the training
necessary for a particular trade or profession, courts
a like misconstruction. "In the natural order," he

[1] *Emile*, ii. 67. [2] *Ibid.*, i. 13.

remarks, "where all men are equal, the common vocation is man's estate; and one well trained for that
will not fulfil badly any vocation pertaining to it. It
is a matter of little concern to me that my pupil should
be destined for the army or the church or the bar.
Prior to the vocation that his parents have chosen
for him is the call of nature to the duties of man.
Life is the business for which I wish to prepare him. I
admit that when he leaves me he will not be a magis-
trate or a soldier or a priest. First and foremost he will
be a man, and all that a man needs to be he is fit to
be when the occasion requires, quite as well as any
one."[1] On a casual reading this certainly seems to
imply that the man of nature is not to follow any
particular vocation, and it has been understood in that
sense by some of Rousseau's interpreters.[2] But a more
careful study of the *Emile* will show that Rousseau had
nɔ intention of making a man who would not also be
a workman and a citizen. When Emile enters his teens
and the time for his introduction to the ordinary social
relations draws near, his tutor is careful to see that he
learns to maintain himself by means of a special craft;[3]
and at a later time when he is about to take a definite
place in the community by becoming the head of a
household, the tutor shows no less assiduity in preparing him to discharge aright all the duties of a
citizen.[4]

What Rousseau is really trying to bring out by

---

[1] I. 29.

[2] *Cf.* Lemaître, *J.-J. Rousseau*, p. 217, " Je ne sais pas, s'il ne serait
pas plus simple et plus sûr de former d'abord l'homme d'un pays,
d'une religion, d'une profession, et si 'l'homme' tout court ne viendrait
pas par surcroit." This is quite true, but is based on a misconception of Rousseau's view.

[3] III. 137 *seq.*   [4] V. 341; *cf.* 472 *seq.*

putting the man in opposition to the workman and the citizen, is not any fundamental antagonism between the individual and society, but the relative antagonism that is inevitable under imperfect social conditions. In any society the man needs to be a workman and a citizen, but there is considerable danger that as society is now constituted the workman and the citizen may not be men.[1] Accordingly, when Rousseau says that it is a matter of indifference to him what the boy's vocation is to be, his words somewhat obscure his meaning; for as a matter of fact he does regard the choice of a vocation as of very great importance, not merely because it is necessary for the boy to have the means of earning his livelihood but even more because of the influence which the choice exercises on the subsequent development of his mind and character. What Rousseau really means to say is that since the man is always more than the worker, an education that is limited to preparing the boy for a particular occupation does him the greatest possible disservice. By nature every man is endowed with infinite capacity.[2] But the merely vocational training imposes on him a single "form" of life, which narrows him down by excluding some of the wide range of interests needed for complete living. In the same spirit, Rousseau looks with suspicion on an exclusive devotion to one country as likely to make a man less a man by rendering him oblivious to those aspects of life which, though rooted in nationality, are essentially supernational. It is this that leads him to insist that the boy is to become a man, not a

[1] *Cf.* Pestalozzi : *How Gertrude Teaches her Children* (Eng. Tr.), p. 178, " We have spelling schools, writing schools, catechism schools only, and we want men's schools."

[2] Cf. *Emile*, i. 132.

citizen. His real object all the while is not to form a man who is not a citizen, but to form a man who is a citizen and more than a citizen.

The idea underlying this phase of thought in Rousseau is most aptly illustrated by a passage in Book IV. of the *Emile*, in which he comments with satisfaction on the fact that Emile has reached manhood without receiving "any particular form," and that he is in the habit of acting independently of the opinion of others.[1] This cannot mean that Emile has not acquired skill in one special vocation, or that he has remained entirely indifferent to the land of his birth; because in point of fact, Emile at this very time had mastered the carpenter's craft, and was well on the way to the discovery that for the realisation of all the possibilities of his nature he must needs be a good citizen. What, then, does Rousseau mean by saying that he has no "particular form"? Surely that the "form" which he has acquired through his education, though in a sense particular, as any actual form must be, does not impose a real limit on his personality. He is not less a man because he happens to be a carpenter and to belong to a particular community. In this respect, in Rousseau's opinion, he differs from most men. The other carpenters who learn their trade by mechanical imitation depend on the authority of their elders and the customs of the trade. The things they know and do are not personal to themselves at all, but depend on tradition. In the same way, the ordinary citizens, who have never asked themselves about the meaning of the State and the nature of their obligations to it, are swayed by prejudices borrowed from their neighbours and from the past. The motives for their civic activities rarely come from what they

[1] IV. 160; *cf.* iii. 135

themselves think and feel should be done, but generally from the opinion they share with the crowd. Now, as a result of his education, Emile is quite different from these fellows of his. He is a worker and a citizen, as they are, but the experience by which he has become so is as much personal as social. Thanks to his education, he has tried everything for himself and thought out everything in a personal way, so that while dependent on society and its institutions as every man must be, he has remained true to his nature, and never acted without finding the reason for action within himself. In this way, the particular forms conferred on him by his training have lost their mere particularity, and do not limit him in any way. Having given them the rational character of his own mind, he is able to look on the particulars as having their worth not in themselves, but as elements in the larger whole of life.

In this view, we reach a new conception of the deficiencies of social institutions. It now becomes evident that the goodness or the badness of an institution is less important educationally than the attitude of mind which the individual, boy or man, assumes towards any institution. It may be true that some institutions are good and some bad, the good being those that are conformable to reason and to nature, and the bad those that are not.[1] The important fact for the educator is that even the best are bad when they are imposed on the individual *ab extra*, and accepted by him, not be-

---

[1] If Rousseau had followed out this line of argument, he would have discovered that the distinction between good and bad institutions is really a distinction between institutions that are good and institutions that have been good. Those that are contrary to nature must at one time have been conformable to it. How else could they have come into being? The real is the rational, as Hegel said.

cause he really finds in them the solution of his own problems as a man, but on the authority of books or of older people or of vague opinion. In this condition of unquestioning faith, all distinctions between good and bad institutions disappear. All stand on a common level of badness.

This whole doctrine is one that needs to be stated with great care to avoid extravagance. The assertion that a man's life is not to be bounded by his interests as a workman or even as a citizen, is apt to change into the quite different assertion· that man would still be man if he were not a workman or a citizen or even a member of society. And the emphasis on the necessity for the conversion of social institutions into the personal experience of the individual man readily leads to a capricious setting up of the self against all authority. It must be confessed that Rousseau does not always escape from these errors. His position as one of the pioneers of modern democratic thought, to whom it fell to translate into political form the Reformation doctrine of the necessity for individual experience as a condition of any worthy spiritual life, made it almost inevitable that much of his work should be exaggerated and one-sided in tendency. In a pioneer indeed this should almost be counted a merit. With the whole trend of the feudal tradition making for a depreciation of individual worth, and putting the political thought of Europe at variance with the individualistic teaching of Protestant Christianity, it needed Rousseau's vigorous statement of the claims of individuality to force men to re-think the practical bases of their political life; and his success in raising the problem should to some extent disarm criticism with regard to his own attempts at solution.

8. *The Problem of Individual Education.* — The difference between national and individual education, as these terms are ordinarily understood, is far-reaching. The one makes individual perfection its primary aim, and subordinates the training in civic and national functions to the making of the complete individual. The other is equally one-sided in its manner of approaching the work of education. It is mainly concerned with the man in his political relations, and is ready to develop or repress individuality in the interests of national well-being. For it, the citizen is always more important than the man.

But, extreme as the opposition is between the two points of view, there is a constant tendency for them to approximate in the actual practice of education. It was not altogether an accident, for example, that when Germany called in the schoolmaster to win back what had been lost in her disastrous war with Napoleon, the new national education should be based on the individualistic methods of Pestalozzi, and make the well-developed individual its first care. The same tendency is evident in Rousseau's speculations about educational method. The stipulation that education must be in accordance with nature compels the broadening of both ideals by bringing in the element neglected or under-stated in each. Individual education for complete manhood cannot ignore the fact that the complete man is a social being; and national education which proceeds on a proper respect for human nature must deal with men, not in the mass, but to some extent at least as individuals. It might almost be said that for Rousseau the difference between the two ideals is largely a difference of emphasis. Individual education aims at producing the man who is also a citizen, national education at producing the citizen who is also a man.

But though there is always this tendency towards a combination of the characteristic features of the two ideals in the practice of either, the difference is one which never wholly disappears, and which continues to affect more or less directly the spirit and the methods of the teaching. An educational system that puts preparation for adult life in the forefront of its endeavour and regards the making of good workers and good citizens as its primary aim, is almost bound to lay more stress on what is taught to the pupil than on his predilections and aptitudes; and if it encourages originality and initiative at all, it is not because it regards them as essential to the cultivation of individuality, but because in their proper place they are valuable attributes of the adult citizen. Where, on the other hand, the right development of the individual child is the main concern, as it is when education is properly conducted in a good home, the distinctive view of life taken by the pupil is generally allowed to count for more than the subjects he learns. In this case, the actual boy gets more attention than the future man; the process of education is of greater immediate interest than its social results; the manner of instruction is at least as interesting as the matter. Even when the future is kept clearly in mind, it is not thought so important that the pupil should acquire the knowledge and skill essential as an equipment for social service at a later age, as that what he does learn should be a personal possession won by his own effort and thought.

On the side of method, then, the problem of individual education differs from that of social or national education. Even when the teacher of an individual child aims at fitting him to play his part in social life, he looks at education from a different point of view from the statesman. He finds the immature human being confronted with the complexities of civilised society and helpless in presence of it; and he makes it his work to bring him *as an individual* into fruitful relation with this society in all its vital phases. For him, the fact of most immediate importance is not what the child will be when he grows up to manhood, but the kind of person he actually is. His interest is not so much in the social material which the child must make part of himself in order to attain the stature of the complete man, as in those characters of body, mind and spirit that condition the process of assimilation. This does not mean that he is indifferent to the ultimate social needs of his pupil. The good teacher always keeps the goal before him; for in the long run it is that which determines the whole course of development and of education. But while he is engaged in the work of teaching, the centre of interest is the actual individual child whom it is his business to teach. Face to face with him, he does not think of his work as merely the imparting of a certain stock of knowledge or the training in certain approved ways of behaviour, but he tries to look at the educative process from the point of view of his pupil.

From this point of view the first thing to be considered is the sex. Is the learner a boy or a girl? The subjects of instruction, still more perhaps the methods of instruction, must be varied accordingly; for the social functions of the two sexes are very different, and their motives of action, their interests, their mental capacities and habits, their methods of acquiring and using experience, are no less so. Age is the second determining factor in an individual education. Apart from the wisdom or un-wisdom of sacrificing the happiness of the present to an uncertain future and forcing the child to learn what he does not want to learn, it is useless to insist on the child studying subjects beyond his present capacity because of their importance at a later time of life. "Each age, and condition of life, has a perfection and maturity of its own," [1] and this ought to be taken into account both in the subjects and in the methods of instruction. The third factor in individual education is the indi-viduality of the pupil, meaning by individuality the distinctive talents and abilities that characterise each person and mark him off from his fellows. As this more than any of the other factors determines the special part that the pupil will one day play in the world of men, the educator cannot afford to neglect it. And finally, the kind of education to be given— whether indeed any education is to be given—depends on the social rank of the pupil. Rank, therefore, is also one of the factors in individual education, not perhaps so important as any of the other three factors, yet not without importance in its own way.

The individual factors in education, then, are four in number—sex, age, individuality, and rank (naming them in descending order of importance for Rousseau). We have now to consider the significance attached to each of them in the natural education of a child.

9. *The Essential Considerations in a Natural Educa-tion*: (a) *Sex.*—On Rousseau's view, the most profound difference between one human being and another, so far as the educator is concerned, is the difference made by sex. The principles underlying an educational scheme for the one sex scarcely apply to the other at all. What

---

[1] *Emile*, ii. 304.

is said about education, for example, in the first four
books of the *Emile*, only refers to the education of boys:
the education of the other sex gets special treatment in
the long discussion of the Fifth Book. So again in the
Letter on Education in the *New Heloïse*, it is the upbringing of Julie's sons which is the sole topic. The
education of their sister is dismissed in a few words.
"So far as she is concerned," says Julie, "her education
is my affair, but the principles on which it is conducted
are so different from those relating to the education of
the boys that they deserve separate discussion." [1]

It is not quite easy to see why Rousseau should make
the sex-difference so fundamental a consideration in
education. If the end and aim of a boy's education is
to make him a man in the fullest possible sense, there
does not seem any reason why the girl, who shares with
the boy all the attributes of humanity, should not also
be prepared for the same full manhood. Is it because
of the different functions of the sexes in the reproduction of the species? In view of the fact that these
differences do not become important till maturity, they
mean as little for the girl as for the boy: and if, on
Rousseau's principles, the boy's future should not be
allowed to dominate his education, neither should the
girl's. In childhood the boy and the girl are very much
alike, as Rousseau himself recognises. "Up to the age of
nubility, there is no apparent distinction between the children of the two sexes. They have the same countenance,
the same figure, the same complexion, the same voice:
everything is the same. The girls are children, the boys
are children. The same name serves for beings so much
alike." [2] On Rousseau's own premises, it would seem

---

[1] Which, however, they do not get.
[2] *Emile*, iv. 2.

as though boys and girls, being "so much alike," should get similar education.

But Rousseau refuses to follow the argument to its conclusion. "In all that does not pertain to sex," he admits, "the woman is a man. She has the same organs, the same needs, the same faculties. The machine is constructed on the same lines and has the same parts. Their appearance is alike, and from whatever point of view they be considered, the difference between them is only one of less or more."[1] But to argue that their education should be the same because of this common possession of human characters is to forget that there is also a permanent diversity of mind and character due to difference of sex. "Everything they have in common belongs to the species, everything in which they differ to sex. From this double point of view, there are so many resemblances and so many contrasts between them that it may well be said to be one of the marvels of nature that two beings could have been made at once so like and so different."[2]

Care is needed, however, in stating the difference. It is so complete that comparisons between the sexes are peculiarly odious.[3] And yet it is not a difference of essential constitution but of complementary constitution. Nature has made men and women different to suit them all the better for each other. The one is active and strong, the other passive and weak.[4] The one has a grasp of principles, the other of details.[5] The one can judge and reason, the other has a keen observation and a sound intuition.[6] Each sex, in fact, has its points of weakness and its points of strength, and only

---

[1] *Emile*, v. 4.　　　[2] *Ibid.*, v. 5.　　　[3] *Ibid.*, v. 6.
[4] *Ibid.*, v. 7.　　　[5] *Ibid.*, v. 74.
[6] Perhaps better, a "practical reason."

when they combine forces is the complete humanity realised in the new unity of man-and-woman. "From the association of man and woman," says Rousseau, "there results a moral personality of which the woman is the eye and the man the arm, but with such a dependence the one on the other, that it is from the man that the woman learns what must be seen, and from the woman that the man learns what must be done."[1]

It is this fact of complementary difference which seems to Rousseau to make a different education for the two sexes essential. "Once it is demonstrated that man and women are not, and ought not to be, constituted alike in character or in temperament, it follows that they ought not to have the same education. Following the directions of nature, they ought to act in concert, but not do the same things."[2] Whatever else education implies, it must always be a training for the right discharge of one's function; and nature having given man and woman their respective functions, the wise educator will follow nature and make education follow function.

Now, what does this imply? For the man, it must be said, not very much; for the woman, everything. Borrowing the language of Byron for the expression of Rousseau's idea, it might be said that sex, which is of man's life a thing apart, is woman's whole existence. "There is no parity between the sexes so far as consequences of sex are concerned. The male is only a male at certain seasons. The female is a female all her life, or at any rate all her youth. Everything is incessantly reminding her of her sex, and for the right discharge of her duties

[1] *Emile*, v. 74. [2] *Ibid.*, v. 25.

she needs the proper temper of body and mind." [1]
This holds good on the social side no less than on
the physical. The man may neglect his domestic
duties without inflicting any very serious harm on
the community. But any such neglect on the woman's
part would be immediately felt by the whole body
politic. It is on the performance of her duties as
wife and mother that the permanence of the family
and the stability of the state depend.[2]

These considerations are for Rousseau decisive in
the discussion of the education to be given to the
two sexes. Sex is a fact of very great importance
in a man's life and must affect his education at
many points, notably in the years of adolescence,
when the major part of the educator's care is directed
to the right regulation of the sex-passions. But after
full account has been taken of all the ways in which
the nature of the boy or the man as a male animal
influences him, the greater part of his interests will
be found to lie outside the sphere of sex.[3] That part
of his life which is not directly concerned with the
sex functions is so much richer and fuller than the
part which is, that we do not think of these functions
as of predominant interest for him. He is a man
first, a sex-being after. With woman it is entirely
different. Her distinctive work as wife and mother
means so much for her that the broader human
characters, though not excluded from her life, are
kept in subordination to those that fit her for wife-

---

[1] *Emile*, v. 18.   [2] *Ibid.*, v. 19.
[3] What is said about the distinction between that part of life concerned with sex and the part outside its sphere, needs to be qualified
with some care. It must be remembered that Rousseau regards all
the higher life of man as having its origin in sex-inspiration. *Infra*,
Chap. IX., section 5.

hood and maternity. She is a woman first, and only in a secondary way, a human being. That being so, it is clear that her education should prepare her directly for her life-work. " Whether I consider the special destination of the sex, or observe its inclinations or take account of its duties," says Rousseau, " everything concurs to indicate to me the form of education most suitable for woman." [1] The only wise, as it is the only natural, education is an education for womanhood. It is possible to train the woman like a man, but there could be no mistake more serious. Trained as a man, she loses many of the charms which give her influence over men, and is spoiled both for herself and for the other sex. Better far in every way than such a mannish education is a simple domestic education under her mother's supervision. If brought up properly in the home she will learn to love all the tasks of her sex; she will acquire the arts of pleasing that serve in the first instance to commend her to men and at a later time enable her to rule both husband and family; she will make herself master of all the domestic arts, and find out " how to look after her household and occupy herself in her own house." In a word, she will become the complete woman.[2]

[1] *Emile*, v. 31.

[2] *Ibid.*, v. 62. Rousseau sometimes expresses the same idea in a way which though characteristic is open to misunderstanding. *Cf.* v. 32 : "The whole education of woman should be relative to men. To please them, to be useful to them, to make themselves loved and honoured by them, to educate them when young, to care for them when grown up, to advise them, to console them, to make life sweet and agreeable for them, these are the duties of women at all ages and should be taught them from their infancy " ; v. 8 : " Woman is especially constituted to please man." If statements like these are read in the light of later day prepossessions about the equality of the sexes (as, for example, in Miss Hodgson's *Studies in French Education*, chap. ix.), they convey the wrong impression that

In this way, though both boys and girls get the best education in the home, education means very different things for them. The boy is left to develop at leisure without undue thought for the future that may never come; and all the motives for learning are found in the impulses proper to his age and not in adult direction. The girl's education proceeds on wholly different principles. Unlike the boy, who is carefully screened from a premature interest in adult life, she lives for her life-work from her youngest days. She is not less an individual than the boy, but in presence of the over-mastering law of her sex-nature, her individuality is kept in constant check. It might almost be said that while he has a characteristic "nature" that marks him off from the grown man at every stage of his boyhood, the girl is never anything but a woman more or less immature, either doing woman's work or preparing for it. It would seem as if either nature or Rousseau were not quite consistent![1]

10. *The Essential Considerations in a Natural Education :* (b) *Age.*—After sex, the most important fact for the person responsible for a child's education is

Rousseau thought of woman as man's inferior, and wished her to spend her whole life ministering to him. Taken in their full context, they plainly are not intended to have any such meaning. Rousseau is careful to insist that the services women and men render to each other are mutual, and that words like "inferior" and "superior" are altogether out of place in describing their relationship. After saying that "women are specially constituted to please men," he immediately adds that "men in their turn have to please women." Moreover, as I have tried to indicate above by a phrase, it is woman's power to please men, which surely is not disputed, that makes them men's masters in their proper sphere.

[1] The inconsistency is the result of an ambiguity in Rousseau's use of the word "nature." Is the "nature" of a person what he now is or what he will ultimately be? In the discussion of the sex-differences in education, Rousseau wavers between the two.

undoubtedly the age of the child. On a superficial reading of Rousseau one might be tempted to think that he pays more regard to age than to sex. But the reason for this is simply that, like his contemporaries, he takes for granted without argument the view that difference of sex calls for a difference in the subjects and the methods of education, whereas he is conscious that in insisting on the necessity for proper recognition of age in the choice of educational matter and method, he is going against all the practices of the schools. There can be no doubt whatever that he regarded the sex-differences as the deepest of all the differences that distinguish individuals. It is to be noted in this connection that his whole discussion of the phenomena of age turns on the difference made in body and mind by the maturity or immaturity of the sex functions.

" My method," he declares, " is based on the measure of the human faculties at the different ages and on the choice of occupations suitable for these faculties. Probably another method that appeared to work better could easily be found; but I doubt whether it would have the same success if it were really less appropriate to the species, the age, and the sex of the pupil." [1] The existing methods of education, in his opinion, go off on wrong lines because they fail to take account of the fact that childhood has ways of thinking and acting as distinctive as those of adult life.[2] Grown-up people never seem to be able to put themselves in the place of children,[3] he says. They are generally so much occupied with what is going on in their own heads that they do not realise the effects of their teaching on their pupils,[4] and consequently they are always making the mistake

[1] *Emile*, iii. 129. [2] *Ibid.*, ii. 53.
[3] *Ibid.*, iii. 28. [4] *Ibid.*, ii. 75.

of trying to turn children into men before their time.[1]
"They do not know childhood," he says in a perspicuous
passage in the Preface to the *Emile*, expository of his
own system as a system that followed nature. "Acting
on the false ideas they have of it, the further they go
the more they blunder. The wisest men pay close attention to what it is important for men to know, without
considering what children are capable of learning. They
are always looking for the man in the child without
thinking of what he is before he becomes a man." For
his part, he is content to let nature be his guide and to
leave the development of body and mind to follow its
proper order. His system is nothing more than an
attempt to let the child's growth keep as near its natural
course [2] as is possible in a world of men who have departed
from nature. Others want to make the man : he is content to let childhood ripen in the child [3] and come to its
appropriate maturity,[4] confident that if this be done
childhood will pass into adolescence and adolescence
into manhood, all in their appointed seasons.

On this view, it is necessary for the teacher to study
the child at the different stages of his progress towards
manhood. "This is the study," Rousseau rightly says,
with reference to the *Emile*, "to which I have applied
myself with greatest diligence, so that even if my
method as a whole should chance to be chimerical and
false, profit may always be got from my observations.
It may be that I do not see very well what needs to be
done, but I think my conception of the child with whom
we have to work is sound." "Begin, then," he says
to the teacher, "by studying your pupils better, for

---

[1] *Emile*, ii. 191.
[2] *Cf.* Preface to the *Emile*: "la marche de la nature."
[3] *Emile*, ii. 68.   [4] *Ibid.*, ii. 304.

assuredly you do not know them. If you read my
book with this object in view, I do not think it will be
without profit for you." [1] The *Emile*, then, is intended
by Rousseau to be a treatise on child study and its
practical applications to the work of education.

This is not the place to go into a detailed account of
what Rousseau regards as the special characteristics of
childhood and youth, or to discuss the educational
superstructure he rears on the basis of his study of the
growing mind and character. It must suffice to indicate broadly the lines on which he treats age as a factor
in education.

Each of the first four books of the *Emile* deals with
a well-marked stage in the development of the boy.
The first treats of infancy, the second of boyhood,
the third of the transition years between childhood
and adolescence, and the fourth of adolescence. But
for a right appreciation of all that Rousseau has to
say about the physical and mental characteristics of the
boy at the different ages one must not attach too much
importance to this fourfold division; or, at any rate,
not let it divert attention from the more fundamental
division that is dependent on the coming of puberty.
Strictly speaking, there are only two periods for the
educator: the time before puberty, and the time after it.
During the one, Rousseau tells us, man merely exists; in
the other, he really begins to live.[2] It is the awakening
of sex that makes the difference. Sex comes as a whip
to hurry forward the growth of both body and soul.
Under its influence the child who has hitherto lived
within the narrow bounds of self-interest, scarcely able
to think of anything outside the immediate physical
needs, is born anew into the great world of human

[1] *Emile :* Preface.   [2] *Ibid.,* iv. 2.

interests, and becomes a living soul. The knowledge of good and evil, the sense of social obligations and duties, the intuition of the oneness of all things in God, all become possible for him for the first time. Needless to say, a change so far-reaching as this is of supreme consequence for education. Rousseau would even say that until it has taken place, education has not begun at all. " The period at which ordinary education comes to an end," he says, " is the one when ours is to begin." [1] Properly speaking, all that the child has learned before the critical change is not education at all, but only a preparation for the real education which endows the soul with the great human interests.

And yet the educator cannot afford to neglect the years before puberty. In a desert island, perhaps, the boy might be allowed to run free from all the trammels of a civilisation beyond his comprehension, and await the time of the soul's quickening before beginning his true education. But this is not possible with a boy growing up in the midst of society. Attention must be paid to him, if only to prevent the incoming of vice and error before reason is present to repel their onset. The need for this negative education makes it necessary to study the boy's progress towards adolescence and to distinguish stages on the way.

Rousseau marks off three stages in the pre-adolescent period. The first is infancy in the literal meaning of the word, ending some time about the end of the second year of life when the power to eat, speak, and walk is acquired.[2] Psychologically, this is the age of sense passivity, when the world is pouring in its impressions on the nascent mind, and meeting but little response in the way of an answering activity. Morally and

[1] *Emile*, iv. 6.   [2] *Ibid.*, i. 193.

socially, it is the time of pure animality without any consciousness of human relations. After infancy comes childhood proper, reaching its most perfect development about ten, and passing into the next stage at twelve. The mind is still immersed in sense, but the senses have acquired capacities that anticipate later intelligence. The boy cannot judge and reason in the ordinary meaning of the terms, and yet he has sense-intuitions which enable him to adapt himself to his actual physical environment in the necessary activities of his life. Morally, and therefore socially, he is still self-contained. He is aware of his own rights and capable of protesting vigorously when they are infringed by other people, but entirely lacking in any sense of obligation to others which would in any circumstances lead him to prefer their interests to his own on the grounds of right or duty. Like the savage, whom he resembles in mind and morals, he has risen above the animal, but is not yet a social being. He lives in society without the least understanding of its ways. The third stage, which lasts from twelve to fifteen, is characterised by an accession of physical strength, greatly exceeding the demands made on it for the purposes of growth. The transmutation of this surplus energy from a physical into a mental form results in a striking development of intelligence. The limitation to the sense-given facts that marked the years of boyhood is to some extent removed. The idea takes the place of the image, things distant in space become real, the past and the future become yoked in ideal union with the present, and the rational connections of things, their causes and their effects, begin to acquire meaning. On the moral side, indeed, the boy in the early teens continues much as he was in childhood, and yet though

conscience has not awakened, the general progress of
mind brings with it a certain moral progress. The
vision of the future, the consciousness of goods to be
gained and evils to be shunned by foreseeing action,
puts a check on impulse, which may not be moral in
the strict meaning of the word, since the motive is
still a merely personal advantage, but which is certainly
on the way to morality. So too in the matter of social
relations, there is a certain progress towards comprehension. Even if the lad's concentration on himself
prevents him understanding why men refrain from
self-pleasing actions in deference to a higher law, his
greater breadth of mind enables him to appreciate the
utility of social combination. Clearly he is well above
the savage in outlook at this stage. If not yet a social
being, he is at any rate on the level of the primitive
farmer or of Robinson Crusoe. Surrounded by society,
he lives in semi-independence of it, capable at need
of sufficing to himself if chance should strand him on
a desert isle remote from his fellows.[1]

This is indeed a notable survey of mental and moral
development, beyond all comparison the most profound
and suggestive of its kind in the whole literature
of pedagogy. Perhaps the most noteworthy feature of
it is its unity of conception. It is an attempt to see
the task of education as a whole. As we follow Rousseau's account of the individual growth through the

---

[1] What is said here about the characteristics of the successive
periods of childhood and youth is based chiefly on the first four
books of the *Emile*, and only applies to the boy. Book V. shows
that Rousseau recognised a corresponding series of gradations in
the case of girls, but it is not possible from the rather meagre account
he gives, to be quite sure that he thinks of the girl as going through
the same stages. So far as I can judge, he did not divide the pre-
adolescent period in the girl into three stages but into two: one
before and another after ten.

different stages of childhood on into adolescence, we see the gradual evolution of man's soul. We begin with the child in the state of animal feeling, and discover that in this undifferentiated feeling is the potency of all that goes to constitute the higher life of the spirit. In the second stage we see the child at home in a world of things, unconnected save by their occurrence within his experience. He perceives them in spatial relations and in a more limited extent in relations of time, but their meaning is wholly hid from him. This is followed at the third stage, by a growing appreciation of the scientific categories which give man the first approximation to the meaning of things. The boy is now able to apprehend relations like those of cause and effect, and begins to form his experience of the world into more or less extensive systems of connected facts. Then finally, at the fourth stage, which is reached at adolescence, he rises still higher, and begins to be conscious of the supreme categories of the spirit, the categories of unity: first in their imperfect social form, as when he comes to some kind of knowledge of humanity as a whole, and later in the form in which they are given through religion, which is essentially the consciousness of the One in whom all things have their being, the completely comprehensive system in which all the contradictions of human life find their solution.[1]

[1] In the summary statement of Rousseau's view of individual development given in this paragraph, I have of set purpose used terms connecting it with Hegel's discussion of the categories in his *Logic*. With reference to this particular paragraph, the reader should consult Welton, *The Logical Bases of Education*, p. 17, where the Hegelian doctrine is translated into an educational view not unlike that which I have attributed to Rousseau.

It may help to bring out with somewhat greater fulness the view of human development held by Rousseau, if I put what has been said in the present section into a tabular form with some supple-

11. *The Essential Considerations in a Natural Education:* (c) *Individuality.* — There can be no question about the necessity for taking account of sex and age in any natural system of education. " All that characterises sex," says Rousseau, " ought to be respected as established by nature " ; [1] and the same may be said with regard to age. When we come to consider the value to be allowed to the native individuality of the pupil, however, we are on less sure ground. It seems to be a fact that this native individuality which marks a child from the hour of birth is also " established by nature." At any rate, it is matter of common belief that even before the influences of society come in to affect initial endowment, children are characterised by idiosyncrasies of bent and temper, of disposition and ability, that may be subsequently modified but not fundamentally changed. Some children, as Rousseau puts it, are

mentary additions, for the interpretation of which the reader must be referred to the *Emile* itself.

The Educational Periods.	Infancy, Birth–2.	Childhood, 2–12	Pubescence, 12–15.	Adolescence, 15–25.
The parallel stages of social development.	The animal.	The savage.	The farmer (or Robinson Crusoe).	The incipient social man.
The moral development.	The physical individual under the law of necessity.		The calculating individual under the law of utility.	The moral individual under the law of virtue (iii. 10).
The intellectual development.	Undifferentiated feeling.	Sense-activity.	Intellect.	Soul (iii. 166).

[1] *Emile*, v. 36.

well born, others are ill born.[1] But even if it be granted
that this diversity of mind and character is original and
underived, and to that extent in the nature of things,
the doubt rises whether the form in which it manifests
itself may not be a social perversion. That, it will be
remembered, was the view taken in the *Discourse on
Inequality*. There Rousseau maintained that it was
society which called forth the diversity latent in human
nature and exaggerated it for its own ends, and he
would fain have had mankind remain in the primitive
condition in which the differences between one man and
another had not arisen.

Thus, even though individuality is in a sense natural,
there is some ground for uncertainty as to the importance that should be attached to it by the educator.
In the *Emile*, however, this doubt is lightly set aside.
Here Rousseau is not discussing education under ideal
conditions, but education under the ordinary conditions
of the modern world; and the question whether it is a
good thing or a bad thing for men to cultivate those
characters in which they differ from their fellows is
really not relevant. If they are to be members of
society at all, they have no option. Society has no place
in it for unspecialised members. The only concern of
one who seeks to make a man of nature is to ensure for
individuality its legitimate development, without detriment to more fundamental characters.

Whether in this Rousseau is altogether consistent
is open to dispute. If society wrought mischief in
making men conscious of their individuality, it is not
quite clear how it can be in accordance with nature to
carry this unnatural process still further in order to
maintain existence under social conditions. The in-

[1] *Emile*, iv. 44, 187; *New Heloïse*, v. 3.

consistency, however, (if it is an inconsistency), is not of any consequence for the educational discussion of the *Emile*. Throughout the *Emile*, it is maintained that one of the gravest evils done by the ordinary methods of education is the repression of individuality under a rigid system that makes no allowance for the endless diversity of minds; and Rousseau claims as a merit of the negative method which follows nature and interferes as little as possible, that it is adapted to "the individual genius of the child." "Each mind," he says, "has a form of its own in accordance with which it must be directed; and for the success of the teacher's efforts it is important that it should be directed in accordance with this form and no other. If you are prudent, you will study nature for a long time, and observe your pupil carefully before saying a single word to him. It is best, to begin with, to leave the germ of his character perfectly free to show itself, and to avoid putting any constraint on him, so that you may the better see his whole nature. . . . The wise doctor is not so reckless as to prescribe at the first sight of his patient, but studies his constitution before prescribing. He takes time in his treatment, but he cures, where the doctor who was in too great a hurry would kill." [1]

Following out his principle, Rousseau insists again and again on the necessity for finding the method of instruction that is most suitable for every pupil. Some are slow to learn, others are quick. "One nature needs wings, another shackles. One has to be flattered, another to be intimidated. One man is made to carry human knowledge to its furthest point; another may find the ability to read a dangerous power." [2] There can be nothing so foolish, then, as a system which treats

[1] *Emile*, ii. 69.   [2] *New Heloïse*, v. 3.

them all alike without regard to their distinctive genius.
Even if it were desirable to teach them all the same
things, it would still be necessary to change the method
with the pupil. " The accomplishments that give
pleasure have been systematised too much," he protests, in discussing the training of girls; "everything
has been reduced to maxim and precept. . . . Why
should this be? Is the art of singing, for example,
restricted to written music? Is the same kind of song
suitable for all voices? Is the same method suitable
for all minds? No one will ever make me believe that
the same attitudes, the same steps, the same movements,
the same gestures, the same dances, equally become a
little brunette and a tall beautiful blonde. So when
I see a master giving exactly the same lessons to both, I
say to myself: This man follows his routine, but knows
nothing of his art." [1]

The whole subject of individuality in its bearings on
education is very fully treated by Rousseau in the Letter
on Education in the *New Heloïse;* indeed, the careful
review of the subject in all its aspects is one of the most
distinctive features of that letter. The discussion begins with the condemnation of a system that forces the
common stock of adult wisdom on children, without
allowance for the genius of the individual child. " In
addition to the constitution common to the species,"
it is maintained, "every child brings into the world at
birth an individual temperament which determines his
genius and character. It is not a question of changing
or restraining this temperament, but of giving it form
and bringing it to perfection." To this statement of
the case—which is Rousseau's—the objector makes a
double answer. In the first place, while accepting the

[1] *Emile*, v. 66 ; *cf.* iv. 378.

view that each man is different from his fellows in virtue of inherited characters, he holds that the ideal of education is to form a typical man by the suppression of idiosyncrasies. "Would it not be infinitely better," he asks, "to form a perfect model of an upright, rational man, and then aim at making each child as like this model as possible by means of education, repressing the passions and perfecting the reason—in a word, correcting nature?" On this view, the encouragement of the individual genius of the child is no part of the educator's work. His business is to impart certain forms of knowledge and skill which society has judged necessary for the equipment of its members, irrespective of what is distinctive and individual in them. Then, in the second place, the objector goes still further in the course of the argument and asserts that individuality is not really native at all, but the result of social influences of various kinds. The diversity of minds, he suggests, instead of coming from nature, may be the result of education, due to the diverse ideas and sentiments excited in us from childhood by the objects that impinge on us, by the circumstances in which we find ourselves, and by all the impressions we receive.

The case for the opponent, it must be admitted, is quite fairly stated. What answer can Rousseau give? The difficulty of giving a satisfactory answer is that the difference in point of view between Rousseau and his critic is one of those fundamental differences that argument can scarcely reach. It is the difference between the spirit of classicism and of individual freedom, of the nations of Southern Europe and the Teutonic nations.[1] Rousseau is to some extent

[1] See Texte : *Jean-Jacques Rousseau.* Introduction.

aware of the difficulty of finding a really adequate
reply, and takes refuge in an appeal to experience.
" Look at these two dogs in the court," he makes
the advocate of inborn temperament say. " They
are from the same litter! They have been fed and
treated alike, and have never been away from each
other. Yet one of them is lively, affectionate, and
full of intelligence; the other is stupid, surly, and
unteachable. The single difference of temperament
has produced the difference of character, just as the
single difference of internal organisation produces the
diversity of minds in our own case." He proceeds to
point the moral by calling attention to the same
phenomenon among men. He will not say that there
is anything original in their sentiments and ideas.
He admits that these have their origin in social experience. But he asserts that behind the sentiments
and ideas held by any one man are certain dispositions
or propensities which have led him to hold these
particular sentiments and ideas, and that these are
primitive and underived, and owe their existence to that
unique personality which is each man's birth possession.
What is the conclusion? " The mind can only be
changed by a change in its internal organisation. A
change of character calls for a change in the temperament on which it depends." It would be as easy to
make a dark man fair as to make a hot-headed man
plegmatic, or a cold, methodical man imaginative. If
that be so, then both objections are met. Diversity of
mind and character cannot be explained by education,
and consequently it is vain to think of making all
children conform to a uniform ideal imposed on them
by adult wisdom, irrespective of initial endowment.
Instead of trying to change the natural dispositions,

the educator should rather seek to develop them to their fullest extent. "It is only in this way that a man can become all that he is capable of becoming, and that the work of nature is made perfect by education."

The critic might easily quote Rousseau against himself at this point; for does not the ideal scheme of national education which he sets forth in his discussion of Polish education involve the imposition of a uniform mode of life and thought on the individual citizens, such as he himself condemns in the education of his day? It is certainly not easy to see what place an education which preserves individuality by adapting its methods to the infinite variations of personality has in the national method Rousseau advocated for the Poles. A national education presupposes common schools and common subjects of instruction; for the cultivation of individuality, as Rousseau seems to understand it, the only possible method would be a system of tuition like that of the *Emile* specially directed to meet the needs of the individual pupil. The obvious line of compromise would be to establish a system which was at once national and individual;[1] but as that would produce "double men,"[2] it is not admissible on Rousseau's premises.

The reason for the difficulty is to be found in the ambiguity of his conception of individuality. About individuality, as we have seen, a doubt always lurks in Rousseau's mind. He is never quite sure whether to ban or to bless, and in the end he does both. If he

---

[1] In the *Considerations on the Government of Poland*, it will be remembered, Rousseau would allow the ordinary lessons to be studied at home under the paternal direction, on condition that the pupil took part in the public exercises and games.

[2] *Emile*, i. 24.

had tried to analyse the implications of individuality further, he might have found the explanation of his double attitude. There is a good individuality and a bad, as he is dimly conscious, without being able to distinguish the one from the other. The individuality of caprice which brings the individual into conflict with law and order merely because they put restraints on the unfettered exercise of his will is unmistakably bad, and is subversive of all social order. The individuality, on the other hand, which enables a man to occupy a distinctive position in the community is totally different in character. So far from being provocative of conflict, it is an organising principle which fits the individual into the moral and social order. Now it all depends on which of these meanings is given to individuality whether the national and the individual ideals of education are incompatible. If individual education implies the cultivation of self-assertion and caprice, it is anti-social; if national education secures uniformity by a ruthless crushing out of all diversity, it is anti-individual. Either of these represents an extreme that makes it impossible to bring about a reconciliation of the two ideals. Rousseau, not having made the meaning of individuality clear to himself, is unable to resolve the apparent contradiction.

12. *The Essential Considerations in a Natural Education:* (d) *Rank.*—The last consideration involved in carrying out a method of individual education according to nature is the subsidiary but not altogether negligible one of the general conditions under which the work is to be done. Rousseau enters into this quite briefly at the beginning of the *Emile* when he defines the relations he assumes to exist between Emile and his tutor. After pointing out that the

father is the natural teacher of the boy, he goes on to
assume exceptional circumstances under which a tutor
(in this case himself) undertakes to play the father's
part. This, he points out, puts him in a different
position from the father. Unlike the father, whose
duty it is to educate the child under any circumstances,
the tutor is free to choose his pupil and to make his
own conditions, and since a wrong choice involves the
mis-spending of his own life, it is only right that he
should do so. What, then, are the conditions he lays
down? Mainly these: that Emile should not be in any
way an exceptional child; that he should be healthy;
that he should live in a temperate country like France;
and that he should be the son of wealthy parents.[1] All
these points are of considerable interest, and have a
bearing on the problem of an ideal education; but we
shall confine our attention to the last of them, for the
special light it throws on Rousseau's view as a whole.

Why this demand for social rank as a condition of a
natural education? Rousseau's answer to the question
is twofold. In the first place, he says: "The poor man
has no need of education. That called for by his condition is forced upon him; and in his case no other is
possible. The education that the rich man receives, on
the contrary, is the one that befits him least, both with
respect to himself and to society." In the second place:
"Natural education ought to fit a man for every human
condition. Now it is less reasonable to educate a poor
man to be rich than a rich man to be poor. That being
so, it is better to choose some one who is rich to be
educated. We shall at least be sure of making one
man more; whereas a poor boy may become a man by
his own efforts."[2]

[1] *Emile*, i. 82-86. [2] *Ibid.*, i. 86.

This passage has been taken to imply that no good purpose is served by giving education to the poor. " It is apparently an aristocratic tendency in the man who has so often been called the prophet of democracy," says Professor Höffding,[1] altogether missing the point that Rousseau is really paying a compliment to the poor man. Why not educate the poor man? Because, says Rousseau, he is already receiving the best possible education from the conditions of his everyday life. It is the business of a natural education to fit a man for his environment. The poor man's life gives him that education. The adaptation to environment, moreover, must not be restrictive. It must leave him with the capacity to fill any position in life. The poor man's life by its very simplicity fulfils this condition. The poor child *may* make a man of himself; there is no such hope for the rich child if he is left among the artificialities of his original sphere. It is not because it is only a man of wealth who can afford to provide his son with a tutor till he reaches man's estate, or because the rich are more worthy of consideration than the poor, that Rousseau wishes Emile to come from the upper classes. It is because only a boy who is so unfortunate as to be rich has any need of the education which Rousseau proposes to give Emile.

It is important to grasp this for the right understanding of the subsequent development of Rousseau's educational principles. Pestalozzi, his immediate successor, accepted most of his views as substantially right, but set aside this restriction of education to the rich at one stroke by asserting the necessity for giving the poor an education which would not merely fit them to earn a living, but would develop every faculty

[1] *Rousseau und seine Philosophie*, p. 150.

needed for complete living. In this Pestalozzi anti-
cipated the point of view of modern democracy which
has consistently regarded the idea of a universal education as one of its first principles. But Rousseau,
though the father of democracy, was himself no demo-
crat; and the claim for an equality of privilege as
between rich and poor would certainly not have been
regarded by him as implying the necessity for the
education of every child—for the good and sufficient
reason that he did not regard education as a privilege
at all. Far better, he says in effect, that men should
continue to live the dull, unintelligent life of the
country poor which calls for no great cultivation of individual capacity but makes for sure happiness, than
that they should enter into the exciting artificial life
of the towns, where, at the cost of happiness and peace
of mind, a man must develop every talent to its fullest
extent in order to hold his own. Education in the
accepted use of the term is not in itself a good thing.
It is an unhappy necessity forced on man, one of the
consequences of his fall from grace.

The system of natural education propounded by
him in the *Emile*, we must repeat again, does not
represent his own ideal, but only such an approximation to it as an unpromising social environment
permits. In some ways the undirected discipline of
circumstances, which is the only education the poor
man gets, is nearer his ideal than the method of the
Emile. It was just such an informal education which
he himself got in boyhood, and he was satisfied that
if ever a boy got a rational education, it was himself.
If every one could get such an education there would
be little need to think about the matter at all. The
trouble is that there are large sections of the com-

munity over whom the circumstances of life exert no
such beneficial influence, people like Emile who have
been born in a class in which convention has well-nigh
stifled nature. In their case an education according
to nature is a most difficult task, which calls for all
the resources of the wise educator. Truly, "much art
needs to be employed to keep social man from
becoming wholly artificial." [1]

Perhaps it is a mistake to lay too much stress on
the reference to Emile's rank. Rousseau nowhere says
that this natural education should be confined to the
children of the wealthy; only that they are the best
subjects for it. They need it most, and they demonstrate its possibilities best. There is actually nothing
in the *Emile* itself to suggest that its methods are
impossible of application to children of every social
rank. It is all a question of whether it is worth applying them in the case of the children of the poor.
Rousseau does not seem to think that it is.

13. *Natural Education (A Summary Statement of
the Preceding Argument)*.—Before going on to consider the means to be employed in giving the child
an ideal education, it may be well to link together the
main points in the argument of the chapter by way of
recapitulation.

A natural education, we have seen, is an education
which forms the Man by developing to the utmost
limits of need all the capacities that enable him to
give effect to the basal impulses of his nature. The
special form assumed by it depends on the level of
development reached. For primitive man it means
simply the gradual acquisition through experience of
the power to adapt himself to the physical environ-

[1] *Emile*, iv. 368.

ment. For civilised man it means the preparation as worker and citizen which enables him to adjust himself, and to keep himself adjusted, to his more complex social environment. But always, whether at low level or high, it involves the satisfaction of personally felt needs by methods that are expressions of personal thought and character. This broadly is the requirement for a natural education for any human being. An education which satisfies it is a natural education, in that it is in conformity with "the constitution common to the species" —that is, with human nature.

In the later stages of human progress, other considerations almost as fundamental as this basal human nature come into view, notably the differences made by sex and age. Though the characters depending on sex and age are not generic human characters in the sense of being common to every member of the human family, though indeed they constitute the basis of the deepest possible differences between individuals, they are so intimately bound up with the common nature of man as to be necessarily associated with it, when the nature of any individual person is under consideration. To educate an individual in accordance with nature in this broader sense, we must take into account not only the fundamental human characters, but also those connected with sex and age.

Finally, there are certain characters of a more individual kind, partly natural and partly conventional in origin, which serve to distinguish one child from another—idiosyncrasies of disposition and ability, and differences of social condition, which are peculiarly the concern of those dealing with the individual child as an individual. These also—but more doubtfully—may be said to pertain to the child's nature, and consequently to come within the province of the educator who seeks to educate in accord with nature.

We have seen further that Rousseau has two different ideals for this natural education, to some extent conflicting with each other. The difference between them really turns on the importance attached to the more individual traits of personality, which depend on idiosyncrasy and on social accident. On the one hand, there is the ideal of a national education that counts individuality well lost in subjection to the law of a higher self than one's own. On the other hand, there is the ideal of an individual education that despairs of finding a higher self worthy of this sacrifice, and seeks to cultivate individuality to its utmost limits with a view to social success under the defective conditions of artificial society. Behind the differences of the two ideals, and deeper than them, is the conviction that any education, whether national or individual, that fails to do justice to the essential human characters as well as to the secondary characters dependent on age and sex cannot be natural; and the consequent demand for a method of upbringing in harmony with the needs of "race, age, and sex."[1]

14. *The Natural Education of the Home.* — It is important to note that though Rousseau is prepared to find a natural education realised either by the national or by the individual method, it is only the individual method which he has been at pains to elaborate with the practical end in view. A national education consonant with nature presupposes a natural society; and as none such exists or is capable of existing in the great states of the modern world, the national ideal must obviously remain of purely theo-

[1] *Emile*, iii. 129.

retical interest. For the practical educator, who wishes
to follow nature and is not prepared to wait indefinitely
for the reconstruction of society, there is really only
one course left. Lacking the opportunity to educate
aright the children of the nation, he can give all his
care to the education of a few chosen pupils, and
so determine the conditions under which their lives
are spent that all the requirements of a natural education will be satisfied in their case. It is an individual method after this pattern that is expounded and
justified at full length in the pages of the *Emile;*
and it is to the *Emile* we must go to get Rousseau's
ideas on the actual practice of a system of natural
education.

The *Emile* is a difficult book to describe. *Emile, ou
de l'Éducation,* is the full name of the work ; and the
double title suggests its twofold character. It is at one
and the same time a romance and a treatise.[1] The
framework of the book, as we have seen, is the life-story
of the boy Emile from birth to marriage ; and on this
framework is constructed an encyclopedic discussion of
an immense variety of subjects more or less connected
with education, usually relevant to the story, though
sometimes digressing from it into by-paths suggested by
Rousseau's versatile interests. "Naturally, theories concerning the constitution of man and of society figure in
it with honour ; philosophy, religion, and morality also
occupy an important place ; politics, political or domestic
economy, literature and science, the arts and handicrafts, hygiene and health, love and marriage, the

---

[1] GRAHAM : *Rousseau,* p. 152. "It is enough of a story to spoil it
as a treatise, and far more than enough of a treatise to spoil it as a
story." Brédif says much to the same effect : "A romance of education is his main work. Rousseau is the most thoughtful of romancers,
and the most romantic of thinkers."

woman—her qualities, her defects, her occupations; agriculture, commerce, finance, luxury and the toilet, the world, manners, travel, even the details of the author's life. All these things and many more besides have a prominent place in the book." [1]

As not uncommonly happens when the romance form is employed as a medium for the exposition of ideas, there is considerable difficulty in distinguishing what is accidental from what is essential; and much of the criticism of Rousseau's educational doctrine has gone on completely wrong lines as a result of the confusion. There are only two characters in the story—the boy Emile and his tutor, who is no other than Rousseau himself. Under ordinary circumstances, as Rousseau maintains in the prolegomena to the tale, the boy's father ought also to be his teacher, but being for some reason or other unable to do the work, he hands over both his duties and his rights to a tutor, who differs from other tutors in being no menial concerned only about his own interests, but a large-hearted philosopher who is willing to undertake the task for the sake of friendship. The moment the child is born this tutor takes charge and lays down the law about food, clothes, baths, and all the other details of infant life to the theoretically objectionable but practically useful nurse. If the child has been born in town he takes him away to a retired country spot, far from the foul air and fouler morals of the town; and there with much art he hedges him in with conditions of his own devising which serve to exclude all the ordinary vices of mind and heart.[2]

Many of Rousseau's contemporaries, enamoured of the

---

[1] Beaudouin, *La Vie et les Œuvres de J.-J. Rousseau*, ii. p. 45.
[2] See especially *Emile*, i. 74-127, ii. 70-114.

idyllic picture of country education that he put before them in the *Emile*, immediately rushed to the conclusion that an ideal education demanded a literal reproduction of the relation of Emile and his tutor, and not a few of them even outdid the *Emile* in the extravagance of their ideas and methods. In a romance entitled *L'élève de la nature*, for example, published the year after the *Emile*, Beaurieu shut up his hero in a cage till he was twenty years of age and then set him free on a desert island, stark naked.[1] Among those who sought to reduce the precepts of the *Emile* to practice, it was generally taken for granted that a boy could only be properly educated if a man with the qualifications of Emile's tutor were willing to spend a considerable part of his life at the task; and further, that teacher and pupil must be cut off from all the ordinary social relationships and live in the isolation of a remote country place. It is certainly a tribute to the magic of Rousseau's powers of persuasion, if not to the clearness of his ideas, that immediately on the publication of the *Emile* a considerable number of people was willing to imitate its method with the utmost literalness, despite the obvious practical difficulties of the undertaking. We of a later generation are no longer tempted to this kind of discipleship, but the misconception of Rousseau's principles that made it possible in his own age still lingers on. The critic of to-day, interpreting the *Emile* to the same effect as his first disciples, still wins easy victories over a Rousseau of his own imagination, and thinks he has exposed the absurdities of his system when he has commented on the impossibility of giving every boy a

---

[1] It is rather interesting to note that Rousseau refers to this work with approval in a letter addressed to M. Panckoucke (May 25th, 1764).

tutor to himself and separating him from the normal
influences of family life. The fact is that in this both
disciples and critics have fallen into error. So far from
the features of the *Emile* which they have regarded as
cardinal elements in Rousseau's educational doctrine
being essential, they are merely the accidents of his
romance.

It must be admitted in extenuation of the misunderstanding that Rousseau himself is to some extent
responsible for it. When an author illustrates his
principles by showing their operation in a particular
case the presumption is that the case he chooses for the
purpose is a typical one; and, indeed, Rousseau expressly says in one passage that he regards *Emile* as a
" model." [1] Moreover, there are one or two passages
in the *Emile* itself which suggest, even if they do not
altogether justify, the views of his disciples. There is,
for example, the striking passage in the Second Book,
to which attention has already been called, in which he
asks how the child is to be saved from the precocious
development that is the result of any contact with
ordinary society, and indicates the moon or some desert
island as the only proper place for the purpose.[2] Apart
from express statements like this, the whole tenor of his
previous writings on similar topics had prepared his
readers to expect an anti-social view, and led uncritical
followers to read into the proposal to educate Emile in a
country village, the more extreme idea of an education
in perfect detachment from all society. There was perhaps less excuse for them considering the self-sacrificing
tutor as an essential part of Rousseau's scheme. In the
First Book of the *Emile* Rousseau says most explicitly
that the true preceptor is the father,[3] and dwells per-

---

[1] *Emile*, i. 82.   [2] II. 70 ; *cf.* ii. 109.   [3] I. 62.

sistently on the very great difficulty of finding any man able to take the place of the father when the father, for any reason, either cannot or will not bring up his own son. A little reflection might have shown that the tutor was introduced into the story, not so much because Rousseau thought it essential to have such a specially gifted person superintending the work of education, but because he wanted to get into the story himself and speak in the first person : he was never very fond of telling a tale in which he himself could not act as the hero.[1] But though Rousseau gave some ground for the mistake, and though at a later time he occasionally fell into it himself when speaking about the *Emile*, there can be no doubt whatever that he regarded the tutor and the isolation of the pupil as unessential parts of the romance. To think otherwise is to miss the real meaning of the *Emile*.

In this connection, the Letter on Education in the Fifth Book of the *New Heloïse*, written probably when Rousseau was busy with the first draft of the *Emile* and representing the identical point of view, indicates most clearly what he regarded as fundamental in his system. The *New Heloïse*, it is true, is also a romance, but just because in it the educational ideas are put in a different setting, it is easy to see at least what is not essential. In this Letter the ideal education is entirely domestic. The implication of the story is that for the best education of a child the whole family group is necessary : the mother to be the nurse and the first director of morals, the father to secure and maintain the right conditions

---

[1] "On verra, pour ainsi dire, Jean-Jacques à cinquante ans précepteur de Jean-Jacques à dix ans, et ce sera tres beau . . . et Jean-Jacques aura l'infini plaisir là encore, d'être toujours en scène et à tous les âges et de ne jamais sortir de lui-même." Lemaître, *J.-J. Rousseau*, p. 216.

of life and to act as teacher as soon as the child is intelligent enough to learn, the brothers and sisters to exert a mutual influence through the ordinary differences of age and sex. Here there is no tutor to play the *deus ex machina* at every turn, and no departure from the normal life of childhood : only a quiet country family living the simple, self-sufficient life which in Rousseau's opinion approaches most nearly the state of nature under social conditions.

It may be said that this too, like the tutorial method of the *Emile*, is only a fiction of the romancer and no nearer the facts of everyday life. But the objection, though quite legitimate if the educational system of the *New Heloïse* stood by itself, is ruled out as soon as a comparison is made between it and those sections of the First Book of the *Emile*[1] in which Rousseau sets forth his ideas of an education according to nature, without reference to and even to some extent in contradiction of the story of Emile. Such a comparison brings out with perfect clearness as the central doctrine both of the *Emile* and of the *New Heloïse*, that the true education of nature is domestic education, that " the proper nurse is the mother, and the proper teacher the father."

The educative function of the family is consequent on the position it occupies, midway between nature and society. On the one side, it is broad based on natural relationships that are prior to any social conventions. And yet, on the other side, there would be no permanent family apart from convention and law. " The most ancient of all societies and the only natural one," says Rousseau in the *Social Contract*,[2] " is the family, and yet the children only remain bound to their father for

[1] I. 32–64.   [2] I. 2.

such time as they have need of him for their preservation. As soon as the need ceases, the natural bond is
dissolved. The children are no longer under obligation
to obey their father, the father is no longer under
obligation to care for the children. Both resume their
independence. If they continue together, it is not because of nature, but because of will. It is only by
convention that the family abides." Putting this in
other words, the life of the family has its origin in a
natural bond, but it is kept together by the development of a spiritual bond, out of the natural. The
necessity of nature gives place to the voluntary relationship of free agents. The law of animal need is
succeeded by the higher unity of a common spirit, that
subjects both parents and children to a new form of law.
It is because of this intimate relation of nature and
spirit in the mutual dealings of parents and children
that the family provides the best possible medium for
the natural education of a child. More obviously in
the family than anywhere else are the conflicting interests of individuality and of social life—both of them
necessary factors in human personality—brought into
harmony. In the more complex economic and political
groups which the child enters at a later time, individuality tends to disappear under the pressure of law
and custom. But in the family, the natural affections
safeguard the individual child from the oppression of
group law, and his natural individuality counts for more
than it does anywhere else in the world. At the same
time, though individuality is encouraged and developed,
there are limits beyond which it is not allowed to pass.
The family, like every other society, has an end of its
own, to which every member must contribute, and a law
that checks errant impulses running counter to this

end; and thus, while the child finds himself encouraged and helped to develop his distinctive powers, he learns the essential lesson that every social being needs to learn—that personal inclination must be brought into willing subjection to the law which springs out of the nature of the group to which he belongs.

Now it is this idea of the family as mediator between the child and society by reason of the happy combination of individuality and ordered life within it, that solves for Rousseau the problem of natural education on its individual side. He sees that the child who lives in a family which is faithful to its own ideals receives a preparation for life that enriches personality, instead of impoverishing it as the ordinary education tends to do; and both in the *Emile* and in the *New Heloïse*, the system of education he sets forth as an approximation to his ideal is based upon the conception of the family as a natural school.

In the *Emile*, this is to some extent obscured by the introduction of the tutor in place of the ordinary home influences; and yet, though the absence of the maternal tenderness and the lack of the mutual discipline which results from the association with brothers and sisters are undoubtedly grave defects in the scheme —graver defects indeed than Rousseau realised—the most significant features of home education are retained. The tutor, it must be remembered, takes upon himself the duties of the father, and fills the part in the boy's life which the father ought to have filled. *In loco parentis*, he rules and orders all the circumstances of the boy's life in such fashion as to bring home to him the necessity that is in things, and to ward off from him the disturbing caprice of unregulated social action. That is to say, he does deliberately and of set purpose what is done fairly well by every father and mother worthy of the name, even when they are not conscious of the significance of what they do. He reveals and administers the law to which every human being is subject, and in doing so, unifies experience for the child who is too immature to unify it for himself. Like the family, he is the representative of the social order, and the social order at its best, comparatively free from admixture with the element of caprice that is characteristic of ordinary social institutions. But he is not merely the spokesman and representative of the law. Otherwise, so far as the child is concerned, the education he gives would have the very defect for which Rousseau condemns society: it would crush out individuality by the exercise of authority. Unlike the common educator, the tutor tempers judgment with mercy by giving his pupil the fullest possible liberty: "well-regulated liberty," he calls it,[1] liberty for the child to follow the promptings of his own heart right up to the point where they meet a check in some natural obstacle or in some necessary social law. Here we might almost say he plays the mother's part, in complement to the law-giving and law-maintaining functions of the father.

The significance of the educative influence of the true home which is concealed by the unfortunate instance adopted for the purposes of illustration in the *Emile*, becomes quite explicit in the ideal family life of the *New Heloïse*. In this work Rousseau shows us the perfect father and the perfect mother, discharging their respective functions in the upbringing of a family. It is the father's part to think and to plan. He is responsible for the right ordering of the external con-

[1] *Emile*, ii. 59.

ditions of life, without which the sense of the unity of experience could not be acquired by the child. But in the early years of life, which are all that are dealt with in this brief sketch of an ideal education, the actual educator is the mother. It is she who, under the guidance of the father, stands by in seeming passivity, watching the gradual unfolding of her children's powers, and all the while taking her own measures to develop the good and to check the bad. It is she who gives the whole household its unity of spirit, so that even the servants, who are usually a disturbing factor in the education of children, help the mother to provide them with ideal social surroundings. In short, she educates much as Emile's tutor does, by combining individuality and law in her children's experience. The only difference between them is that she carries on her work with a less definite consciousness of its meaning. She simply does her duty as a woman and a mother, and everything else seems to follow of itself.[1] In her humility of soul, she is ready to ascribe her success to good fortune rather than to any wisdom or virtue of her own. Wisdom, she remarks, depends greatly on good fortune. "Say rather," replies the friendly critic to whom she has expounded her views, "that good fortune itself depends on wisdom. Do you not see that the working together of all things

---

[1] *Cf.* Pestalozzi: *How Gertrude Teaches her Children*, Eng. Tr. p. 145. "The mother, weak and untrained, follows Nature without help or guidance, and knows not what she is doing. She does not intend to teach, she intends only to quiet the child, to occupy him. But nevertheless, in her pure simplicity, she follows the high course of Nature without knowing what *Nature* does through *her*." The difference between Rousseau and Pestalozzi is, that while Pestalozzi believes in the educational potencies of the ordinary untrained mother, Rousseau speaks as though the good influence of the mother was only to be reckoned on in exceptional cases where the mother was a woman of high character and broad culture.

on which you congratulate yourself is your own achievement, and that every one who comes near you is constrained to be like you." Surely the wise mother is a truer type of the natural educator than the philosophical tutor, and the family education of the *New Heloïse* a higher expression of Rousseau's ideal than the isolated tuition of the *Emile*.

CHAPTER VIII

THE LAST PHASE

1. *The Closing Years.*[1]—The years of comparative
calm and happiness which followed Rousseau's departure from Paris in 1756, and gave opportunity for
the writing of the three great works with which we have
been mainly dealing in the last two chapters, were
brought to a rude and violent end by the storm that
arose on the publication of the *Emile* in 1762. In all
probability, the free discussion of religious questions in
the *Confession of Faith of the Savoyard Vicar* would
have been sufficient to endanger the freedom of its
author under any circumstances. It was all the more
unlucky for him that the Parliament of Paris[2] was
busy attacking the Jesuits at the time of its appearance,
and was glad of the opportunity to prove its impartiality, as well as its orthodoxy, by condemning the
new heretic. "My book has appeared at an unfortunate
time," remarks Rousseau in a letter written the day
before he was unexpectedly driven to flight by the
threat of immediate arrest. "According to report, the
Parliament of Paris, to justify its zeal against the
Jesuits, means to persecute those who differ from them
in opinion as well; and the only man in France who
believes in God is to be the victim of the defenders of
Christianity."[3]

[1] 1762–1778.   [2] The supreme judicial tribunal of Paris.
[3] *Correspondance:* à M. Moultou, June 7, 1762.

Thanks to the good offices of powerful friends, however, Rousseau was able to escape from France without the least difficulty. Like the hunted animal that makes straight for home, his first thought was to get to Geneva ; and he had reached the Canton of Berne on his way thither, when he got the bitter news that the aristocratic Council had followed the example of the Parliament of Paris by ordering the *Emile* to be burned (along with the *Social Contract*), though as yet no copy of the book had reached the town. Scarcely had he recovered from the shock of this unexpected blow, when the Council of Berne ordered him to quit its territories at once. Thereupon he fled into the domain of Frederick the Great, and by his good graces was allowed to reside in Motiers, in the principality of Neuchâtel, for some three years. Then once again he was forced to set out on his travels by reason of the ill-will of the fanatical populace, and after another vain attempt to find an asylum nearer home, he was persuaded by David Hume, a warm friend and admirer, to pay a visit to England. Here he was received with every honour by people of all ranks, and might have found a refuge free from care and trouble. But by this time, the condemnation of his books and the persecutions which followed had completely upset a brain not very stable at the best, and in less than six months he quarrelled violently with Hume, and returned to France to resume his mad wanderings in a more familiar land.

There is no need to enter into further details about the last sad years of his life with their ever-increasing burden of infirmities. Suffice it to say that, after repeated change of abode under the impulse of maniacal fears, he finally returned to Paris in 1770, and though the decree of arrest was still in force, he was allowed to settle down unmolested. Here he remained for about eight years, leading a quiet, obscure life. Then, with dramatic appropriateness, the old longing for the open country laid hold on him, and he retired from the city to a little cottage at Ermenonville, ten miles away, and there, some two months later, he died suddenly in the same utter loneliness in which he had lived.

He was buried in the Isle of Poplars in the gardens of Ermenonville, at a spot which he himself had chosen but eight days before. "By the serene moonrise of a summer's night, his body was put under ground on an island in the midst of a small lake, where poplars throw shadows over the still waters, silently figuring the destiny of mortals. Here it remained for sixteen years. Then, amid the roar of cannon, the crash of trumpet and drum, and the wild acclamations of a populace gone mad in exultation, terror, fury, the poor dust was transported to the national temple of great men."[1]

2. *After the Emile.*—There is substantial truth in the paradoxical statement made in one of the *Dialogues* that the *Emile* was the last of Rousseau's writings. The two parts of the profuse *Confessions*, the *Dialogues* in which Rousseau is made judge of Jean Jacques, the *Reveries of a Solitary Stroller*, were certainly written after the *Emile*, and make up a very considerable body of work of high merit. But though these productions of his later years are not lacking in originality—the *Reveries*, for example, represented a quite new *genre* in literature—there was none of them of the same epoch-making character as the *Social Contract* or the

[1] Morley, *Rousseau*, ii. 327.

Emile. They were in the main expository in character
rather than creative. They grew out of Rousseau's
personal experience or related to some phase of his
major writings, and constitute as it were an exposition
of himself or his previous works. Their interest is
consequently of a secondary rather than a primary
order. They affect very considerably our estimate of
the man, without adding to or detracting from our
estimate of the thinker.

Apart from autobiography, which forms the great
bulk of these later writings, the subjects mainly under
discussion are the ideas on politics and education
previously expounded in the *Social Contract* and the
Emile. No sooner was the *Emile* published than
criticisms and questions began to pour in upon
Rousseau from every quarter. First came refuta-
tions of one kind or another in large numbers. A
year or two later, but before the flow of these had
dried up, would-be disciples wrote asking for further
information and for guidance on particular points of
conduct. It was impossible for Rousseau to defend
himself against all his detractors or answer all the
queries of his friends; but he could not remain
altogether silent, and he was led by way of general
answer to restate his views on various topics. It
cannot be said that this supplementary discussion
added much that was really new to what he had
already said more formally, but it is interesting
enough in its own way, and helps to bring out more
clearly certain aspects of his teaching. It will serve,
then, to complete our account of Rousseau's educational doctrines to consider quite briefly his defence
of his ideas against opponents and his further exposition of them to friendly questioners.

3. *Letter to the Archbishop of Paris*.[1]—The most
notable, if not the most powerful, refutation of the
Emile was one contained in the Episcopal Charge
(*Mandement*) of Mgr. de Beaumont, the Archbishop
of Paris,[2] and Rousseau chose to make reply to it
as the one most worthy of his answer.[3] Taken all
in all, even with a somewhat petty strain of self-
pity running through it, which makes him pose as a
victim of calumny and misunderstanding, the Letter
to the Archbishop is "a masterpiece of dignity and
uprightness," and an effective enough reply to the
criticism directed against the *Emile* on religious
grounds.

After a somewhat lengthy apology for himself,[4] he
plunges into the heart of the discussion with a summary statement of those views about human nature
which are at the root of the difference between himself
and the Archbishop. The fundamental principle of
all morality, the principle underlying the *Emile* and
all his writings, he declares, is that "man is a being
good by nature, who loves justice and order," and
that "there is no original perversity in the human
heart." "I have shown," he adds, "that self-love
(*l'amour de soi*), the only passion born with man, is
in itself indifferent to good or evil, and that it becomes

---

[1] 1763.

[2] *Mandement de Mgr. l'Archevêque de Paris portant condamnation d'un
livre qui a pour titre : Émile, ou de l'éducation, par J.-J. Rousseau,
citoyen de Geneve.*

[3] M. Beaudouin compares with this his previous choice of King
Stanislaus as opponent on the *Discourse of the Sciences and the Arts.*

[4] The *apologia pro vita sua* on which he enters here is written in a
strain of the most complete self-satisfaction. "I do not hesitate to
say," he remarks toward the end of the *Letter*, "that if there were
a single government in Europe that was really enlightened, it would
have done public honour to the author of *Emile* and reared statues
to him." Little wonder Voltaire scoffed at this!

good or bad according to the accident of circumstances. I have shown that none of the vices imputed to the human heart are natural to it. I have, so to speak, followed out their genealogy and shown how, by progressive departure from original goodness, men finally became what they are." In keeping with this, the *Emile* has as its main object to find means to prevent men becoming bad.

What is there wrong in all this? The Archbishop's *Charge* had not left that in doubt. According to him, the *Emile* ignored facts of life to which not merely religion but the experience of all ages has borne witness. "Yea, beloved brethren, there is in us a strange mixture of greatness and meanness, of ardour for the truth and fondness for error, of virtuous inclination and vicious tendency. . . . Man feels himself dragged down by a hateful propensity, against which he would struggle in vain were it not that his childhood was directed by wise, virtuous, and watchful masters, and that he himself, by the grace of God, maintained a strenuous, unceasing fight all through life." [1] Rousseau, in short, has forgotten the initial corruption of man's nature.

To this Rousseau replies with a peremptory refusal to accept the doctrine of original sin. Not only is the scriptural basis of the doctrine less sound than Augustine and the theologians have maintained, but it offends against all our ideas of the justice and goodness of God. But, says Rousseau, with fine dialectical skill, what does it matter whether we accept the idea of original sin or not? The *Emile* is a book calculated to be of service to the whole human race, but intended in the first instance for Christians, who,

[1] *Mandement* 3.

according to this doctrine, have all been cleansed
from original sin and its effects by baptism. In
their case, if not in the case of the heathen, there
is need for some such explanation as the *Emile*
gives, of the fact that, after having been purified from
sin, they should yet have become bad; and all the
more need in view of the fact that they have received
their education at the hands of those "wise, virtuous,
and watchful masters" commended by the Archbishop.

The Archbishop's condemnation of the educational
method proposed in the *Emile* and his approval of
the one commonly practised—to quote Rousseau's
paraphrase of him—really amounts to this: "We see
that men are wicked in spite of the most rigid discipline from their very infancy. If, then, this discipline
were not exercised, how could they be made wise,
seeing that incessant discipline fails to make them
so?" A very obvious begging of the question!
Rousseau has no faith at all in the ordinary education as a force making for righteousness. It is the
education that the Archbishop regards as the most
virtuous which, in his opinion, is responsible for all
the vices of children.

This section of the *Letter* concludes with an admirably lucid statement of the distinction between negative
and positive education, on which is based Rousseau's
objections not only to clerical education [1] but to all

---

[1] It should be noted that though Rousseau does not esteem the
priests in their *rôle* of teachers very highly, there is an unexpected
calmness and restraint about his judgment of them. Even in this
Letter, when he is face to face with the opposition of the Church,
his view is quiet and sane. He does not like clerical teachers,
and he says so. Then he goes on: "All this is of no special consequence, seeing that I do not exclude priests. Let them educate
the young, if they are competent. I have nothing to say against
that."

forms of education that are over-zealous in seeking
the man in the child. "If man is good by nature,
as I think I have shown, it follows that he will
continue good so long as he is not changed by something external to him; and if men are wicked, as
people have been at pains to teach me, it follows
that their wickedness comes to them from elsewhere.
Shut the door against vice, then, and the human heart
will always be good. On this principle, I establish
negative education as the best, or rather as the only
good education. . . . By a positive education I mean
one that tends to form the mind before the proper
age and to acquaint the child with the duties of the
man. By negative education I mean the education
that aims at perfecting the organs which are the instruments of knowledge, and prepares for reason by the
exercise of the senses. A negative education is far from
being a lazy one. It does not impart the virtues, but
it keeps out the vices. It does not teach truth, but it
preserves from error. It inclines the child to all that
can lead him to truth when he is fit to understand it,
and to goodness when he is fit to love it."

There is no need for us to follow the course
of Rousseau's answer further. He takes up the
Archbishop's *Charge* point by point, and makes
detailed reply to it. In particular, he restates
with care the theological doctrines that he had expounded in the *Savoyard Vicar's Confession of
Faith*,[1] which he now declares to be the most valuable
work of the age. But all this is outwith our
immediate interest.

4. *Correspondence with the Duke of Wirtemberg*

[1] This was also the subject of his *Letters from the Mountain* (1764).

about the Education of his daughter Sophie.[1]—In some ways, Rousseau was happier in dealing with his foes than with his friends. He had a positive genius for controversy, and never appeared to better advantage than when engaged in dialectical fence with an opponent.[2] With his friends, he was more ready to be carried away by his own moods. They came to him seeking advice, and he was apt to let his judgment be affected by their expectations. This is probably the simplest explanation of the varying views he held about the attempts of disciples to carry the ideas of the *Emile* into practice.

If the general interpretation of the *Emile* given at the end of the last chapter is sound, it is clear that at the time the *Emile* was written Rousseau did not intend to suggest that a boy could only be properly educated if exiled from polite society in the company of an omniscient tutor. In fact, the relation of pupil and tutor in that work did not express his conception of the best educational method at all, but was merely a romantic device for the effective presentation of his ideas about domestic education. But his disciples immediately accepted the romance as reality, and proceeded to convert its fantastic method into such practical forms as the exigencies of social life permitted. In less than two years there were to be

---

[1] For Rousseau's Letters, see the long series in his collected *Correspondance*, especially those of Nov. 10, 1763 (which is the letter quoted in the present section), Jan. 21 and Sept. 3, 1764. The first of these is translated in my *Minor Educational Writings of Rousseau*. For the letters of the Duke, see Streckeisen-Moultou: *Rousseau, ses amis et ses ennemis*, vol. ii. The two quotations made are from pp. 161 and 165. For another letter on the education of an infant, see the letter to Madame Roguin (March 31, 1764) in the *Correspondance*.

[2] "C'est son vrai genre de ferraillier avec ceux qui attaquent ses écrits." Grimm, commenting on the *Letter to the Archbishop*, in *Correspondance Littéraire*, v. 284.

found in every country in Europe fathers and mothers bold enough to attempt to give their children the very training that Emile and Sophie got. "Though Sophies and Emiles are rare, as you rightly say," Rousseau writes complacently to Madame Roguin, "nevertheless, there are some children being brought up like them in Europe, even in Switzerland and your own neighbourhood; and already there is promise of success to reward their worthy fathers and mothers for the devotion that leads them to endure the troubles of so arduous an education."

From later expressions of opinion by Rousseau, it may be doubted whether he was ever completely satisfied with the interpretation given to the *Emile* by the zeal of his followers; but to begin with at least, he did not repudiate it, and even talked at times as though he believed that the meaning they read into the story was the one he himself intended it to have. In another man, this kind of acquiescence in a dubious position might have been hypocritical. But Rousseau had the impressionable mind that found belief easy at any time, and there is every reason to think that for a season he was quite convinced that he had meant from the beginning what his followers took him to mean.

The situation thus created was certainly an interesting one. Rousseau had depicted a fictitious tutor and pupil, without any thought of the fiction being made a model in real life. Now that there was an evident desire to try the experiment suggested by the fiction, there was need to define the limits within which the actual facts could be made to approximate to the imaginary ones. The problem was one to appeal to Rousseau; and we find him busy with it in the correspondence he began with the Duke of Wirtemberg in the autumn of 1763.

The Duke wrote asking advice from him about the upbringing of his infant daughter, Sophie. Rousseau, evidently much flattered by the request of " His Most Serene Highness," [1] expressed his willingness to answer any queries that might be put to him on the subject. A month later the Duke wrote again, telling Rousseau that his wife and he were trying to put the methods of the *Emile* into practice. " Every morning," he told him, " we bathe the little one in the coldest spring water, and after drying her lightly we leave her naked a good part of the morning. . . . We never put any covering on her head, and she wears neither gloves nor stockings." His main difficulty was that his circumstances did not permit him to retire from his office of state, and he was uncertain about the practicability of any scheme of natural education which did not begin with the separation of the child from the ordinary social life. " If my situation permitted me to isolate my child, I should have less difficulty, for then I should follow you point by point. But it is exceedingly difficult to avoid departing from your wise plan in circumstances completely different from those you have chosen."

In reply, Rousseau wrote a long letter dealing with the various questions which the Duke had raised. " If I had the misfortune to be born a prince," he begins, " and yet had a soul noble enough to wish to be a man despite my rank and fulfil the great duties of father, husband, and citizen of the world, I would soon be conscious of the difficulties of the double task, and more especially the difficulty of educating my children for the state in which nature placed them, in spite of that which they

[1] The phrase is repeated rather frequently in the correspondence.

occupy among their fellows. In that case I should begin by saying to myself: I must not seek contradictory things. The difficulty I wish to overcome is inherent in the situation, and if that cannot be changed, then the difficulty must remain. I will follow the right course as far as it is in my power. And having done that I shall be content, whatever my success."

What mainly prevents education being natural in the household of a man in the Duke's position is that the head of the household has so much to occupy him that he cannot look after his child himself; and Madame the Duchess is in almost the same position. The duties of state are too exacting to permit them to discharge their duties as father and mother, and so they must find some one else able to discharge these duties for them. The problem, it will be noted, is to all intents and purposes the problem of the *Emile*, but in this case unfortunately there is no heaven-born tutor ready to play the friendly part and come to the aid of the parents. Obviously enough, some substitute must be found for him.

Following out this line of thought, Rousseau evolves a scheme to meet the needs of the situation. He sums up its cardinal features in three rules.

I. *Make sure that the child is dear to some one person.*—It is essential on any method of natural education that there should be some person charged with the duty of co-ordinating and directing all the circumstances of the child's life, and if the parents who would naturally do this under normal conditions are not able to do it, some one who is prepared to look at life from the child's point of view, as they would have done, must be got to take their place. The child being a girl, this person should be a woman, a widow for preference rather than a maid, but at any rate not young and pretty, since it is above all things important that she should be perfectly trustworthy. She will be all the better fitted for the task if she is uncultured. She ought to be perfectly natural, and culture is apt to make people hide their real characters.[1] The only difficulty is to give her some motive for seeking the well-being of her pupil as she would her own. That, Rousseau thinks, can be managed easily enough by appealing to her self-interest, and making her understand that the better the child gets on, the better it will be for herself.

II. *This person, when chosen, should get her course completely marked out for her.*—This is the method that Rousseau would take to overcome the practical difficulty of finding any one wise enough for the work of education. An ordinary woman, such as this one would be, cannot be expected to direct the child's education aright if left to herself. Consequently, she must work to a plan made by the father. A memoir of instructions should be put into her hands, and this should be her constant study.[2] Doubtless unforeseen difficulties will occur for which no provision has been made in the memoir. In that case, the mother is always at hand to resolve them. Her own education and culture give her the advantage over the governess of being able to think out general principles and to see their applications in practice. This maternal supervision indeed is

---

[1] Rousseau makes an elaborate analysis of the right kind of woman for the post.

[2] This is a most interesting anticipation of the method adopted by Pestalozzi at a later time, when he sought to make every mother an educator, and had to get over the difficulty caused by the ignorance of the ordinary mother. Instead of a memoir, he wanted to put in the hands of the mother what he called his *Mother's Book*, that would enable her to teach the child just what the child should be taught. Probably Rousseau would have found it quite as difficult to draw up his Memoir as Pestalozzi did the *Mother's Book*.

indispensable if the method is to succeed. The mother should know the memoir as well as the governess, but know it in another fashion. The mother works by principle, the governess by rule.

III. *The governess should have absolute control of the child.*—The mother's supervision of the educative process must not mean a division of authority. That would be a fatal defect in the system. There must be one person, and only one, responsible for the child, to whom the child owes obedience. But does this not commit too much to the care of this governess ? Not at all, answers Rousseau. Properly understood, this rule really means that everything should be regulated in accordance with the memoir. The governess exercises her authority only as its interpreter.

It would almost seem as though it were this wonderful memoir that was to do the work of the tutor of the *Emile.* The memoir, Rousseau goes on to urge, should determine the whole life of the household, so as to insure the absence of any disturbing influences on the part of the servants. But evidently enough, a mere memoir, however excellent, cannot take the place of personal government. What the whole scheme implies is really the setting up of an ideal household like Julie's in the *New Heloïse;* and Rousseau indicates this quite explicitly by excusing himself from the necessity of discussing household conditions which he had already discussed in that work. In a word, the attempt to elaborate the tutorial method of the *Emile* with a view to ordinary life leads Rousseau directly back to the conception of natural education as the education that goes on in a well-ordered family, and is a virtual condemnation of the method of isolation suggested in the *Emile* or any method that reproduces its central feature.

5. *Rousseau's Later Views about the Emile.*—The
letter to the Duke of Wirtemberg which we have just
been studying ends with a curious note of self-distrust.
"Perhaps the things I have written," he says, "are only
the ravings of a fevered brain. The comparison of the
real and the ideal has given me a romantic mind and
put me at a distance from the actual world. But you
give your orders, my lord, and I obey. It is my ideas
you ask. Here they are. In submitting them to so
competent a judge, I am not afraid of them doing any
harm."

If this stood by itself, it might be regarded as an
example of the rhetorical depreciation of himself, which
is not uncommon in Rousseau's later writings and which
is specially characteristic of the *Confessions.* But in
point of fact, it is repeated often enough in expressions
of opinion on matters of education at this period to
make it plain that there is more than rhetoric in it.
There is a passage in one of the later letters to the
Duke,[1] for instance, expanding the same idea, which has
all the appearance of sincerity. "You inspire me with
all the esteem for M. and Madame de Gollowkin that
you feel for them yourself," he writes; "but though
flattered by the approval they express of my precepts,
I am not without fear that their child may one day be
the victim of my errors. To do them justice, I ought
to assume from the picture of them you have given me,
that they are enlightened enough to discern the truth
and to put only what is good into practice. Yet there
always remains a certain dread, because of the extreme
difficulty of such an education. The fact is that it is
only good when taken as a whole and carried on with
perseverance. If they come to relax their efforts or

[1] 21st Jan. 1764.

change their system, all that they have done up to that
point will spoil all that they subsequently do. If they
do not go on to the end, it will be a great misfortune for
them ever to have begun."

The same idea recurs in a letter written six years
later to an *abbé* who had informed him that he had
adopted the plan of the *Emile*.[1] He expresses his admiration for the courage shown in doing so, but warns
him of the immense labour he has undertaken and
the great difficulty of keeping it up for twenty years.
"One moment of impatience, negligence, or forgetful-
ness may deprive you of the fruit of six years of toil,
without the possibility of recovering it by the work
of ten years more."

In both of the cases instanced, as well as in the Letter
to the Duke of Wirtemberg, it is assumed that the
method of the *Emile* is perfectly practicable when circumstances are propitious, and that whatever defects
reveal themselves in working it out are not to be
attributed to the method but to the people who use it.
At the same time, it does not seem to be reading too
much into what Rousseau says, to infer that he was
really ill at ease when brought face to face with the
people who were trying to carry out his ideas in this
fashion, and that he would fain have shown them the
error of their ways if it had not seemed to involve a
confession of error on his own part.

This is borne out by a curious incident recorded about
his visit to Strasburg in 1765. "You see before you,"
said a M. Angar whom he met there, "a man who has
brought up his son according to the principles which
he had the good fortune to find in your *Emile*." "So

---

[1] *A l'Abbé M.*, 28th Feb. 1770. It is translated in *The Minor Educational Writings of Rousseau*.

much the worse, sir, for you and your son," was Rousseau's reply. "I had no wish to prescribe a method," he adds by way of comment; "I merely wanted to prevent the harm that was being done in education."

Here he has obviously shifted his ground and is no longer willing to give even a cautious blessing to the educating of Emiles. Not content merely to disclaim responsibility for the interpretation of the *Emile* which made a special tutor absolutely necessary for a right education, he goes the further length of asserting that he had intended the *Emile* to be merely a criticism of the ordinary methods of education. The same repudiation of the literal view takes an even more exaggerated form in a letter written in 1764. "You remark very truly," he says to his correspondent, "that it is impossible to make an Emile. But you surely do not think that that was my object, or that the book with that title is really a treatise on education. It should rather be regarded as a philosophical work on the principle put forward by the author in other writings, that man is naturally good. To bring this principle into harmony with the equally certain truth that men are wicked, it was necessary to demonstrate the origin of all the vices in the history of the human heart. This is what I have done in the *Emile*." [1]

In both cases we must get behind the words to the spirit of what is said. It is not true that he had no wish to prescribe a new method of education when he published the *Emile*. In the Preface he expressly

---

[1] *Lettre xxiii.* (to Philibert Cramer) in *Œuvres inédites de Rousseau* par M. G. Streckeisen-Moultou, p. 408. Cf. *Letters from the Mountain*, v. : "The subject of the *Emile* is a new system of education, which I submit to philosophers for examination, and not a method for fathers and mothers, to which I have never given a thought."

states his intention of being constructive where other critics had been negative. Nor is it true that the *Emile* is an abstract treatise on the genesis of evil in man. So far as it had its origin in his views about natural goodness and social badness at all, it was intended, as he himself said in his *Letter to the Archbishop,* "to be a search for the means to be taken to keep men from becoming wicked." Perhaps we get at the significance of both statements best by not laying too much stress on their positive profession. He is right in his statement of what he did not mean, but somewhat perverse in his statement of what he did mean. A sure proof, if proof be needed, that he was not quite clear about what he really intended to do when he wrote the *Emile.*

6. *Considerations on the Government of Poland.*[1]— The important chapter in the *Considerations on the Government of Poland,* which has already been discussed at length,[2] was Rousseau's last published utterance on the subject of education.

There was a certain fitness in Rousseau's pronouncements on education ending with a scheme of national education. He had appeared in the *Emile* as the champion of individuality and freedom, and had been understood both by friends and foes to advocate education in detachment from the everyday relations of home and nation. It was well that it should be made plain for those who could understand, that the *Emile* did not represent his full educational doctrine, and that the man who had sought to show how each child could be developed to the height of his powers was also able to appreciate the fundamental position occupied by educa-

[1] 1772.   [2] Chap. vii. 4.

tion in the life of the community. There could have been no more effective refutation of the narrow view taken of the *Emile* by disciples and critics alike.

That this last book should be in certain essential respects irreconcilable with the *Emile* was almost a matter of course. The contradiction that had vexed Rousseau's thought about man throughout was too deep to be lightly overcome in the last years of his life. It was his merit that he should have held faithfully to the truth in the conflicting views, leaving the task of reconciling them to the men of a later age.

CHAPTER IX

ROUSSEAU'S PERMANENT CONTRIBUTION TO EDUCA-
TIONAL THOUGHT: A CRITICAL ESTIMATE

1. *Rousseau and his Age.*—Now that we have completed our survey of the various factors contributing to
the development of Rousseau's educational doctrine and
have seen the form that it finally assumed, it is time to
attempt a critical estimate of its worth.

In beginning this part of our task, it may be
necessary to remind ourselves of the difficulty of
passing on Rousseau a simple judgment of approval
or of disapproval, such as it is sometimes possible to
pass on a contemporary thinker. Barely three half-
centuries have elapsed since the *Emile* first appeared.
But these three half-centuries have been among the
most momentous in the history of mankind. The
violent breaking up of feudal government which took
catastrophic expression in the French Revolution would
in itself have been enough to change the current of
human thought. But, added to the political upheaval,
there was the greater economic upheaval which had its
beginnings in what is sometimes called the Industrial
Revolution, and which continues to affect profoundly
the evolution of humanity. With these great changes
operating in countless ways, the whole outlook on life
is completely different from what it was in Rousseau's
age. To us it is strange beyond comprehension that
there ever was a time when his writings won the

passionate adherence of men of every social rank and every grade of intellectual power. The ladies of fashion waiting with the greatest impatience for the opportunity to read the first copies of the *New Heloïse*; Kant, most regular of men, missing his daily walk because he had lost count of time in reading the *Emile*; Pestalozzi renouncing his prospects as a professional man to become a farmer of the Rousselian type—these, and all their unnumbered fellows who in diverse ways came under the mighty spell of Rousseau, so obviously belong to a different world from ourselves that it is only with the greatest difficulty that we understand them even a little. The *Discourse on Inequality*, which with the *Social Contract* made mad revolutionaries of common men, offends against our sense of historic continuity and seems fanciful and far-fetched. The *New Heloïse*, consisting of interminable letters filled with false sentiment and with passions torn to shreds, appears stilted and wordy, and refuses to ring true for us. The *Emile* irritates us with its paradoxes and exaggerations and vain repetitions. It is possible, indeed, to overcome the unfamiliarity of the first impressions and to win our way to the elemental truths that these distracting features conceal. But even when we have done so, the heart remains unmoved and we are no nearer discipleship. Do what we will, Rousseau is in some ways further off from us than many of those who lived centuries before him. Such is the change in the temper of men's minds since his time.

The difficulty of appreciating Rousseau is largely due to the fact that he lived in an age of transition. Halfway on in the eighteenth century, when he was busy writing, there was a spirit of unrest abroad in Europe. The speculative scepticism about all things divine and

human which showed itself first in Bayle (and to a less
degree in Locke), and which reached its consummation
in Voltaire, was but one symptom of a more general un-
settlement of life. The new spirit of the Renaissance,
which had called modern civilisation into being by the
creation of new nationalities and a new church, was still
at work, slowly leavening the political institutions of the
different nations ; but except in one or two phases (of
which the most outstanding was the English Revolution
of 1688), the impulse towards social reconstruction was
still spending itself in seemingly vain protests against
feudal conditions. There was a sense of impending
change, but when or how the change was to come, no
one had any clear notion. The train had already been
laid for the upheaval of 1789, and there were dull
mutterings foreboding revolution ; but to all outward
seeming the existing institutions appeared destined to
go on till the crack of doom.

The effects of such an age on a mind like Rousseau's
must always be remembered in studying his works.
Considered out of their setting, as one expression of a
brief phase, one might almost say a mood, through
which European life and thought passed on the way to
more modern forms, his writings are apt to appear
perverse and bizarre. The overwrought sentimentality,
the persistent individualism never far removed from
cynicism, the delight in paradox and contradiction for
their own sake, the fretful revolt against convention
and custom, all repel our sympathy and make it
difficult for us to appreciate the truth behind them.
We seem to see in them only the idiosyncrasy of a
morbid soul that had drifted from its moorings in
ordinary human relations.

Not till we get beyond the individual man, and realise

that in him the *malaise* of a whole age found utterance,
do we reach the right point of view for the understanding of Rousseau. Then we discover that the very ex-
travagances which appear deserving of condemnation
in the individual become the supreme distinction of the
thinker. For we hear voiced in them the deep heart-
yearnings of an unhappy generation, coming to consciousness of its own state and finding that consciousness
bitter. It is indeed a strange paradox that this man,
who seemed both to himself and to his fellows out of
touch with the ways of ordinary men, should express
the inner meaning of his age better than any of them;
but so it was. The very alienation from society which
made him a solitary in the midst of men enabled him
to experience more completely than his contemporaries
some of the deepest tendencies of an age which had
outgrown its social forms and seemed to itself to have
exhausted all that made life worth living. The secret
of his power lay in the fact that when most alone he
really came nearest the common condition. The divorce
between institutional and individual life that was so
patent in his case was characteristic in greater or less
degree of the whole age, and it only needed the definite
statement of it by one who had felt it more deeply than
other men to bring it home to the general consciousness.
" He it was who became the interpreter of those burning
hearts that, in the words of Chateaubriand, 'have felt
themselves strangers in the midst of mankind': he who
'with a full heart dwelt in an empty world.'"[1]

If this be kept in mind it will prevent us going to
Rousseau with the expectation of finding in him a
solution for any of the problems of the modern world.
It was the inevitable result of the part he played in a

[1] Texte, *J.-J. Rousseau*, p. 300.

time of transition that he should never come near
finality in dealing with the subjects on which he spoke
with most assurance. He was essentially a pioneer, to
whom it fell to venture out into the unexplored territories of the future; and his thought, like that of most
pioneers, had the defects of its qualities. It was generally over definite towards the past from which it had cut
itself loose. It was always indefinite in the direction of
the future towards which it set itself, in faith of attainments yet unrealised. If, then, we try to measure his
greatness by the new ideas and plannings to be found in
his writings, the chance is that we will do him less than
justice. New ideas are undoubtedly present in abund-
ance—for Rousseau was a man of extraordinary originality [1]—but they are ideas in bud rather than in fruition,
promises rather than fulfilments. Indeed, when taken
apart from their subsequent growth and unfolding in
the systems and methods of successors and opponents,
they are apt to appear rather insignificant. It is only
when we think of them as germinal elements in the
developing thought of Europe that we appreciate them
at their proper value. We see then that the service that
Rousseau did to all later philosophers and statesmen was
not to solve problems but to set them. " The tragedy of
revolution which was necessary to the new birth of
European civilisation was enacted in his breast before it

---

[1] *Cf.* Amiel's *Journal* (*Journal Intime*), Eng. tr. by Mrs. Humphry
Ward, p. 111: "J.-J. Rousseau is an ancestor in all things. It
was he who founded travelling on foot before Töpffer, reverie
before René, literary botany before George Sand, the worship of
nature before Bernardin de S. Pierre, the democratic theory before
the revolution of 1789, political and theological discussion before
Mirabeau and Renan, the science of teaching before Pestalozzi, and
Alpine description before De Saussure. . . . He formed a new French
style, the close, chastened, passionate, interwoven style we now use
well. . . . Nothing indeed of Rousseau has been lost."

passed on to the stage of society"; [1] and it is possible
that if it had not first been Rousseau's tragedy it might
not have been Europe's. For it was the estrangement
of man from all the great human institutions, embodied
in his experience and expressed in his writings with un-
exampled fervour, that forced on his age the fundamental problems of the modern world, both on the side
of theory and of practice. With him the democratic
view of life with its manifold puzzles and contradictions
made its first definite appearance, and a new cycle of
thought began.

2. *Rousseau's General Criticism of the Ordinary
Education.*—From what has been said, it will be evident how important it is for the right understanding
of Rousseau's views on education to see them not only
in relation to his philosophy of life, but also in relation to
the whole historical situation of which that philosophy is
but one expression. To do this, we shall first consider
them on their negative side as a criticism of education
as it has usually been practised, and then go on to
define as well as may be the merits and the defects of
his own attempts at reconstruction, especially in their
bearings on later thought and practice.

We note, as a matter of course, that Rousseau's view
of education is determined by his general attitude to
society. The protest against social institutions, made
and maintained in the name of nature, necessarily
involves a protest against those institutions which are
concerned with the preparation of the young for social
life—and on the same grounds.

---

[1] E. Caird, *Essays on Literature and Philosophy*, vol. i. p. 106.
See also essays on Goethe and Wordsworth, pp. 76 *seq.*, 171, for
illuminating comments on Rousseau's doctrines.

Rousseau's complaint is not that society and its institutions are antagonistic to nature—though in his unguarded moments he speaks as if they were. On the contrary, he recognises quite clearly that man needs to be a member of society in order to be truly man and to realise all the possibilities of his nature; and that this calls for a directive education.

But this does not mean that he is at all satisfied with the actual society in which men live to-day, or with the ordinary methods of education by which they are fitted for this society. It is in his view the condemnation of most existing communities that the men who grow up in them run grave risks of becoming citizens and ceasing to be men. The reason for this unhappy state of matters is to be found in an excessive stability, characteristic of social institutions, that is dangerous for individuality. If new conditions called forth new institutions, or if the members of a society could be made to re-experience the old institutions into which they enter as they grow up, this would be avoided. The trouble is that customs and laws once called into being to minister to the needs of man's nature are apt to linger superfluous on the stage after their part has been played, and to pervert men by claiming deference and obedience which has ceased to be their due. The individual man, on his side, is too weak to withstand this claim, and submits to it, often against his better judgment. When that happens, the impulses to a fuller personal life which are ever welling up in human nature, and which appear with fresh vigour in every new generation, are crushed down by the weight of tradition and precedent. For the time being, the age-long conflict between the established order with its permanence, and the individual life that must change and grow if it is to find satisfaction for itself, pauses with a seeming victory for the established order. Instead of society adapting itself to man, man is forced to adapt himself to society.

Now this contradiction between stability and change, inherent in all social life, is specially manifest in the educative process. "We teach the child to write, and every style that is not original is not style. We teach him to think, and every thought he gets from another is not a thought but a formula. We teach him to feel, and a borrowed feeling is an affectation, an hypocrisy, a declamation. By its very definition, then, teaching (*l'enseignement*) defeats its own end." [1] This contrast runs all through education. It appears in the opposing interests of teacher and pupil, in the antithesis of the curriculum and the child, in the difference between training for future station and education to satisfy present need, in the conflict between social uniformity and individual initiative.

Rousseau's objection to the ordinary education is that when choice has to be made it sacrifices the child to the school, the individual to society, the present to the future. With a "pedantic mania for instruction" that magnifies the teacher's share in the work of education at the expense of the pupil's and forgets that learning is more fundamental than teaching, it forces the growing child to acquire knowledge and skill that have no relation to his dispositions and answer to no needs of his nature. Obsessed with the thought of adult requirements, it takes no account of the essential originality of the child, and is content if only it can bring him by its own way to the common end of disciplined manhood, whether it is his way or not.

[1] Abridged and translated from Faguet, *Dixhuitième siècle*, p. 360.

3. *Rousseau's Criticism of Contemporary Education.*
—It must not be thought that this view of education
was merely an abstract deduction from Rousseau's
general doctrine of social relations. No doubt, as he
himself maintained, it was the logical sequel of his
whole criticism of society. In actual fact it took
shape, not in the form of general principles, but as a
criticism of what he conceived to be the malpractices of
contemporary education; and it is understood best when
seen in relation to the system which it condemned.

It is difficult to realise the low ebb that education had
reached throughout Europe by the middle of the eighteenth century. With the growth of luxury and the
decay of ideals towards the end of the previous century,
the life of a large section of the community in all the
great nations had become exceedingly artificial; and as
generally happens in an artificial age that distrusts
spontaneity, childhood, which is nothing if not spontaneous, suffered worst of all. Here is the account of
the state of matters given by one historian: "Youth
was then for most children a sorrowful period: the
instruction hard and heartlessly severe. Grammar was
beat into the memory, and likewise portions of scripture
and poetry. The common punishment at school was to
learn by heart the 119th Psalm. Schoolrooms were
gloomily dark. No one thought that children could
find pleasure in work or that they had eyes for anything
but reading and writing. The profligate age of Louis
XIV. imposed on the poor children of the higher classes
hair curled by the barber and smeared with powder and
pomade, laced coats, knee breeches, silk stockings,
and a dagger at the side, for active, lively children the
severest torture." [1]

[1] Raumer, quoted in Painter's *History of Education*, p. 274.

The dressing of the child as a miniature man indicates the view generally taken of childhood and of education at this time. Just as the boy was made to wear the same dress as his elders, so he was furnished with the same learning. In the theory of the schools, Latin and Greek were regarded as necessary for the equipment of the man of culture, and so the child was set betimes to the study of Latin and Greek. The method followed in instructing him introduced him to the classics by the adult method of formal grammar. That he did not want to learn the grammatical rules, or did not understand them when he did, was a fact to which no one paid any attention. Most people had too much respect for the educational tradition to consider the child's likes and dislikes at all; and the few who gave thought to such things found in the crude faculty psychology, with its demand for an appropriate discipline for each faculty, sufficient justification for the compulsory learning of the languages. It was the firm conviction of the pedagogues of the age that the master faculty of reason was best cultivated by the memorising of the grammar and the reading of the classical authors; and that even if by any chance reason were not developed, the memory, which is the faculty that serves all the other faculties, was certainly benefited.[1] What more could any one want?

This neglect of the child's point of view and the faith in methods of repression which was the inevitable outcome of it in a sophisticated age, were aided and abetted by the clerical instructors who had long enjoyed a virtual monopoly of the work of education in France and other Catholic countries. The religious teacher is always more

[1] Rousseau deals at some length with this doctrine in the *New Heloïse*, v. 3.

or less suspicious of human nature. He is prone to look on the inclinations and the instincts of the child as essentially evil, and to distrust the untutored operations of the senses and the affections as likely to lead astray. Education, for him, means the remaking of the child's nature, by crushing out the original tendencies and dispositions, and putting in their place the higher impulses of the spirit. So far from the pupil's unwillingness to learn a subject being an argument against its study, it is, in his view, an argument for it; for, quite apart from the acquisition of more or less valuable knowledge, the effort called forth in learning serves as a preparation for the constant struggle with the passions which is the lot of every good man.

"Education," says the Abbé Galiani, the ablest of all Rousseau's critics, in a letter written to Madame d'Epinay in 1770, "is the same thing for man and for beast. It can be reduced to two principles, to learn to put up with injustice, to learn to endure *ennui*. What does one do when one breaks in a horse? Left to himself, the horse ambles, trots, gallops, walks, but he does it when he wishes, as he pleases. We teach him to move thus or thus, contrary to his own desire, against his own instinct—there is the injustice : we make him keep on at it for a couple of hours—there is the *ennui*. It is just the same thing when we make a child learn Latin or Greek or French. The intrinsic utility of it is not the main point. The aim is that he should habituate himself to obey another person's will (and so bore himself): that he should be beaten by a creature born his equal (and so learn endurance). When he has learned all that, he can stand on his own feet, he can go into society. . . . All pleasant methods of teaching children necessary knowledge are

false and ridiculous. It is not a question of learning
geography or geometry : it is a question of learning
to work, of learning the weariness of concentrating
one's attention on the matter in hand. . . . Develop
these ideas, and then you will have a book the precise
opposite of the *Emile* and worth very much more." [1]
From all this, it will be evident that Rousseau had
undertaken a formidable task when he ventured to
question the worth of the educational system of his
time. It meant putting himself in opposition both
to the teachers, rendered confident by an educational
tradition going back to the Renaissance, and to the
Church which stood behind the teachers and sanctioned
their repressive methods as means of grace. And the
task was all the harder, because he could look for little
help from the spirit of the age. A conventional age
could scarcely be expected to view with favour a
scheme of education that proposed to deal with children as children. It was a clear case of Rousseau
contra mundum.

Another man might have shrunk from a combat so
unequal, but Rousseau was not the man to be distressed at finding himself alone in criticising any
social institution. It was enough for him that he
saw humanity suffering hardship and oppression in
the persons of the children. All the weight of
authority on the side of the established order, all
the sophistry of interested parties or of people who
loved the old ways because they were old, counted
for nothing with him. His dissatisfaction must out.

In one sense, he came to the work of criticism with
an open mind. He himself had no personal cause

---

[1] *Lettres*, vol i. pp. 118, *seq.*, quoted and translated in Hodgson,
Studies in French Education, pp. 232-4.

for complaint in the matter of education. For good
or for evil, the chances of life had brought him through
boyhood and youth without any experience of what is
commonly called "schooling." Further, until the publication of the *Savoyard Vicar's Confession of Faith*
embroiled him with both Catholic and Protestant
theologians, there was no hostility on his part to
clerical teachers : rather the reverse. Though the
Emile was written at the very time when there
was a general outcry against clerical education, one
looks in vain for any reference to the subject in
its pages. His dissatisfaction, then, was quite impersonal.

In educational matters, as we have seen, his first
master was Locke. The reading of the *Thoughts on
Education* at an impressionable age seems to have
been the first thing that made him realise the badness
of contemporary education. At any rate, it was after
he had studied Locke that he first showed himself
antagonistic to the degenerate Renaissance tradition
which had long dominated France and the north of
Europe ; and on the negative side he continued his
disciple to the end. Like Locke, he denounced un-
sparingly a system that made knowledge an end in
itself. The man who seeks knowledge for its own
sake, he says in the *Emile*,[1] enters a sea without
bottom or shore : there is no hope of escape for him.
The education that takes mere scholarship as its aim
is not in any sense of the word a preparation for life.
It is what Pestalozzi, quite in the spirit of his master,
dismisses contemptuously as a "monkish education,"
the kind of education that might be adequate enough
for one whose days were to be spent within the four

[1] III. 32.

walls of a cell, but perfectly useless for the ordinary purposes of life.[1]

But though he accepts what may be called the utilitarian view that education should keep in close touch with everyday life, he does not want the child to be educated with direct reference to the future. Here he parts company with Locke, who was at one with those teachers he criticised, in thinking of education as mainly a preparation for later achievements. Rousseau, for his part, sees in this sacrifice of the present to the future the fundamental sin of the teacher against the child. Each period of life, he insists, has its own perfection and maturity, and should stand by itself. To make it a mere stepping-stone to the periods which lie ahead is to rob the child of all that makes life good for him as a child. Even if it were possible to use up childhood and youth in accumulating experiences for use in manhood, it would be wrong, on Rousseau's principles, to do it. Every age has rights of its own, that should no more be infringed than the rights of manhood. A child is a child and a man a man, and the only one way for either child or man to be happy is to live true to his nature. The nature of the child being different from the nature of the man, the child ought to be allowed to remain full time at the level of his immediate life; for only so can he realise all the happiness that is possible for him.

"What are we to think of the barbarous education," he asks, "that sacrifices the present to an uncertain future, and begins by making the child miserable in order to prepare him a long way ahead for an alleged

---

[1] IV. 146. "The pretence is made that we are being formed by society, and yet we are instructed as though we were to spend our lives in solitary meditation in a cell."

happiness he will probably never enjoy ? Even if I believed this education to be reasonable in its object I could not but be indignant at seeing poor, unfortunate children forced under an intolerable yoke, and condemned like galley slaves to never-ending toil, with no certainty that all these troubles will ever serve any good purpose. The age of gaiety is passed amid punishments, threats, and slavery. Who knows how many children die victims of the absurd wisdom of a father or a tutor ? " [1]

As a matter of fact, the sacrifice is made in vain. Do what the teacher will, it is utterly impossible to make a man of the child before his time ; and the only effect of the attempt to do so is to indoctrinate the child with all the errors and vices that mar social life. The teacher is generally too grown-up to put himself in the child's position, and realise how limited is his outlook. It seems to him a matter of course that the child should feel and judge and reason as he does himself ; and he usually deals with him as he would deal with another grown-up person. He argues with him, he suggests consequences in the remote future, he appeals to his sense of right and wrong— ignorant of the fact that the child is not a rational being, that only immediate consequences mean anything for him, and that conscience is not yet developed. What is the result ? The child is forced prematurely into the world of adult concerns, and led to acquire a veneer of culture that has no value whatever as a preparation for the future. Though totally unable to distinguish between good and evil, he is compelled to speak and act as though he could distinguish between

[1] II. 10 ; *cf.* also iii. 62 *seq.* For a curious reproduction of this argument, see Lecky, *The Map of Life*, p. 223.

them, and his whole intellectual sanity is compromised by the sham. The prejudices and habits acquired by untimely education before the age of reason, retain their hold all through life, and destroy, beyond all hope of later restoration, the individuality which is the only sound foundation for the upbuilding of personal character.

If there is any truth in this view, it would seem that the best way to educate a child would be to leave him as free from adult interference as possible, so as to allow the capacities proper to his years to develop to their utmost extent, without regard to what the future holds in store for him. It is a difficult doctrine to accept, but Rousseau boldly accepts it with all its consequences. Children, he says, should do nothing with their soul till it has all its faculties. The most dangerous period in human life is from birth to the age of twelve. It is then that errors and vices take root before there is any instrument to destroy them. When the instrument does come, the roots are so deep that it is no longer possible to tear them up.[1] The first education, therefore, should be purely negative. It should not consist in the teaching of virtue or of truth, but in preserving the heart from vice and the mind from error. If only that could be managed, the boy would come to the teacher at twelve without a single habit or prejudice to counteract the effect of his teaching.[2]

In practice, the doctrine is easier to apply in a negative way than in a positive, and Rousseau has to admit not a few exceptions in his scheme. Indeed it proves to be of greater service in the criticism of the ordi-

---

[1] *Emile*, ii. 66. The "instrument" to which he refers is reason.
[2] *Ibid.*, ii. 67.

nary education than in determining his own method.
No sooner has he enunciated the principle than he
directs it against the ordinary education. "Do the
very opposite of what is usually done," he says, "and
you will almost always be right,"[1] an extravagant
maxim which turns out to mean that the boy should
never be treated as though he were a man. In the
moral sphere it involves a prohibition of rebukes, corrections, threats, punishments, and, above all, of argumentation and reasoning. Most people, he says, try
to convince children of their errors. Even the wise
Locke would reason with them for this purpose.[2] But
there is a better plan. Let the teacher be rational
himself and avoid reasoning with children, especially
to make them approve of what is disagreeable to them.
There is no argument he can use that will ever make
them regard a disagreeable course of action as right.[3]
They may feign agreement to please the teacher, but
it will only be a pretence. The premature introduction of moral considerations always does produce some
such immorality. In the intellectual sphere, the idea
of a negative education leads to the postponement till
a later age of such studies as history, geography, literature, and foreign languages—the humanistic studies
that call for powers of intellect and experience of life
beyond the child's range. Away with all the lessons
learned from books! "I hate books," he remarks.
"They only teach us to talk about what we do not

---

[1] *Emile*, ii. 68 ; *cf.* Froebel, *Autobiography* (Eng. tr.), p. 116.

[2] *Ibid.*, ii. 51. If Rousseau had read his Locke more carefully, he
would have found that Locke's view did not differ substantially from
his own.

[3] Note that here Rousseau is only speaking of children. Some of
his critics make the mistake of reading the sections of the *Emile*
relating to children as though they applied to people of all ages.

know." [1] They are of doubtful use for men : they are
worse than useless for children.

But does this mean that the child is to learn nothing
at all till he grows up ? By no means. Though the
soul lies fallow in the first years of life, the senses are
then reaching their maximum vigour, and should
receive training to prepare for the later ripening of
judgment and reasoning. For that, however, nothing
in the way of ordinary lessons is required. Childhood
is the time for play, and should be spent in play.
Without ceasing to be play, the boy's games can be used
by the tutor to teach him all that he is capable of
learning at this period of life. [2]

From the ordinary man's point of view, this leisurely
method of education seems open to objection at various
points. It might be said, for example, that if childhood
is spent in play, there will not be sufficient time to
acquire the knowledge and skill needed in later life.
To this objection Rousseau makes an eminently sane
reply. " Try to teach the child all that is useful for one
of his years, and you will find that his whole time will
be more than taken up. Why are you eager to set him
to the studies of an age which he may never reach, to
the prejudice of the studies that suit him to-day ?
But, you will ask, will there be time for him to learn
what he ought to know when the moment comes to

---

[1] *Emile*, iii. 96. *Cf.* iv. 332, v. 352 (especially the former). From
these passages, it will be evident that Rousseau distrusts book knowledge at every period of life. In this connection, a remark of
M. Lanson, one of the most sympathetic of Rousseau's critics, is
well worthy of quotation. " I am quite of the opinion of M.
Faguet, that in certain moments in advanced civilisations, rich in
literary masterpieces, the best pedagogic maxim that can be given
is to put books aside. The acquisition of knowledge inevitably tends
to take the place in education which the formation of judgment
and character ought to take." *Histoire de littérature française*, p. 786.

[2] *Ibid.*, ii. 269, 287, 319.

make use of it? That I do not know. What I do
know is that it is impossible to learn it sooner; for our
real masters are experience and personal feeling, and a
man never really appreciates what is proper to manhood till he is actually in its relations. A child knows
that he will one day become a man, and all the ideas
he can have of man's estate are occasions of instruction
for him; but concerning the ideas of that estate which
are beyond his comprehension, he ought to remain in
absolute ignorance. My whole book is one long proof
of this educational principle." [1]

But there is another objection of a more serious kind.
Even if we agree with Rousseau that the child can
know nothing about the concerns of manhood, and
limit instruction to what lies within his present range
of mind, it does not seem right to allow him to grow
up, doing only what he pleases. Are there not evil
tendencies in his nature that need to be checked and
corrected, or even rooted out? Surely "it is in the age
of childhood, when pains are least felt, that they should
be multiplied with a view to restricting them in the
age of reason."

Rousseau's first answer turns back the objection on
the hypothetical opponent. Are you sure, he asks,
that these tendencies to evil which you pretend to cure
in him, are not the results of your own misapplied
efforts rather than defects of nature, as you seem to
think? [2] In itself, this suggestion is no real answer to
the critic. The question is one of fact. Is it true, as
the theologians say, that the child is naturally prone to
evil? If so, then it is the plain duty of the teacher, as
the defenders of the traditional view maintain, to
repress the natural impulses and to put good habits

---

[1] *Emile*, iii. 64.   [2] *Ibid.*, ii. 13.

in their place. Strong in the faith that nature does all for the best, Rousseau meets the doctrine of innate depravity with an absolute denial. " Let us lay it down as an incontestable principle that the first movements of nature are always right. There is no original perversity in the human heart. There is not a single vice in it of which we cannot say how it entered and whence it came." [1] No one ever does evil as evil.[2] Badness, whether in child or adult, is but misdirected good, and for the misdirection in the case of the child, it is the parent or teacher who is responsible.

There is no need to enter at any length into this age-long controversy. In the form in which it rises in the *Emile*, it is very evidently a conflict of two half-truths, neither of which is adequate.[3] It is not true to say that every tendency in the child is sinful, and needs to be repressed : neither is it true to say that every tendency is good and worthy of cultivation. The new light thrown on child life by the doctrine of evolution makes it impossible for us to hold either view in its extreme form. Looking on man's inheritance from the past, we see a strange mixture of good and evil traits. Some are evidently rudimentary survivals from a stage of life outgrown by the human race. Others have still a part to play in the life of to-day. Others, again, seem to point beyond the present attainments of humanity to still higher phases. For the educator, therefore, it is not a question of wholesale repression or indiscriminate encouragement of the native impulses, but of wise

---

[1] *Emile*, ii. 62.
[2] *Ibid.*, iv. 127. See also the *New Heloïse*, v. 3.
[3] This remark has a wider application than that given to it in the text. It might be made equally well about the difference between the old education which Rousseau attacked, and the new education of which he was the pioneer.

selection and furtherance of the best, combined with the regulation or even in some cases the extinction of the worst.[1]

But though it is no more possible for us to accept Rousseau's view than that of the educators he criticised, it would be a mistake to think of the two views as standing on the same level of worth. There is a world of difference between the dead half-truths of tradition and the living half-truths of the seeker after the ideal. The errors of the seeker—and such are Rousseau's errors —are the splendid errors on which the hopes of human progress depend, and they must be judged accordingly. At the time when the *Emile* was written there was indeed urgent need for the proclamation of the essential worth of man. Under the shelter of the theological exaggeration of human depravity, there had grown up and become firmly established a harsh repressive system of education which ignored childhood and did violence to all that was best in human nature; and there was no possibility of any better education until the fundamental conceptions of the method had been challenged and made suspect. It was the main merit of the *Emile* that by putting in the forefront the idea of natural goodness it made most effective protest against all the evils of the ordinary education which sprang out of contempt for human nature. Even though men were not prepared to follow Rousseau in the new way he had indicated for them, it was impossible for them henceforth to go back wholeheartedly to the old. By a counter dogmatism, he had shaken to its foundations the established dogmatism, and set a problem that all future educators must attempt to solve.

Though the conflict of opposing ideas which was

---

[1] *Cf.* Dewey, *The School and the Child*, p. 28.

begun by the publication of the *Emile* is still in progress, there is increasing evidence of the worth of
Rousseau's doctrine of the child.   The new education
which makes the child its central consideration, is
in the direct line of descent from it.   The modern
educator certainly does not think of treating every
random impulse of the child as though it were in
the nature of things.   But he gives adherence to
the basal principle of the *Emile*, in recognising that
these primitive mind elements in the child to which
Rousseau was the first to call attention, need to be
taken into account in all his work.   The Dark Ages
of education, when the subjects learned counted for
more than the child, have been left behind for ever.

4. *Rousseau's Constructive Work in Educational
Theory.*—When we think of Rousseau's place in the
history of education, our thoughts turn most readily
to his destructive criticism of the methods in vogue
in his time.   In this we reverse his own judgment on
his work.   In the Preface to the *Emile* he expressly
disclaims any intention to dwell on the defects of the
ordinary education.   He will not stop, he says, to
prove that it is bad.   A thousand others have done it
before him, and he has no desire to fill his book with
what every one knows.   "I will only remark," he adds,
"that for a very long time there has been an outcry
against the established practice, and yet no one sees fit
to propose a better.   Both in literature and in learning,
the tendency of our age is towards destruction rather
than construction.   In spite of all the writings pro-
fessing to deal with matters of public utility, the most
important of them all—which is the art of forming
men—is still overlooked."   For his part, he adds, he

intends to follow in the footsteps of Locke in the proposals he made for educational reform, though he has no hope that any more attention will be paid to what he says than was paid to Locke.

To some extent the failure to recognise the constructive part of Rousseau's educational projects at its true value is due to his own imperfect presentation of his ideals. The reader of the *Emile* passes from the promises of the Preface to the detailed exposition of method in the text, expecting to get information on "the art of forming men." He finds the greater part of the book occupied with the story of the boy Emile and his tutor, and probably concludes from this that the main point of Rousseau's new method is tutorial instruction sustained over the first twenty-five years of life in greater or less detachment from society. This conclusion, as we have seen, is quite wrong. A more careful reading would have shown that the tutor acts on behalf of the father, and that a well-ordered family education represents for Rousseau the nearest approach to a real natural education that is attainable under the conditions of modern life.

The whole course of thought about education since Rousseau's time has gone to prove that it was a sound instinct that led him to regard the family as the fundamental educational institution. Later educators, differing from Rousseau in doing more justice to the claims of the great communities to which every man belongs, are yet at one with him in recognising that we must always look to the family for the best adjustment of the relations of individual and society in early education. There is general agreement that there is no other social institution in which the individuality that is so important in a democratic state counts for so much, or is

so safely and so wisely brought into subordination to
the wider law and order; and that consequently the educational foundations must always be laid in family life.

At the same time it must be confessed that Rousseau
himself did not appreciate his own conclusion at its
proper worth, as his readiness to abandon it in the tale
of the *Emile* plainly shows. He saw in a general way
that the child grows up to manhood best within the ring-
fence of the family, but he had no clear idea of the way
in which the influence of the family operates. Consistently with his idea of boyhood as the non-social
period of life, he views the family as a set of external
conditions. The boy is in the family but not of it. It
provides him with food and clothing and security from
evil influences, both physical and social, and so he is
able to develop himself as an individual within its
borders. But the various activities that are necessary
for this development have no relation to the activities
by which the family as a whole maintains itself. The
end that the boy sets before himself is not the promotion of the common life, but the promotion of his own
life. He never realises that he has an interest in what
is being done in the little community or co-operates
with its members in its work. Like the man of nature,
he lives alone, even when not alone.

But though the idea of family education, in spite of
this defective form, is one of the chief contributions
made by Rousseau to educational theory, it must
not be imagined that tutorial education or domestic
education or national education or any single form
of education is essential to his ideal. In a modern
nation-state with its special type of social organisation, the family is no doubt the best educator. But
it is quite conceivable that in another type of society

the ideal might be realised in other ways. In a state like Plato's Republic or the Poland of Rousseau's dream, for example, where all individual wills are subservient to the general will, the best education would certainly be a national education. The domestic method is only a relative best.

What, then, is this ideal that seemed to Rousseau capable of being attained under the very different conditions represented by the tutor of the *Emile,* the good family of the *New Heloïse,* the guardians of Plato's *Republic,* the reconstructed Poland ? The answer is indicated, in part at least, in the Preface of the *Emile.* After asserting that he has a new method of education to propound, he goes on with seeming abruptness to commend the study of the child to the teacher, the implication plainly being that the new method is one that depends on just such knowledge as this child study would give. Then he adds : " With regard to what may be called the systematic part, which in this book is nothing but the course of nature . . . " : meaning, as I take it, that whatever else it is, the ideal education which is in accord with nature is one that begins with a sound knowledge of the course of physical and mental growth in childhood and youth, and adapts its method to it.

5. *Negative and Positive Education.*—On this interpretation of his intention Rousseau invites us to find the essence of his system not in any particular method, such as that employed with the boy Emile, but in the general view he gives of child life and its proper nurture. To get this view we must begin by separating what is merely particular and local in any one scheme of education he puts before us from the more general ideas that

underlie all his schemes. Confining our attention to the *Emile*—because it is at once the most complete and the most systematic presentation of his educational theory—we find these fundamental ideas in the account given of the successive stages of human life from birth to maturity, and in the general treatment of the child based on the characterisation of the several stages.

The periods of childhood as marked off by Rousseau have already been indicated, and there is no need to do more than recall them. First, there is the asexual period from birth to the age of twelve, including infancy and childhood. Then there is an intermediate period which lasts in the case of the boy from twelve to fifteen. Finally comes the period of adolescence, extending from fifteen till the age of marriage, sometime in the early twenties. If we regard the second of these as but a phase of the first (as it is, if only manifest sex function be considered), then we have two periods, childhood and adolescence.

In this division of the periods of pupilage there is nothing specially new, unless perhaps the recognition of the distinctive character of the years between childhood and adolescence. What is new is the masterly analysis of the characteristic features of the different periods which Rousseau made on the basis of the physiological changes connected with the sex functions. Recognising, as no one had done adequately before, the supreme importance of the beginnings of sex-activity at puberty for the spiritual life of man, he divided the life of the immature human being into two great periods, according to the absence or the presence of sex-life, and further sub-divided these periods according to their degree of remoteness from the pubertal crisis.

The fact is that his whole account of education turns

on his conception of the effects of the sex functions on body and soul.[1] The child, on his view, is a mere neuter, not merely in the matter of sex, but of everything truly human, and lacks passion, reason, conscience, and every other adult faculty. The real beginnings of life (and of education) await the first activities of the sex functions. When sex awakens there is an almost catastrophic irruption of the passions into the sphere of conduct, and a period of emotional stress and strain, lasting over many years, is ushered in. Not less momentous are the indirect results: the nascence of imagination, the first relating activities of intellect, the quickening of conscience, the new birth of the soul, the change of a solitary into a social being to whom nothing human is alien.[2] Changes so vast and far-reaching cannot but be of vital moment for the educator.

In the first place, if the consciousness of right and wrong only develops after the altruistic sentiments, which, *ex hypothesi*, are absent before puberty—the child must be devoid of all morality. There is nothing in his nature to enable him to attach any meaning to the distinction between good and evil, or to prompt him to any form of action that does not bear obviously and directly on his own well-being.[3] In the second place, if appreciation of the beautiful depends on the capacity

---

[1] Behind all that Rousseau says about adolescence and adolescent education is the somewhat vague theory, which has received prominence in recent educational speculation from Dr. Stanley Hall's advocacy of it, that the appreciations of goodness, beauty and truth that create for man the spiritual universe are but glorified forms of the inspiration or afflatus which is one of the secondary results of the maturing of the sex functions. See Stanley Hall, *Adolescence*, ii., chaps. 12, 14.

[2] *Emile*, iv. Rousseau was the first to discuss the subject from the educational point of view, and his discussion is still one of the best.

[3] *Ibid.*, ii. 50.

for emotion, and the emotions are essentially the sex-glow transmuted into new forms, the whole world of beauty, whether in nature or art, is closed to the child. It is vain to expect him to admire fine scenery or to appreciate good literary form. He can see and understand the facts immediately before his eyes and nothing more.[1] In the third place, until he is able to think connectedly and rise by an effort of abstraction to the consciousness of the whole of things—which capacity is wanting before adolescence—God is nothing but a name, or is imaged in some sensuous form that gives no true knowledge of Him. He is therefore incapable of religious experience of any kind.[2] And finally, since the mind of the child is sense-bound, all abstract words, such for example as those applying to human conditions, are unintelligible to him. He is utterly unable to understand the meaning of life, whether presented in the guise of history or in more speculative forms. In short, the whole world of the spirit, all of morality, art, religion, philosophy, that enriches human experience and raises civilised man above the level of the savage, is completely beyond the ken of the child till the time of the pubertal wakening.

For the educator these premises admit of only one conclusion, and Rousseau draws it. It is impossible to make a beginning with the real work of education till the pupil reaches adolescence. The end of education, as Rousseau is careful to insist, is to prepare the child for the full life of a social being. But up to "the age of reason" (at fifteen ?) all the great spiritual interests are totally incomprehensible to him. They may be put before him with all the skill that the teacher possesses, but they mean as little to him as colour means to a man born blind, for there is nothing in his experience to

---

[1] *Emile*, iii. 18, 19.   [2] *Ibid.*, iv. 161 *seq.*

give the slightest clue to their significance. His mind moves wholly on the physical plane. If he has not been screened from the natural reaction of his physical environment by the unkind kindness of his parents, he is quite at home in the orderly world of "things," and has come to know from personal experience what to expect from them in all the common contingencies of action. But men and their ways are a mystery to him, and continue a mystery until the gradual nascence of his own spirit after the pubertal crisis gives him the key to it. Then slowly and painfully, needing all the help he can get from wise elders who have gone the road before him, he acquires the varied experiences that finally make him as much at home in the social world as he is in the physical. This is his proper education.

But what about the years before adolescence? Is there nothing for the educator to do then? That, Rousseau would answer, depends on the community to which the child belongs. If he has been born among savages or even among peasants, there is no need for him to have any education at all. In that case life itself is his educator and requires no help from blundering man. If, however, his lot has fallen among civilised people, the policy of *laisser faire* is impossible. To leave him to his own devices in a community whose ways are altogether above his level is to expose him to the constant temptation of premature experience; and that is of all things most fatal to a personal view of life, since it means that long before he knows what he is saying or doing, he is aping his elders and acquiring all their conventions without any conception of their meaning and worth. In these circumstances the best thing, according to Rousseau, would be to prevent him coming under social influences, or, failing that, to reduce them to the smallest amount and give them the forms least likely to be injurious to the immature mind.

If we call this attention that is paid to the boy "education," we must be careful to distinguish it from the real education which becomes possible in the years of adolescence. Compared with that it is only a negative kind of education which has fulfilled its purpose when it has prevented error and vice getting into the soul, and has left it free for the later influences. The distinction is fundamental in Rousseau's pedagogy.[1]

The difference in content between the two educations is clearly indicated in a passage in the Second Book of the *Emile* relating to the first education. "There are two kinds of dependence: natural dependence, the dependence on things, and social dependence, the dependence on men. . . . If you keep the child dependent on things alone, you will follow the order of nature in the stages of his education."[2] On this view, the first business of the child is to make the acquaintance of the world in which he lives. The world, as Rousseau says elsewhere, is the book from which all the lessons of childhood are to be learned. In the first feeble years, according to the ideal scheme of the *Emile*, the child sees and touches all the objects immediately around him, and gets a sensuous knowledge of their weight, their shape, their colour, and all their other physical qualities.[3] In the succeeding

---

[1] I have some hesitation in speaking of the adolescent education as positive. Rousseau himself, so far as I can remember, only uses the phrase "positive education" on one occasion (in the *Letter to the Archbishop of Paris*), and there he means by it the ordinary education. In spite of this, I have used the phrase "negative education" as implying comparison with the later education rather than with the ordinary education, and should like to appropriate "positive education" for that later education.

[2] II. 35. *Cf.* iv. 15.   [3] Book I.

years, up to the age of twelve, he continues this experimental examination of the properties of things, and
not merely trains the five senses, but acquires the power
to judge and reason intuitively about all that comes
within their scope.[1] From twelve to fifteen his acquaintance with the world of things assumes the form of knowledge. The sense-reasoning of the earlier years develops
into the scientific reasoning that discerns causes and
effects and groups its ideas in orderly systems.[2] All this
acquisition of experience, it is to be noted, is quite
different from the lessons got in schools. The boy learns
when he likes and as he likes, and is never conscious
that he is learning. The sole motive for learning is the
desire for self-activity. He must be doing something,
and in doing he learns.[3]

The positive education which begins when the young
adolescent becomes conscious of his dependence on men
differs from this " education of things " in many respects.
The social world is a more complex world than the
physical, and there is always room for doubt (Rousseau
thinks) whether it is so well ordered. In any case it is
not possible to leave the learner so much to himself as
in the earlier years. He has need of the teacher, to a far
greater extent than before, to act as mediator between himself and society, and to bring society down to his level of
understanding. In the first education the teacher's action
was as far as possible confined to determining environment, and direct interference with the boy was avoided.
Now the teacher comes more into the open and gives explicit direction very much in the fashion of the ordinary
educator. The result is that more importance is attached
to the results of the teaching than in boyhood. So

[1] Book II.   [2] Book III.
[3] This applies even to the highest of the three stages. See iii. 11.

long as the pupil was only a boy, it was a matter of little consequence what he acquired in the way of knowledge, or whether indeed he acquired any knowledge at all. "You give the child knowledge at an early age," says Rousseau to the educator who objects to the time wasted by the method of negative education; "for my part I am busy preparing the instrument for acquiring it."[1] In other words, Rousseau does not wish the educator to give the child any particular form of knowledge or skill, but merely to cultivate the faculties already in season, so that the mind may be ready for its proper work in the years of adolescence. When that time comes, the youth must be made fit to enter into the world of men, and the mere training of faculty is no longer sufficient. To be a man he must be able to earn his bread by doing some useful work. That implies the acquisition of some form of specialised ability. He will meet men of all kinds, both good and bad, and he must know their ways if he is to bear himself aright among them. He will one day marry. He must have an ideal of womanhood to enable him to choose well, and some acquaintance with the obligations of domestic life. Once married, he will have a definite standing in the community, in preparation for which he must acquaint himself with the duties of a citizen. These and all the manifold relationships of social life call for an education quite different from the education of boyhood. The perfecting of practical capacity is still an important part of the educator's work. Rousseau calls attention to that when he insists on the desirability of acquiring taste or tact (*goût*) for the ready discernment of the right course of action in any set of social circumstances. But far more important is the forming of right sentiments and ideas with respect

[1] *Emile*, ii. 189.

to all the common situations in which a young man may find himself. The sentiments of purity, for example, which are best acquired in the simplicity of rural life, are needed to keep him upright if chance throws him into the company of men of dissolute lives. The "circle of ideas"[1] appropriate to any particular state of life—to use a phase that anticipates Herbart—should be formed with the help of the teacher, to provide a standard of reference in future contingencies[2] and to prompt to right action.[3] This upbuilding of systems of sentiments and ideas with a view to the proper conduct of life is the central feature of adolescent education.[4]

6. *The Defects in Rousseau's Account of Individual Growth.*—The view of child life on which the "system" of the *Emile* is based may be summarily stated in two propositions. (1) In its progress from birth to its first maturity, the individual life passes through an unbroken succession of stages—infancy, childhood, pubescence,[5] adolescence. (2) There is an absolute difference between adolescence and the asexual stages preceding it, which compels an absolute difference in educational treatment.

These are fundamental ideas by which Rousseau's educational theory must stand or fall. What are we to say about them ? Are they substantial truths that the educators of all time must reckon with ? The surest

---

[1] *Emile*, iv. 161.   [2] *Ibid.*, iv. 301.   [3] *Ibid.*, iv. 83.

[4] This view of adolescent education is well illustrated by the preparation for the meeting of Emile with the ideal Sophie. Long before he meets her he has perfectly clear ideas about the kind of woman she should be, and has nothing to do but to fall in love with her at first sight, as the one who completely satisfies all his expectations. See iv. 410.

[5] There is no popular name for this period, and Rousseau does not give it any name.

answer is that for the most part they have already
passed into commonplaces and become the guiding
principles of those concerned with the business of
education. Schmidt bears witness to this in summing
up his account of Rousseau : " The beginning of human
education at birth, the organisation of the child's environment with a view to giving him knowledge of
things by means of direct experience and self-activity,
the reason of the senses before the reason of the
intellect, love for children and for the pleasing instinct
that shows itself in their games, consideration of the
man in the man and the child in the child : these are
the great truths which Rousseau proclaimed with inspiration, and which from that time have been accepted
as axioms in pedagogy." [1]

And yet though both ideas have affected the development of educational theory, they do not stand on quite
the same level of influence. There has been a very
general acceptance of the idea of an orderly sequence of
stages in education ; but the sharp distinction made by
Rousseau between the education of the child and the
education of the adolescent has found but grudging
recognition. The difference between the two educations has been admitted, much on the lines laid
down by Rousseau, but there has been no disposition
anywhere to follow him in treating the difference as a
discontinuity.

It is not difficult to see the reason for this discrimina-
tion between the two ideas. It points straight to a
serious weakness in Rousseau's view of education as
growth. Thinking in terms of the category of growth,
he represents each period of the child's life as passing
into the next by the same inner necessity that is

[1] *Geschichte der Pädagogik*, iii. p. 501.

manifest in the growth of the plant. But in spite of all he does to give the impression that each period as he represents it is an outgrowth from an earlier one, he never manages to satisfy us that it is really an outgrowth, and not a new phenomenon making an abrupt appearance unrelated to its predecessors. Consider, for example, his doctrine of educational evolution as it is stated by one of the greatest of his disciples : " The boy has not become a boy, nor the youth a youth, by reaching a certain age, but only by having lived through childhood, and further on through boyhood, true to the requirements of his mind, his feelings and his body ; similarly adult man has not become an adult man by reaching a certain age, but only by satisfying the requirements of his childhood, boyhood and youth." [1] In this passage (which represents very closely Rousseau's own view) we seem to have an assertion that true education is an unbroken evolution. But a more careful examination will show that it is rather the *distinction* between the different stages of life than their *unity* in the experience of one growing personality that is emphasised. The boy lives so many years "true to the requirements of his mind, his feelings and his body," and then somehow or other ceases to be a boy and becomes a youth ; but in spite of the disclaimer, there is nothing beyond the fact that he has reached a certain age to account for the change. If there is anything in the boyish activities that after a certain time brings about the development into youth, it is certainly not indicated here. Rather we are left with the idea of each stage as a distinct phase that merely happens to be a member of the same series as the others.

In Rousseau's case, the defect is more pronounced

---

[1] Froebel, *Education of Man* (Eng. tr.), p. 29.

because of the use of the terms of the faculty psychology
to characterise the periods of pupilage. The child is
spoken of as a creature of sense, altogether lacking
reason and conscience; then we are informed that about
the age of twelve there has appeared a reason of the
intellect to take the place of (or to be an addition to ?)
the sensuous reason of the previous stage, but no
suggestion of any genetic relation is given. Then at
fifteen, conscience appears still more abruptly, without
any predecessor even remotely resembling it. That is
to say, Rousseau's account of mental growth makes soul
the result of a series of additions, as though it consisted
of the senses *plus* the intellect *plus* the conscience, a
building of three storeys reared at three separate times.
For anything that he has to say to the contrary, there
is no reason why a sensuous being should ever become
an intellectual being, or why again, an intellectual being
should ever become conscious of good and evil. It just
happens to be so; presumably it is in the nature of man
that it should be so.[1]

The difficulty appears in its acutest form in the
absolute distinction made between childhood and
adolescence. In terms of that distinction, we must
regard as purely adolescent phenomena all the higher
activities of soul—the power of judgment and reason-

[1] It should be added that though this aggregational conception
of growth is the one most obvious in the *Emile*, there are many
indications that the faculty psychology on which it depends is
breaking down in Rousseau's hands. Note, for example, the connection between sentiment (that is, determinate feeling) and idea, to
which attention has already been called in chap. vi. (p. 166). If ideas
are preformed in sentiments, then the transition from the child
stage before twelve when sentiments are the main content of mind,
to the stage from twelve to fifteen when ideas succeed them is a
true evolution. See also the statement in ii. 186, with reference to
the relation between the sensuous reason and the intellectual reason,
for a further example of the same tendency to abandon the sharp
distinction between faculties.

ing, the impulse to unselfishness and the ability to appreciate it in others, the capacity for personal religious experience. We must believe that there is no glimmering of rationality, no altruistic impulses or judgment concerning good and evil, no consciousness of God and immortality, before the pubertal crisis; and that all these enter into the life of the boy for the first time with more or less abruptness sometime after the fifteenth year. It is little wonder that Rousseau has found few disciples willing to go this length with him, or that at times he finds it difficult to remain faithful to his own principles.[1]

The reason for the over-definite demarcation of the different periods of life on Rousseau's part is obvious enough. It was an exaggeration consequent on his reaction against the view commonly taken of the child. On the whole educational system, whether of family or school, the adult has imposed his own standards of life and thought, assuming tacitly that the immature human being is such another as himself, with capacities similar to his own and differing only in degree.[2] The ordinary parent, for example, makes his child say his prayers and his catechism, evidently thinking that the religious modes and ideas which are good enough for himself are good enough for his child.[3] Against this grave error Rousseau protests by asserting that the child is not moral or religious or rational in the way that his elders are; and it must be said that if (as the

---

[1] See, for example, the difficulty he has in holding to his statement that children cannot reason. *Emile*, ii. 118 (especially the note).

[2] In this connection it is interesting to note that the Shorter Catechism, faithfully learned by many generations of Scotsmen, was appointed by the Westminster Assembly of Divines for the use of those " of weaker intellect " (that is, of children).

[3] See *Emile*, iv. 171, v. 80 *seq.* ; *New Heloïse*, v. 3.

ordinary methods of education seem to imply) the
developed morality or religion or reason of the adult
is the *only* morality or religion or reason, Rousseau
is amply justified in his protest. It is true, as he
maintains, that each age has a distinctive character
and maturity of its own which marks it off equally from
those that have gone before it and those that are to
come after it. Where he errs is in attributing to the
different ages an independence of each other and of
adult life which is not conformable with the facts. He
challenges the static view of childhood held by all
parents and teachers who have not learned the profound
difference between child and adult, and insists on the
significance of the fact of growth. But in combating
their one-sidedness, he fails to do justice to the idea of
growth himself. Growth is at once a process of differentiation and of integration: it implies a series of
distinct stages which yet are but phases of an identical
being. Rousseau throws all the emphasis on the fact
of difference, the fact neglected by those whom he was
criticising, and contents himself with saying that one
stage actually follows the other, without seeing that
on his statement of the case there is no reason why
it should.

Clearly, then, before the account he gives of the
child's progress from infancy to manhood can be accepted, it must be re-stated to show the connection
that exists between the separate members of the series
of stages. Especially is this necessary with regard to
transition from childhood to adolescence. Even if we
grant Rousseau's contention that the adolescent mind
and character have undergone a fundamental change
subsequent to puberty, and agree that the beautiful, the
good and the true are then for the first time compre-

hended with comparative adequacy, we must yet insist that the spiritual life which now becomes manifest is not really a new creation but the perfection of what lay hid in child life. If it be asked—as Rousseau might ask— how experiences that depend on the activity of sex function can have any equivalent in the asexual period of life, the answer would seem to be that the child is not merely the son of his parents but the son of his race, and that characters which were at first only the possession of individual adults and have afterwards passed into the racial equipment, must subsequently appear in some form or other in the children of the race. This is illustrated plainly enough in the case of the secondary physical characters of sex, and there seems no reason why it should not hold good in like manner of the moral and intellectual characters. At any rate, it is true that we find in children some anticipations of all the later feelings and thoughts; and even if this does not warrant us in dealing with children as we would with adults, it certainly forbids us cutting off the present from the future in the absolute manner that Rousseau seems to prescribe. In short, while agreeing with him to treat the child as a child, we must never forget that the child will one day be a man, and that his present capacities do not exhaust their virtue in providing for the present need, but contain the promise of the future; and so far as may be, without doing violence to the rights of childhood—to speak in Rousseau's dialect—we must always be seeking to direct the childish experiences towards manhood.

7. *The Defects in Rousseau's Account of the Social Factors in Education.*—The prime flaw in Rousseau's account of individual growth may perhaps be found in

the fact that he looks on the growth of the child as a
natural process like the growth of a plant. A plant
seems to pass from one stage to another in consequence
of some inner impulse which operates unceasingly from
the first germination of the seed in the spring till the
ripening of the fruit in the autumn; and so, Rousseau
seems to imply, is it with human growth. This is the
idea that underlies his faith in the goodness of the first
impulses of nature, and his advocacy of liberty for the
development of the child apart from adult restrictions.
Now it cannot be denied that there is some justification
in fact for the suggestion of an ordered progress in the
development of man's powers, which is conveyed by the
analogy of human growth to plant growth. But if this
is taken for more than a partial truth, it leads to the
essential difference between man and all other organisms
being overlooked. Man belongs to the natural world,
and never more obviously than in the earlier years of
life which Rousseau has specially in mind when using the
analogy. But even then he is more than natural. He
is spiritual, and therefore not a simple product of
growth but the outcome of a free activity which curbs
and checks the natural impulses in the interests of a
higher life. A view like that of Rousseau "leaves out
of account the truth that a man must die to live . . .
and . . . have the caprice of nature subdued in him in
order that he may attain to true freedom." [1]

The analogy of child and plant shows its weakness
most evidently in the view of social relations it implies.
If the dependence of the child on its parent or its
teacher is really comparable with the dependence of
the plant on the gardener, as the introductory sections
of the *Emile* would seem to indicate, then the child is

[1] Caird, *Essays on Literature and Philosophy*, i., p. 127.

by his nature a self-contained unit, who may be helped
by society to develop his potentialities but does not
really owe any of his essential characters to society.   If
the analogy stood alone, it would not be justifiable to
read as much as this into it.   But as a matter of fact,
the implication suggested is confirmed by everything
that Rousseau says about the relation of the child and
society.   He recognises that by nature the adult man is
in some sense a social being, but he is never quite convinced that to be man at all he must be a social being
his whole life through.   The boy he constantly regards
as pre-social man.

On this view, the child's relation to society is very
different from the man's.   The man's life is but a
fraction of which the community is the whole : the boy's
life is a unity in itself.   In the case of the man, it is
right that the necessary restraints should be imposed
on the passions and the self-seeking impulses, either
by the individual himself or by society, in order that
the full stature of manhood may be attained; for man
is only truly man when he finds his life by losing it in
willing subjection to some higher common life.   But
with the boy it is different.   Until the sex awakening,
society means nothing for him whatever, and social
restraint can never be anything but an external interference with the native impulses of his "nature."

The criticism of this conception of childhood has
already been suggested in the last section.   It is not
possible to think of human life as cleft in two in this
fashion.   If man is a spiritual being when mature, he
cannot be merely a natural being in the first years of
life.   Unless we are to think of the life of man that is
above nature as coming into existence in consequence
of a change of physical state—which would be a purely

natural change—we must postulate a continuity between childhood and manhood. That implies that even
when the child seems most a creature of nature, there is
something of spirit in him. If this be so, then there is
need in his case as in the man's—though not perhaps
as much as in the man's—to control the impulses
proper to his age, so that on his own level he may
learn the first lessons of the higher life and grow
into man's estate.

This failure of Rousseau's to recognise the child's
need of society for the growth and development of his
nature from the earliest days is responsible for some of
the most serious defects in the working out of his educational ideal. In conjunction with a deep distrust of all
actual social institutions which outlived his cynical condemnation of society, and persisted even after he saw
that man is by nature a social being, it led him to completely wrong views of the social factors in education.
The weakness of his educational system on this side
appears most markedly in his misconception of the
educational value of social institutions, in his doctrine
of rewards and punishments, and in his treatment of
the humanistic subjects of the curriculum. These are
important enough to be worthy of consideration in some
detail.

(a) *The Educational Value of Social Institutions.*—
Consistently with the idea that the child represents
man at a pre-social stage, Rousseau regards the problem
of education as the making of a social out of a non-
social being. On this view, he thinks of education as a
preparation for society, but fails to see that it is of
necessity also a preparation by society. Consider, for
example, his conception of the educational function of
the home as it is presented in the letter on education

in the *New Heloïse*. The relation of the boy undergoing education to his parents is largely negative.
Their interests and occupations mean nothing for him;
the common ends of family life which are their concern
are not his concern. He pursues the even tenor of his
way at the promptings of his own impulses, and seemingly the only advantage which his membership of the
family brings him is that he is able to do so without
other let or hindrance than that due to the necessity in
things. On the parents' side, the relationship is almost
as limited. In the years of infancy they feed him and
clothe him, and at a later stage this care for the physical
well-being is extended to his mental and moral well-
being, and they provide education as they provided food
and clothing. But the education is not regarded as the
result of the ordinary home life, so much as the outcome of special conditions brought into being by the
deliberate and exceptional action of the parents.

This individualistic conception of domestic education,
which ignores the educative influence of the family as
an institution and makes the conduct of the child's education the special business of the father and mother as
individuals, reveals its true character in the story of the
Emile. In that book, as we have noted already,
Rousseau begins by asserting that the father is the
proper teacher, and yet he is so little conscious that it is
not the father in his individual capacity but the father
as part creator of the little community to which the
child also belongs, that he takes Emile out of the
family group and entrusts him to a tutor who only
resembles the father in directing the external circumstances of the boy's life. He is not unaware of the
difficulties that attend this view of education. "Who,"
he asks, "can hope to have complete control of the

speech and actions of all the people about a child ? " [1]—
as if the teacher had to fight a single-handed battle
against a hostile world. A truer insight into the
manner in which the boy's life is organised for him
by the share he takes in the daily life and work of the
family—such an insight as came to Pestalozzi when
he discovered a potential educator in every mother and
a school in every home—would have prevented the
difficulty arising, or at least would have provided the
solution when it did arise.

It is precisely the same weakness that is evident in
Rousseau's account of the social education of the adolescent in the Fourth Book of the *Emile*. The direct
preparation for society there set forth is achieved for
the most part by the special machinations of the tutor.
It is true that there is explicit recognition of the need
for actual participation in social life to make the youth
a social being. But all Emile's relations with society
are of the most casual kind. He learns the carpenter's trade by spending occasional days at the bench,
but never feels the constraint of economic need. He
wanders about as a knight-errant seeking grievances
to redress and vindicating the law of nature, but he
never occupies a definite station in the community,
and never experiences the moral discipline got by performing duties exclusively one's own. According to
Hegel, "there are five instruments of education—viz.
the family, the school, rank or social class, people or
nation, the church." [2] Rousseau knows only one : that
is society in general, not society in any definite institutional form. In practice, this reduces itself to the tutor

---

[1] *Emile*, i. 8.
[2] Mackenzie, *Hegel's Educational Theory and Practice*, p. 3. See
also chap. ix.

giving Emile a special training for his future relations with his fellows. That membership of some of the minor communities is necessary, if the individual is to be socialised and made fit to discharge his obligations to the great community, is an idea which comes to Rousseau in a casual criticism of Plato,[1] but finds no place whatever in his own educational scheme.

(b) *The Doctrine of Rewards and Punishments.*— Rousseau's individualistic principles find curious illustration in his views on the subject of rewards for children. "The most suitable way of governing children," he remarks, "is to lead them by the mouth."[2] If they are indisposed to do some task, he sees no objection to the teacher tempting them to zeal by offering them cakes or other eatables.[3] The fact that taste is the only sense that is wholly "physical and material" makes this appeal to the palate the one method of reward that is morally safe. All other methods call the social motives into play, and in the case of children the only social motive that is effective is the dangerous motive of vanity, the sentiment of pride that rises in the heart on comparing one's self with others. The choice, it seems to him, must be made between "the motive impulse of gluttony" and that of vanity, and he has no difficulty in deciding for himself. "The first is a natural appetite connected with sense, the second is a work of opinion, subject to human caprice and open to all kinds of abuses."[4] Any method is better than the method of comparing one's own work with that of other people. The only

---

[1] *Emile*, v. 24.   [2] *Ibid.*, ii. 286.

[3] The method taken by Rousseau to get a lazy boy to run, which is narrated at length in the *Emile*, ii. 245–251, is a case in point. The same idea is repeated in different forms in the *Emile*.

[4] *Emile*, ii. 286.

comparison admissible is comparison with one's self. To-day's drawing is better or worse than yesterday's; this jump is so much longer or shorter than some previous jump; and so on. That there is a legitimate place for approval or disapproval of the same kind when expressed, not by the boy himself, but by his peers or by his tutor—in other words, for a judgment that is social and not individual—Rousseau will not admit. He does not see the inconsistency of recognising the possibility of a bad social motive and denying the possibility of a good.

The same point of view appears in his doctrine of punishments. Punishment, he says, "should never be inflicted on children as punishment. It should always come to them as a natural consequence of their evil-doing." [1] In this Rousseau thinks to follow the method of nature. When the child falls, he hurts himself When he touches fire, he gets burned. In all such contingencies there is the invariable reaction that leads the child in course of time to avoid those actions which have painful consequences. The case is somewhat different in an educational discipline, since it is the intervention of the tutor that turns the boy's evil-doing back on himself. So far as the boy is concerned, however, the two cases are identical. When he tells a lie, he is not punished expressly for lying, but is made to suffer such consequences of deceit as not being believed when he tells the truth. Or, again, if he is malicious and breaks windows, he is allowed to catch cold and suffer all the miseries attendant on open windows in inclement weather. "Being devoid of any sense of right and wrong," he makes no moral distinction between the mistake of touching fire and the evil

---

[1] *Emile*, ii. 94.

of lying; but he avoids both because of the unpleasant results that follow.

It is to be noted that this doctrine of rewards and punishments is chiefly to be found in the early Books of the *Emile*, and there the reason given for it is that the boy is too undeveloped to be capable of being rewarded or punished in a *moral* way. So considered, it must be judged along with Rousseau's whole view of childhood. At the same time, it is impossible to deny that behind the doctrine are all Rousseau's anti-social prepossessions, leading him to favour a view that finds the essence of reward and punishment in the existence of a state of feeling in the individual, rather than in the communal approval and disapproval expressed by it. But whether we regard it as simply the corollary of a particular conception of childhood, or as following from an individualistic view of social relations, the doctrine is peculiarly open to criticism. The question to be raised in the one case is whether a merely physical pleasure or pain, such as that which determines the child's actions, can even ultimately have a moral effect: or, putting the question in reverse form, whether in view of the admittedly moral effect on the man of this treatment of him as a child, these pleasures and pains can be said to be merely physical in their effects. The question in the other case concerns the *status* of the tutor as dispenser of rewards and punishments. Rousseau represents him as the administrator of natural law. But by what right does he act? If he acts as an individual, then the caprice that attends all individual actions affects his direction of the child's life, and he acts contrary to nature. If he acts as the representative of a community—which is surely the only justification for any one taking the responsibility of rewarding and punishing upon him-

self—then the expression of the praise or the blame
of the community is an essential part of the act
of requital done by him. He cannot confine himself
to merely natural reactions.[1]

(c) *The Humanistic Subjects of the Curriculum.*—
Pre-adolescent education, as we have seen, is negative
in Rousseau's scheme. That means that history, literature, and religion,[2] each in its own way dealing with and
expressing a phase of the common life of humanity, are
entirely excluded from it. It is maintained by Rousseau that all that is vital in these subjects is totally
beyond the comprehension of the child; and that, apart
from that altogether, they have no proper place in the
experience of one who is by the limitations of his
nature a non-social being.[3] It is difficult to avoid at
least partial agreement with him on the first score
and admit that the humanistic subjects are largely
(though surely not altogether) beyond the scope of the
child. But again—as in the question of rewards and
punishments—we have to object to the drawing of a
hard-and-fast line of separation between childhood and
adult life. The needs of the future require at least a

[1] For a valuable criticism of the doctrine of punishment by consequences as it appears in Herbert Spencer—which does not wholly
apply to Rousseau—see Laurie, *Educational Opinion from the Renaissance*, chap. xvi. Perhaps I should add at this point that I do not
wish what I have said about Rousseau's doctrine of rewards and
punishments to be taken as wholly condemnatory of the method he
suggests. On the contrary, I think that there is much to be said for
it within proper limits in dealing with young children. My objection is to the interpretation of the method as implying natural and
not social reactions. The method is no more and no less a social
method than any other.

[2] I have confined my remarks in this section to history and
literature. To have entered on a discussion of the place of religion
in education would have lengthened the section quite unduly without
adding much to the illustration.

[3] Rousseau deals with the matter very thoroughly in the *Emile*,
ii. 116–147.

beginning to be made in childhood with the study of
the humanities.

It is in the education of the adolescent, which on the
theoretical side is exclusively devoted to the human
sciences, that Rousseau's social philosophy declares itself
most evidently. When the youth Emile attains the age
of eighteen, his tutor concludes that the time has come
to acquaint him with the ways of men, but he hesitates
about introducing him abruptly into a society of doubtful moral character, in which perhaps he will be corrupted before he has had time to find himself. "This
is the time for history." In the records of human
affairs he can study men at a safe distance. "By
means of history, he will read the hearts of men without the lessons of philosophy, and see them as a simple
spectator without personal interest and passion." [1] Unfortunately, the study of history is not easy. Many
things conspire to make the stories it tells of doubtful
worth. The most serious defect—the defect which would
seem to rob it of all value for education—is the fact
that it is always biassed. Do what he will, the historian
cannot pass the facts through his mind without altering
them in the process: "they change form in his head,
they shape themselves according to his interests, they
take on the hue of his prejudices." [2] Rousseau recognises the difficulty of using such material for the purposes of education, and tries in vain to escape from it.
"I shall be told," he says, "that the accuracy of the
history is of less importance than the goodness of its
morals or of its characters, and that so long as the
human heart is truly depicted, the exact narration of
events is of little consequence. Provided the pictures

---

[1] *Emile*, iv. 103. See the whole discussion, iv. 103–125.
[2] *Ibid.*, iv. 106.

are skilfully and naturally drawn, that is true enough;
but if most of them have only their models in the
historian's imagination, do we not get back to the
inconvenience we are trying to avoid, and accord to
the historian the authority we want to take from the
teacher? If my pupil is only to see fancy pictures, I
prefer them to be traced by my own hand rather than
by that of another. They will at least suit his case
better." [1] But the device of making the teacher the
final authority is really of little avail. If history is only
"fancy pictures" (or, as Rousseau says in a previous
paragraph, "the one lie among several lies which looks
most like the truth ") it cannot by any chance serve the
purpose he wants it to serve. It will not really intro-
duce the pupil to the ways of men, but to the point of
view of the man who narrates or teaches it. The truth
is that history can only give guidance to the youth who
seeks knowledge of mankind, if it is not merely the
record of human affairs from particular standpoints,
but the embodiment of the spirit of society in the
writings of particular men; and Rousseau is too much
of an individualist ever to get behind the individual
historians to the spirit of nationality or of humanity
which must in greater or less degree possess them if
they are to write educationally valuable history.[2]

In his scheme of studies the study of literature comes

---

[1] *Emile*, iv. 108.

[2] Rousseau is aware, however, of the existence of a spirit of the
crowd or the nation. Cf. *Emile*, iv. 116: "It is true that the genius
of crowds or nations is very different from the character of the
individual man, and that the human heart would be very imperfectly known if it were not also examined in the multitude." (See
also iv. 459.) He then points out that the converse is also true,
and that for a right knowledge of the multitude it is necessary to
know its constituent individuals. As an individualist, it is the study
of the individual (*e.g.* in biography), rather than of the nation, that
he himself prefers.

at a later stage than the study of history. The knowledge of affairs through the historical record precedes actual acquaintance with the world: literary study comes after it, to perfect the taste (or tact) acquired from experience of the ways of men. Taste Rousseau defines as "the faculty of judging what pleases or displeases the greatest number of people."[1] The man of taste is the man who knows just what should be done in the various social situations in which he may chance to be; and that knowledge, it need scarcely be said, is not got in books so much as from intercourse with men in some great city. That is not to say that books have not got their place. By the study of good books (especially, Rousseau thinks, those of the ancients) and by the study of the drama, the youth may make his taste surer and more catholic. This is indeed a very restricted view that Rousseau takes of the function of literature in education, but within its limits it is quite sound. The literature of an age undoubtedly expresses its distinctive temper, and there is no surer way of getting at what Rousseau calls "the spirit of societies" than through the study of their literature. If we are to criticise Rousseau's doctrine at all, it must be with regard to the pettiness of the aim which he prescribes for the teacher. Here in literature we have an instrument capable of making youths worthy men and good citizens, and all the use Rousseau proposes to make of it is to render them more facile in the ordinary converse of social life. It is no wonder that he attaches little importance to this study, and does not care whether Emile "succeeds with the dead languages, the *belles lettres*, and poetry or not."[2] From the individualistic point of view, the humanistic learning is of comparatively little significance. It is only

[1] *Emile*, iv. 450.   [2] *Ibid.*, iv. 470.

when we think of the individual as finding his true life in what he has in common with the human kind—his neighbourliness, his citizenship, his supernational ideals —that history and literature take their proper place in education.

8. *The Development of Rousseau's Educational Doctrine in the Nineteenth Century.*—A survey of the discussion of the points of weakness and of strength in Rousseau's educational theory will show that all the most characteristic features of his system depend on the importance which he attached to the child as a child. The great germinal truth which made the *Emile* quick and living was the simple idea that the child is the one positive fact in education. It was the effective proclamation of this that made Rousseau the pioneer of the New Education, and the *Emile* the most important work on education produced by the modern world.

The supreme merit of Rousseau is that he brought about the Copernican change in educational thought and practice. Before his time the first interest of those responsible for the work of education was the adult interest in the knowledge to be imparted. The educator looked on learning as a Procrustean bed on which the child had to be stretched for his ultimate benefit. After Rousseau the whole temper of men's minds changed, and in theory, if not always in practice, it came gradually to be realised that the centre of educational interest is not the curriculum but the child. Where the old educational system tried to fit the child to the school, the new began to try to fit the school to the child.

But, as we have seen, much error mingled with the truth. The value of childhood is a theme which readily lends itself to exaggeration, and Rousseau undoubtedly overstated his case. In this way he fell into a double error. In the first place, the emphasis on the child as he is, apart from what he is to be, led to a wrong view of individual growth by encouraging a too sharp distinction of the different periods of life from each other and from the period of maturity; and, in the second place, the emphasis on the child as he is, apart from what he becomes under the cultural influences of society, made him underrate the social factors in education.

Both merits and defects, it should be added, are bound up with his political philosophy, and are not incidental results of his peculiar temper of mind. For one like Rousseau, quick to appreciate individuality and sensitive with regard to its wrongs, the view of the child as the victim of the educator was simply a special case of the view of the individual man as the victim of society. Individualism in theory, especially when informed by the spirit of humanitarianism, inevitably leads to these very doctrines that are to be found in the *Emile*. Any one who doubts this has but to turn to Herbert Spencer's *Education*, written a hundred years later from a similar standpoint. There he will find, in spite of some differences,[1] the same depreciation of the humanistic studies, the same insistence on punishment by physical consequences, the same regard for the child's point of view. So close, indeed, is the resemblance that he learns with the utmost surprise that Spencer had never heard of the *Emile* or read a word of Rousseau's writings when he wrote his book.[2]

This dependence of Rousseau's educational doctrine

---

[1] The most striking difference appears in the attitude of the two men to the child. The child in Rousseau's discussion is a creature of flesh and blood: in Spencer's he is a pale ghost, known by deduction rather than by experience.

[2] Hudson, *Rousseau*, p. 206 (note).

on his individualism is worth keeping in mind when attempting to form an estimate of its permanent value. From the time of the Sophists individualism has always stood on an intellectual plane of its own. From the logical point of view, it has almost always been conspicuously weak, and yet it has generally appealed to some very acute minds and exercised an influence far beyond its logical deserts. Tried by the logical test of consistency, it has made but a poor show : tried by the pragmatic test of practical influence, it has proved itself one of the most potent forces in the direction of the life of man.

This disparity of theory and practice appears most markedly in Rousseau's case. Never was there a thinker who counted for so much in the progress of thought and life, and yet was so open to attack on the score of inconsistency. It would not be difficult for an opponent to make Rousseau appear intellectually contemptible. But after he had done so there would still be need for explanation how one who was so poor a thinker could have influenced his fellow-men so much as Rousseau did. For it is simple fact that Rousseau has left his mark on the course of human affairs in a manner permitted to but a few of the world's greatest men. "We have never seen in our own generation— indeed the world has not seen more than once or twice in all the course of history—a literature which has exercised such prodigious influence over the minds of men, over every cast and shade of intellect, as that which emanated from Rousseau between 1749 and 1762." [1]

<hr/>

[1] Sir Henry Maine, *Ancient Law*, p. 76. In the same passage Maine speaks of Rousseau as "that remarkable man, who without learning, with few virtues, and with no strength of character, has nevertheless stamped himself ineffaceably on history by the force of a vivid imagination, and by the help of a genuine and burning

In face of an influence like this, the ordinary criticism which dwells on defects is apt to appear carping. To estimate Rousseau at his true worth we must seek the judgment of history upon him. There is no sounder criticism of a man's work than that implicitly passed by those who come after him either as disciples or as opponents. When rightly interpreted, the omissions, the modifications, the new developments, which they make in going over the same ground, reveal both his strength and his weakness. How do Rousseau's principles and schemes stand this test?

To answer the question in the matter of education we need only recall the extraordinary influence of the *Emile* on his own age.[1] From the day of its issue it created disciples in every civilised country. Women of all ranks, breaking away from an evil fashion, began to nurse their own children; fathers adopted its method in the training of their sons; the noble families took warning from it and fitted up workshops for their youthful scions in preparation for a time of revolution; a new literature for children sprang up.[2] In these and many other ways it immediately manifested its power. Even more important was the influence it exerted on Basedow, Pestalozzi, and all the others who were seeking to establish a system of elementary education for the common people.[3] Through

love for his fellow-men, for which much will always have to be forgiven him."

[1] See Chuquet, *J.-J. Rousseau*, p. 132 *seq.* For its influence on England, see Graham, *Rousseau*, p. 154; Emile Legouis, *The Early Life of Wordsworth*, p. 55 *seq.*

[2] Emile Legouis, *The Early Life of Wordsworth*, p. 38 *seq.*

[3] Lack of space has prevented any reference to the work done in Germany by Basedow and his followers in carrying out Rousseau's doctrines. A good brief account will be found in Munro's *History of Education*, p. 577. A full account appears in Pinloche, *La Réforme de l'éducation en Allemagne au dix-huitième siècle.*

them its ideas passed into the great current of progressive thought flowing in the direction of democracy, and it is by its effect on them and their successors that its worth is most adequately measured.

Heinrich Pestalozzi (1746–1827).—Pestalozzi towers head and shoulders above all the other disciples of Rousseau. A native of Switzerland like Rousseau himself, he was sixteen years of age when the *Emile* was published, and the reading of the book proved the turning-point of his life. With all the fiery zeal of adolescence he embraced the gospel of nature, and sought to put it into immediate practice by abandoning a professional life to turn farmer. His first experiment in educational work was made with his own son, and this was followed shortly afterwards by an attempt to educate some pauper children whom he had hired to help with the work of his farm. Neither of these experiments was a great success, but they set his mind to work on the possibility of effecting social reform by means of a new method of education. The first public expression of his ideas was made in a didactic tale entitled *Leonard and Gertrude*, published in 1781. The heroine of the tale is the good house-mother Gertrude, whose method of educating her children embodies Pestalozzi's ideal. Stated briefly, the main ideas of the book were these : (1) The best education for the children of the poor is the education got by taking part in the ordinary work of the peasant home. (2) The best educator for such children is the good mother (herself, it may be, quite uneducated), who encourages her children to think about what they are doing, and to put their thoughts into words. (3) This education follows the order of nature most closely when the children's experience advances gradually from the simpler facts to the more complex. (4) The school established to supplement the mother's education must be modelled on the methods of the home. It was not till Pestalozzi was fifty years of age that the opportunity came to put his theories to the test of practice. In the year 1798—the year of the *Lyrical Ballads*—the Swiss Revolution took place, and Pestalozzi being offered a Government post, elected to become a schoolmaster. First at Stanz and then at Burgdorf he conducted large classes with marvellous success; and on the basis of this experience wrote his chief book, which he named *How Gertrude Teaches her Children* (though there is not a single reference to Gertrude in the book), to indicate the fact that he was only developing the domestic ideal of his earlier years. The main advance made in this book lay in the attempt to systematise, or as he put it himself, to " psychologise " education. That is, he tried to express knowledge and skill in terms of certain elementary experiences (*Anschauungen*), which the child could acquire by a series of steps, following the order of natural development of the race.

Though in this book Pestalozzi speaks somewhat disparagingly of Rousseau's "dreams," the extent of his indebtedness to the dreamer will be evident from what has already been said. From him he borrowed the idea of an education following the natural growth of the child's faculties, as well as the method of basing all learning on first hand experience. From him too he got the suggestion of the educational possibilities of the home, and of the cosmopolitan ideal which has as its prime aim the making of men. In a word, Pestalozzi is at one with Rousseau in all fundamental respects.

Yet there were deep differences between the two men. Pestalozzi was quite as conscious as Rousseau of the existence of those grave social wrongs that put society at enmity with nature. But the antithesis of nature and society which Rousseau regarded as an unhappy condition of things from which there was no escape, presented to Pestalozzi a problem by no means insoluble. In spite of its defects, he saw in society the culmination of a long natural development; and the idea gave him hope that by means of education the same development might be repeated in the life of every child. Again, perhaps because the peasantry with whom he was acquainted were more degraded than those whom Rousseau had met, he had not the same satisfaction in contemplating their condition as his predecessor. For him, the problem of reconciling nature and society assumed its most difficult form in the case of the poor, condemned as much by their own vices as by barbarous social conditions to a mean brutish life; and he sought to provide for the many the soul-making education which Rousseau regarded as possible only for the favoured few. The solution he found in the life of the good home. The idea came from Rousseau, but Pestalozzi's was the faith that saw in the common manual tasks the means to an education for the development of human faculty, and in the ignorant mother who loves her child the best educator. Consequent on this difference in point of view was the greater importance attached by Pestalozzi to the method of education. Rousseau could leave much to the wisdom of Emile's tutor. Pestalozzi knew that if the house-mother was to fulfil the educational function he looked to her to fulfil, she must get detailed instructions as to procedure, and it was his ambition (only partly realised) to write a *Mother's Book*, so simple that the most ignorant woman could use it in the upbringing of her family.

It was this that led him to search unweariedly for the
elements of instruction. But though Pestalozzi sought
to have education begin from birth under the guidance
of the mother, he saw the need for supplementing the
home training by means of the school; and here he
seemed to break away most completely from the individual ideal of Rousseau. Yet the departure from
Rousseau was in the nature of an evolution. The school
after Pestalozzi's heart was not the old-time school
which ignored individuality, but a school that carried
out the best traditions of the home and sought to
combine common instruction with the right development of each pupil.

Johann Gottlieb Fichte (1762–1813).[1]—The evolution
of Rousseau's educational ideal entered on a new phase
when Fichte (himself a disciple of Rousseau) in his
Addresses to the German People advocated the methods
of the Pestalozzian school as likely to provide a firm
foundation for a national system of education. Fichte's
own view of national education followed closely the
scheme of Plato's *Republic,* and it found little favour
with the more practical leaders of the new Germany
which was re-making itself after the disaster of Jena.
But his commendation of Pestalozzi ultimately led to
the adoption of his methods in the national schools.
The significant fact about the experiment — for at
first it was only an experiment—was that it combined
the two ideals which Rousseau had held without being

---

[1] See Paul Duproix, *Kant et Fichte et le Problème de l'Éducation.*
This book calls attention to the very great influence of Rousseau on
Kant. See chap. iii. Perhaps I ought to say at this point that I
have passed over Kant's views on education (collected from students'
notebooks, and published under the title *Über Pädagogik*), because they
have had no particular significance in the evolution of educational
theory.

able to bring them into harmony. As a national system, it sought to produce good citizens. Following Pestalozzi's methods, it aimed at making good men. Implicitly, it was an assertion of the possibility of educating for manhood and for citizenship, and a denial of the worth of any system that failed to educate for both.

Friedrich Froebel (1782–1852) and *Johann Friedrich Herbart* (1776–1841).—One important result of the educational revival in Germany was a great activity of speculation on all aspects of school work. Froebel and Herbart, the two outstanding figures of this movement, were both in direct relation with Pestalozzi : Froebel as a disciple, Herbart less a disciple than a critic, and yet owing much to the Swiss pioneer. Partly through Pestalozzi, partly from personal contact with the Rousselian tradition which in their day was still alive though diminished in vigour, both came under the influence of the *Emile*. To some extent this is disguised by the fact that in both cases the principles of Pestalozzi were forced into combination with a system of philosophy—very different in the two men—which had the effect of modifying these principles and making some additions to them.[1] But in spite of Froebel's idealism and Herbart's monadism, the individualistic point of view in education, which had its origin in Rousseau, is still evident in their works : Froebel dwelling on the importance of the individual child very much as Rousseau had done, though more conscious than he that the individuality which does not find its place in a higher unity is worthless : Herbart giving a fundamental place

[1] The combination was fairly easy to make, because Pestalozzi's implicit philosophy was Kantian, and both Froebel and Herbart represented developments of Kant, though in diverse directions.

to the subjective category of interest, which was as important in Rousseau's system as in Herbart's. In fact, it is most striking to note that despite the emphasis laid on the national element in education by the circumstances of the time, the ideals of both men are strongly tinged with individualism. This individualism, if not directly due to Rousseau, certainly owed something to him.

But the continuation of Rousseau's doctrine is even more evident on the side of method than of principle. Pestalozzi, we noted, was compelled to take more thought on questions and method than Rousseau had done. But in the main, it was Rousseau's methods he expanded and put into practical shape. His insistence on the need for *Anschauung* (first-hand experience of things), for example, was but Rousseau's demand that the culture of mind should begin with personal feeling (*sentiment*). If fault is to be found with Pestalozzi at all on this score, it is in the departure from Rousseau's principles, which led him to put the elements of an analytical process before children as the rudiments of learning. This and similar defects of his treatment of method compelled his successors to devote much attention to its problems. Froebel, confining himself to the education of young children, virtually went back to Rousseau. He still emphasised *Anschauung*, but he supplemented Pestalozzi's doctrine by laying stress on the idea of the development of faculty through self-activity. Herbart, on the other hand, more interested in the problems which arise in the education of older children, when the ideas of the mind are being built up in preparation for the future, elaborated a theory of educational method, in which the process of directing and consolidating experience was analysed with minute care for the guidance of the teacher in the work of the school.

On the practical side, Rousseau's methodology is crude and fragmentary compared with that of Froebel or of Herbart, but making due allowance for its incompleteness, it is truer to the facts of child-life over its entire extent than that of these two or any later thinkers. Froebel's method is a generalisation of the method properly applicable to young children; it emphasises self-activity and self-expression, forgetting that a stage comes when what is received is more important than what is given out, when the material of knowledge garnered in the wisdom of the past counts for more than the personal element in mental response. Herbart's method, on the other hand, is a generalization of the method properly applicable to older children, especially to adolescents. It emphasises the great interests of life which come to the learner from the social environment through the teacher, rather than the activities of personal appropriation, forgetting that in childhood what the child does for himself is far more important than what others do for him, and the process of acquisition of greater consequence than what is acquired. Rousseau is broad enough to comprehend both of these conflicting views, and yet escape the limitations of either by means of the fundamental distinction between negative and positive education which both educators, to their loss, failed to appreciate at its true worth.

Recent Educational Theory.—With the passing of Froebel and Herbart, the direct influence of Rousseau came to an end. Sometime about the middle of the Nineteenth Century, the rise of evolutionary methods of thought and the remarkable increase in industrial activity in all the great nations brought about a change in the centre of gravity of educational interest; and under the conditions of a new age less interested in theory than the age that had preceded it, Rousseau almost ceased to be an active force in the educational world. But though he thus suffered eclipse, it was not the eclipse that attends failure. Rather the opposite. The Nineteenth Century neglected Rousseau, not because it had discarded his individualistic way of thinking, but because it had largely assimilated it.

In this connection, it is noteworthy that of the few contributions made to educational thought in Great Britain during the last half century, the most outstanding have been markedly individualistic. Chief among these is Herbert Spencer's much discussed work, *Education*, a book written from much the same political standpoint as the *Emile*, but inferior to it both in depth and range. Then in more recent years we have had Professor Armstrong's proclamation of the Heuristic Method, the logical supplement of Spencer's *Education*, in which the demand is made for scientific method in education as well as for a scientific material. Most of what has been said by these two writers had already been said in the *Emile*. That it needed to be said again proves how little we have advanced beyond Rousseau in spite of our progress in educational organisation.

But it is to the United States that we must turn if we would see the re-incarnation of the Rousselian spirit at its best and at its worst. There the new education which makes the child its dominant consideration has had a warmer welcome than in the more conservative countries of the old world; and according to Professor James, the schools are being devastated by a "soft pedagogy," which forgets the place of effort in life and education in the desire for interest. However that be, it is in America that Rousseau's ideas are being reproduced to an extent that has no parallel with us.[1] They appear, for example, in a book like Mrs. Gilman's *Concerning Children*, with its depreciation of obedience as a child's virtue; and most of all, they appear in the Child Study Movement. Rousseau desired some judicious man to provide the teacher with a treatise on Child Study; and to-day, many people in America, both judicious and injudicious, are busy trying to provide the schools with the necessary knowledge of the child.

Whatever the immediate practical value of this re-crudescence of Rousseau's point of view in America— about which there is room for doubt — there is no question as to its importance for the ultimate educational synthesis towards which all the nations are making in their several ways. So long as the present economic system continues, the educator is not likely to be allowed to forget the need for the education of workers; and the fervour of patriotism safeguards the civic and national elements in the educational ideal. But there is real danger that between citizenship and industrialism, the schools may be tempted to forget their higher function as the makers of worthy men. It is not the least of the virtues of the New Education, advocated by Rousseau and by all those who consciously or unconsciously have become his disciples in America and elsewhere, that it is a constant reminder to all concerned with education that the main business of the educator is to produce not merely citizens and workers but, above all, Men.

As yet this synthetic education, which has as its aim the making of the complete man, is only in process

[1] *Cf.* Bagley, *Craftsmanship in Teaching*, p. 208 *seq.*

of evolution; but here and there—as for example in the writings of Professor John Dewey,[1] a thinker in the line of descent from Rousseau through Froebel, and a wise advocate of the claims of the child—there are some indications of the course likely to be followed on the way to the education of the future. Without entering on any speculations as to its final form, however, we may confidently say that to the end it will bear the impress of the master-mind of the first New Educationist, Jean Jacques Rousseau.

[1] See especially his *School and Society*, in which is set forth his ideal school in the concrete form of a discussion of the Chicago University Elementary School and its methods. The view presented is that the ideal school is simply "the organisation and generalization of the best elements in home life." For his view of the relation of the Child and the Curriculum, see an admirable essay by him under that title in *The School and the Child* (Blackie's Library of Pedagogics).

BIBLIOGRAPHY

D'ALEMBERT, J.—*Jugement sur Emile.* 1782.

BAKITSCH, W.—*Rousseau's Pädagogik, wissenschaftlich beleuchtet.* Leipzig, 1874.

BARNI, M. J.—*Histoire des Idées morales et politiques en France au dixhuitième siècle.* Vol. ii. Paris, 1867.

BEAUDOUIN, H.—*La Vie et les Œuvres de J.-J. Rousseau.* Paris, 1871.

BOYD, WILLIAM.—*The Minor Educational Writings of J.-J. Rousseau (selected and translated).* London and Glasgow, 1911.

BRÉDIF, LÉON.—*Du caractère intellectuel et moral de J.-J. Rousseau.* Paris, 1906.

BROUGHAM, LORD.—*Lives of Men of Letters in the time of George III.* London, 1855.

CAIRD, EDWARD.—*Essays on Literature and Philosophy.* Glasgow, 1902.

CAJET, DON JOSEPH.—*Les plagiats de M. J.-J. Rousseau de Genève sur l'éducation.* A la Haye, 1766.

CHUQUET, A.—*J.-J. Rousseau.* Paris, 1893.

COMPAYRÉ, G.—*Rousseau and Education from Nature.* (Eng. Tr.) London, 1908.

DAVIDSON, THOMAS.—*Rousseau and Education according to Nature.* (Great Educators.) London, 1898.

ESPINAS, A.—*Le système de J.-J. Rousseau in La Revue internationale de l'enseignement,* vols. 30, 31. 1895–96.

FAGUET, E.—*Dixhuitième Siècle—Etudes littéraires.* Paris, 1890.

FORMEY.—*Anti-Emile.* Berlin, 1763.

FRITSCHE, E. und Vogt, Th.—*Bibliothek pädagogischer Klassiker,* vi., vii. Langensalza, 1873.

GABERAL, J.—*Rousseau et les Genevois.* Paris, 1858.

GEHRIG, HERMANN.—*J.-J. Rousseau, sein Leben und seine Schriften.* (*Schroedels pädagogische Klassiker.*) Halle a. d. Saale, 1905.

GEIGER, LUDWIG.—*J.-J. Rousseau, sein Leben und seine Werke.* Leipzig, 1907.

GERDIL, S.—*Anti-Emile ou reflexions sur la theorie et la pratique de l'éducation.* Turin, 1763.

GIRARDIN, ST. MARC.—*J.-J. Rousseau, sa Vie et ses Œuvres.* Paris, 1875.

GÖRLAND, A.—*Rousseau als Klassiker der Sozialpädagogik.* Gotha, 1906.

GÖSGEN.—*Rousseau und Basedow.* Burg bei M., 1891.

GRAHAM, HENRY.—*Rousseau.* (Foreign Classics for English Readers.) Edinburgh, 1882.

GRÉARD, O.—*L'éducation des femmes par les femmes.* Paris, 1886.

GRIMM.—In *Correspondance littéraire . . . par Grimm, Diderot, &c.* Vol. 5.

GROTZ, A.—*J.-J. Rousseau et l'éducation.* Strasburg, 1874.

HÉRISSON, F.—*Pestalozzi, élève de J.-J. Rousseau.* Paris, 1886.

HODGSON, GERALDINE.—*Studies in French Education from Rabelais to Rousseau.* Chaps. viii., ix. Cambridge, 1908.

HÖFFDING, H.—*Rousseau und seine Philosophie.* Stuttgart, 1902.

HUDSON, W. H.—*Rousseau and Naturalism in Life and Thought.* Edinburgh, 1903.

HUNZIKER, O.—*Rousseau und Pestalozzi.* Basel, 1885.

KRAMER, G.—*Francke, Rousseau und Pestalozzi.* Berlin, 1854.

LANSON, G.—*Histoire de la littérature française.* Paris, 1903. Eighth Edition.

LEMAÎTRE, JULES.—*J.-J. Rousseau.* Paris, 1907. (Eng. Tr. London, 1908.)

MACDONALD, MRS. F.—*J.-J. Rousseau, a new criticism.* London, 1906.

MAHRENHOLTZ, R.—*J.-J. Rousseaus Leben, Geistesentwicklung und Hauptwerke.* 1889.

MONROE, PAUL.—*A Textbook in the History of Education.* Chap. x. New York, 1905.

MORLEY, JOHN.—*Rousseau.* London, 1873. (First Edition.)

MÜLLER, P.—*J.-J. Rousseau, der pädagogische Irrstern unsrer Zeit und die christliche Erziehungsaufgabe.* Hannov. 1875.

MUSSET-PATHAY, V. G.—*Histoire de la Vie et les Ouvrages de J.-J. Rousseau.* 1821.

NOÏKOW, PETER M.—*Das Activitätsprinzip in der Pädagogik J.-J. Rousseaus.* Leipzig, 1898.

OLTRAMARE, A.—*Les Idées de Rousseau sur l'éducation* in *J.-J. Rousseau jugé par les Genevois d'aujourd'hui.* (Centenary Lectures.) 1878.

PAYNE, W. H.—*Rousseau's Emile.* (Abridged and translated, with an Introduction, in the International Series.) New York, 1892.

PRECHTER, J. J.—*Briefe über den Emil des Rousseaus.* Zürich, 1773.

QUICK, R. H.—*Educational Reformers.* Chap. xiv. London, 1868. (First Edition.)

SALLWÜRK, E. v.—*J.-J. Rousseaus Emil.* (A German translation, with Biography and Commentary.) Langensalza, 1907. (Fourth Edition.)

SCHLÖSSER.—*History of the Eighteenth Century* (especially vols. i., ii.).

SCHNEIDER, K.—*Rousseau und Pestalozzi. Der Idealismus auf deutschem und französischem Boden.* Berlin, 1895. (Fifth Edition.)

SCHWARZ, F.—*Rousseau's Entwicklung zum pädagogischen Schriftsteller.* Basel, 1879.

SPLITTGERBER, F.—*Die moderne widerchristliche Pädagogik, nach ihren Bahnbrechern Rousseau und Basedow.* Leipzig, 1878.

STAËL, MADAME DE.—*Lettres sur les ouvrages et la caractère de Rousseau.* 1788.

STEEG, JULES.—*Emile.* (Extracts from the first three Books.) Eng. Tr. London, N.D.

STOY, K. v.—*Rousseau, Considérant und die Idee der Erziehung.* Jena, 1850.

STRECKEISEN-MOULTOU, M. G.—*Œuvres et correspondance inédites de J.-J. Rousseau.* Paris, 1861.

STRECKEISEN-MOULTOU, M. G.—*Rousseau, ses amis et ses ennemis.* Paris, 1865.

TEXTE, JOSEPH.—*J.-J. Rousseau and the Cosmopolitan Spirit in Literature.* Eng. Tr. London, 1899.

VILLEMAIN, M.—*Cours de littérature française—Dixhuitième siècle.* Paris.

WIER, S.—*Emile, the Key to Rousseau,* in the *Educational Review,* xvi. New York, 1898.

ZOLLER, F.—*Pestalozzi und Rousseau.* Frankfurt a.M., 1851.

INDEX

365